GO MATH!

HOUGHTON MIFFLIN HARCOURT

HOUGHTON
MIFFLIN
HARCOURT

Printed in the U.S.A.

ISBN 978-0-547-58779-0

9 10 1421 20 19 18 17 16 15

4500523344   C D E F G

Dear Students and Families,

Welcome to **Go Math!**, Grade 1! In this exciting mathematics program, there are hands-on activities to do and real-world problems to solve. Best of all, you will write your ideas and answers right in your book. In **Go Math!**, writing and drawing on the pages helps you think deeply about what you are learning, and you will really understand math!

By the way, all of the pages in your **Go Math!** book are made using recycled paper. We wanted you to know that you can Go Green with **Go Math!**

Sincerely,

The Authors

Made in the United States
Text printed on 100% recycled paper
By using this paper in a typical print run, we
achieved the following environmental benefits:*
Trees Saved: 463
Air Emissions Eliminated: 28,074 pounds
Water Saved: 311,402 gallons
Solid Waste Eliminated: 35,816 pounds

*Environmental impact estimates calculated using
 the Environmental Defense Fund Paper Calculator.
 For more information, visit www.papercalculator.org

GO MATH!

Authors

Juli K. Dixon
Professor of Mathematics Education
University of Central Florida
Orlando, Florida

Miriam A. Leiva
Founding President, TODOS:
    Mathematics for All
Distinguished Professor
    of Mathematics Emerita
University of North Carolina Charlotte
Charlotte, North Carolina

Matt Larson
Curriculum Specialist for Mathematics
Lincoln Public Schools
Lincoln, Nebraska

Thomasenia Lott Adams
Professor of Mathematics Education
University of Florida
Gainesville, Florida

Operations and Algebraic Thinking

COMMON CORE **Critical Area** Developing understanding of addition, subtraction, and strategies for addition and subtraction within 20

1 Addition Concepts   9

Domain Operations and Algebraic Thinking
Common Core Standards CC.1.OA.1, CC.1.OA.3, CC.1.OA.6

2 Subtraction Concepts   49

Domain Operations and Algebraic Thinking
Common Core Standards CC.1.OA.1, CC.1.OA.6, CC.1.OA.8

DIGITAL PATH
Go online! Your math lessons are interactive. Use iTools, Animated Math Models, the Multimedia eGlossary, and more.

Math Story

Animals in Our World

Science

Look for these:

REAL WORLD

H.O.T.
Higher Order Thinking

GO MATH!

Use every day for Standards Practice.

v

© Houghton Mifflin Harcourt Publishing Company

5 Addition and Subtraction Relationships 181

Domain Operations and Algebraic Thinking
Common Core Standards CC.1.OA.1, CC.1.OA.6, CC.1.OA.7, CC.1.OA.8

Number and Operations in Base Ten

COMMON CORE **Critical Area** Developing understanding of whole number relationships and place value, including grouping in tens and ones

6 Count and Model Numbers 237

Domain Number and Operations in Base Ten

Common Core Standards CC.1.NBT.1, CC.1.NBT.2, CC.1.NBT.2a, CC.1.NBT.2b, CC.1.NBT.2c, CC.1.NBT.3

DIGITAL PATH
Go online! Your math lessons are interactive. Use iTools, Animated Math Models, the Multimedia eGlossary, and more.

Math Story
Around the Neighborhood
Social Studies

Look for these:

REAL WORLD

H.O.T.
Higher Order Thinking

GO MATH!

Use every day for Standards Practice.

Measurement and Data

COMMON CORE **Critical Area** Developing understanding of linear measurement and measuring lengths as iterating length units

9 Measurement 365

Domain Measurement and Data
Common Core Standards CC.1.MD.1, CC.1.MD.2, CC.1.MD.3

DIGITAL PATH
Go online! Your math lessons are interactive. Use iTools, Animated Math Models, the Multimedia eGlossary, and more.

Math Story

All Kinds of Weather
SCIENCE

Look for these:
REAL WORLD

H.O.T.
Higher Order Thinking

Use every day for Standards Practice.

© Houghton Mifflin Harcourt Publishing Company

xi

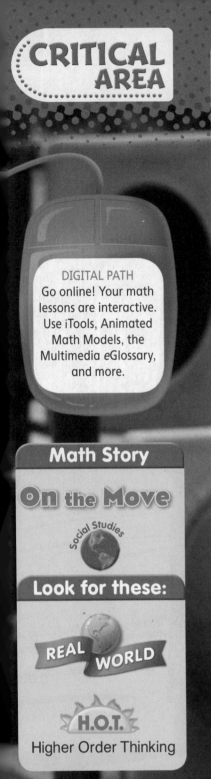

DIGITAL PATH
Go online! Your math lessons are interactive. Use iTools, Animated Math Models, the Multimedia eGlossary, and more.

Math Story

On the Move

Social Studies

Look for these:

REAL WORLD

H.O.T.

Higher Order Thinking

Use every day for Standards Practice.

Geometry

COMMON CORE **Critical Area** Reasoning about attributes of, and composing and decomposing geometric shapes

11 Three-Dimensional Geometry 453

Domain Geometry
Common Core Standards CC.1.G.1, CC.1.G.2

12 Two-Dimensional Geometry 481

Domain Geometry
Common Core Standards CC.1.G.1, CC.1.G.2, CC.1.G.3

CRITICAL AREA

Animals in Our World

written by Martha Sibert

COMMON CORE

CRITICAL AREA Developing understanding of addition, subtraction, and strategies for addition and subtraction within 20

Two parrots sit on the branch of a tree.

How many beaks do you see? ____

© Houghton Mifflin Harcourt Publishing Company

Science

Where do parrots live?

Four elephants walk. They are all the same kind.

How many trunks can you find? _____

Science

Where do elephants live?

3

Three penguins stand. One is very small.

Each has two feet. How many feet in all? _____

Science

Where do penguins live?

Four lions rest happy as can be.

Look at their ears. How many do you see? ____

Science

Where do lions live?

Five giraffes stand straight and tall.

How many small horns do they have in all? _____

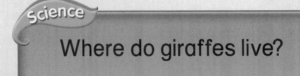
Science

Where do giraffes live?

6

Write About the Story

Write Math ▶ Draw more bears. Then write an addition story problem or a subtraction story problem.

Write the addition or subtraction sentence.

How Many Ears?

Look at the picture of the pandas.
What if there were five pandas?
How many ears would there be?

Draw to explain.

Five pandas would have _____ ears.

 Make up a question about another animal in the story. Have a classmate draw to answer your question.

Addition Concepts

Curious About Math with

Curious George

How many kittens can you add to the group to have 10 kittens? Explain.

Name _____

Explore Numbers 1 to 4

Use to show the number.
Draw the ⬤.

1. 1 ☐

2. 3 ☐

Numbers 1 to 10

How many objects are in each group?

3.

_____ chicks

4.

_____ eggs

5.

_____ flowers

Numbers 0 to 10

How many spots are on the ladybug?

6.

_____

7.

_____

8.

_____

9.

_____

Family note: This page checks your child's understanding of important skills needed for success in Chapter 1.

GO Online

Assessment Options
Soar to Success Math

© Houghton Mifflin Harcourt Publishing Company

Name _____

Vocabulary Builder

Visualize It

Draw to show I more.
Draw to show adding to.

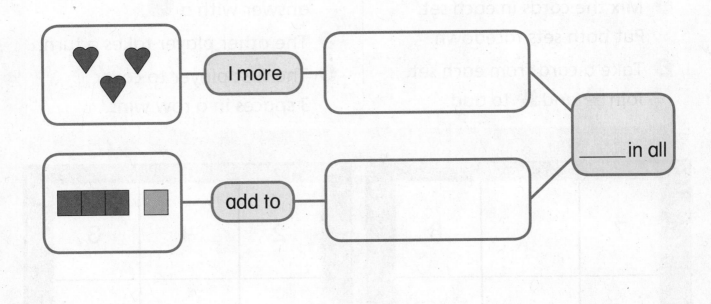

I more

add to

_____ in all

Understand Vocabulary

Complete the sentences with review words.

1. Sue wants to know how many counters
   are in two groups. She can _____
   to find out.

2. Pete has 2 apples. May has 3 apples.
   May has _____ apple than Pete.

Game Addition Bingo

Materials

- 2 sets of Numeral Cards 0–4
- 18 ⬤ • 4  • 4

Play with a partner.

1. Mix the cards in each set. Put both sets facedown.
2. Take a card from each set. Join  and  to add.

3. The other player checks your answer.
4. If you are correct, cover the answer with a ⬤.
5. The other player takes a turn.
6. The first player to cover 3 spaces in a row wins.

7	1	8
3	6	5
0	2	4

Player 1

2	4	3
7	5	0
1	8	6

Player 2

Name _____

Algebra • Use Pictures to Add To

Essential Question How do pictures show adding to?

COMMON CORE STANDARD CC.1.OA.1
Represent and solve problems involving addition and subtraction.

Listen and Draw  REAL WORLD

Draw to show adding to.
Write how many there are.

_____ ladybugs

FOR THE TEACHER • Read the following problem. Have children draw a picture to show the problem. There are 3 ladybugs on a leaf. 2 more ladybugs join them. How many ladybugs are there?

Math Talk
How does your drawing show the problem? **Explain.**

MATHEMATICAL PRACTICES

© Houghton Mifflin Harcourt Publishing Company

Model and Draw

2 cats   and   I more cat   __3__ cats in all

Share and Show

Write how many.

✓1.

3 fish   and   I more fish   ____ fish

✓2.

4 bees   and   4 more bees   ____ bees

Name _____

On Your Own

Write how many.

3.
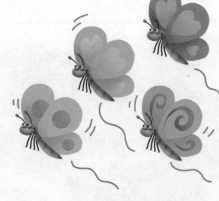

2 butterflies   and   4 more butterflies   ____ butterflies

4.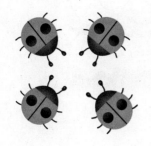
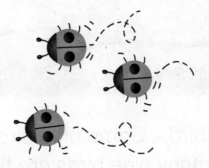

4 ladybugs   and   3 more ladybugs   ____ ladybugs

5. H.O.T. Draw one way to show 9 worms.

____ worms   and   ____ more worms   9 worms

PROBLEM SOLVING REAL WORLD

Write Math

H.O.T. Color the birds to show how to solve.

6. There are 3 red birds. Some blue birds join them. How many blue birds are there?

There are _____ blue birds.

7. ⭐ **Test Prep** How many bees?

2 bees	and	5 more bees	_____ bees
3	5	7	8
○	○	○	○

TAKE HOME ACTIVITY · Have your child use stuffed animals or other toys to show 3 animals. Then add to the group showing 2 more animals. Ask how many animals there are. Repeat for other combinations of animals with totals up to 10.

FOR MORE PRACTICE:
Standards Practice Book, pp. P3–P4

Name _____

Model Adding To

Essential Question How do you model adding to a group?

COMMON CORE STANDARD CC.1.OA.1
Represent and solve problems involving addition and subtraction.

Listen and Draw

Use ▪▪ to show adding to.
Draw to show your work.

FOR THE TEACHER • Read the following problem. Have children use connecting cubes to model the problem and draw to show their work. There are 6 children on the playground. 2 more children join them. How many children are on the playground?

Math Talk
Explain how you use cubes to find your answer.

MATHEMATICAL PRACTICES

Chapter 1

seventeen **17**

Model and Draw

5 turtles   and   2 more turtles

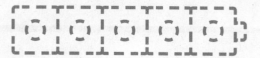   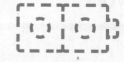

$$5 \quad + \quad 2 \quad = \quad \underline{7}$$

plus   is equal to   sum

$5 + 2 = 7$ is an **addition sentence.**

Share and Show

Use  to show adding to.
Draw the . Write the sum.

1. 3 cats and 1 more cat

2. 2 birds and 3 more birds

$$3 + 1 = \underline{}$$

$$2 + 3 = \underline{}$$

⊘ 3. 4 bugs and 4 more bugs

⊘ 4. 4 fish and 2 more fish

$$4 + 4 = \underline{}$$

$$4 + 2 = \underline{}$$

Name _____

On Your Own

Use 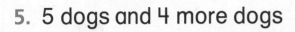 to show adding to.
Draw the 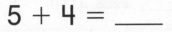. Write the sum.

5. 5 dogs and 4 more dogs	6. 4 bees and 3 more bees
5 + 4 = ___	4 + 3 = ___
7. 4 frogs and 1 more frog	8. 3 ants and 5 more ants
4 + 1 = ___	3 + 5 = ___

9. **H.O.T.** Corey drew cubes to show
adding to. Draw to show how Corey
should fix his picture. Write the sum.

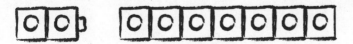

2 + 8 = ___

PROBLEM SOLVING REAL WORLD

Write Math

Use the picture to help you complete
the addition sentences. Write the sum.

 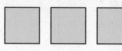

10. _____ + _____ △ = _____ △ in all

11. _____ ● + _____ ● = _____ ● in all

12. _____ ■ + _____ ■ = _____ ■ in all

13. **H.O.T.** Circle the picture that shows 3 + 1 = 4.

14. ⭐ **Test Prep** What is the sum of 4 and 3?

    1   6   7   8
    ○   ○   ○   ○

 TAKE HOME ACTIVITY · Put 3 pennies in one group and 2 pennies in another
group. Have your child write an addition sentence to tell about the pennies.
Repeat for other combinations of pennies with sums of up to 10.

FOR MORE PRACTICE:
Standards Practice Book, pp. P5–P6

Name _____

Model Putting Together

Essential Question How do you model putting together?

COMMON CORE STANDARD CC.1.OA.1
Represent and solve problems involving addition and subtraction.

Listen and Draw  REAL WORLD

Use ⬤ to model the problem. Draw the ⬤.
Write the numbers and addition sentence.

____ red crayons   ____ yellow crayons

____ ⊕ ____ ⊜ ____

There are ____ crayons.

Math Talk

Describe how the drawing helps you write the addition sentence.

MATHEMATICAL PRACTICES

FOR THE TEACHER • Read the following problem. There are 2 red crayons and 3 yellow crayons. How many crayons are there?

Chapter 1

Model and Draw

Add to find how many books there are.

There are 2 small books and 1 big book. How many books are there?

____ books

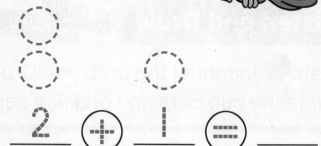

$$\underline{\ 2\ } \ (+) \ \underline{\ 1\ } \ (=) \ \underline{\quad}$$

Share and Show

Use ● to solve. Draw to show your work.
Write the number sentence and how many.

1. There are 4 red pencils and 2 green pencils. How many pencils are there?

   ____ pencils

   $$\underline{\quad} \bigcirc \underline{\quad} \bigcirc \underline{\quad}$$

2. There are 5 blue scissors and 3 yellow scissors. How many scissors are there?

   ____ scissors

   $$\underline{\quad} \bigcirc \underline{\quad} \bigcirc \underline{\quad}$$

Name _____

On Your Own

Use ● to solve. Draw to show your work.
Write the number sentence and how many.

3. There are 4 girls and 4 boys running. How many children are running?

____ children

_____ ◯ _____ ◯ _____

4. There are 3 small cats and 4 big cats. How many cats are there?

____ cats

_____ ◯ _____ ◯ _____

5. There are 6 red cubes and 3 blue cubes. How many cubes are there?

____ cubes

_____ ◯ _____ ◯ _____

6. There are 2 red flowers and 8 yellow flowers. How many flowers are there?

____ flowers

_____ ◯ _____ ◯ _____

PROBLEM SOLVING

REAL WORLD

Write Math

7. **H.O.T.** Write your own addition story problem.

_____

_____

_____

_____

_____

8. Use  to solve your story problem.
Draw to show your work. Write the
number sentence.

___ ○ ___ ○ ___

9. ⭐ **Test Prep**
There are 7 red apples and
3 green apples. How many
apples are there?

    11   10   7   4

    ○   ○   ○   ○

TAKE HOME ACTIVITY · Have your child collect a group of up
to 10 small objects and use them to make up addition stories.

FOR MORE PRACTICE:
Standards Practice Book, pp. P7–P8

Name _____

Problem Solving • Model Addition

Essential Question How do you solve addition problems by making a model?

COMMON CORE STANDARD CC.1.OA.1
Represent and solve problems involving addition and subtraction.

Hanna has 4 red flowers in a .
She puts 2 more flowers in the .
How many flowers are in the ?
How can you use a model to find out?

🔑 Unlock the Problem REAL WORLD

What do I need to find?

_____

flowers Hanna has

What information do I need to use?

__4__ red flowers

__2__ more flowers

Show how to solve the problem.

4	2

_6_

$4 + 2 = \underline{}$

HOME CONNECTION • Your child can model the concepts of adding to and putting together. He or she used a bar model to show the problems and solve.

Try Another Problem

Read the problem. Use the bar model to solve. Complete the model and the number sentence.

- What do I need to find?
- What information do I need to use?

1. There are 7 dogs in the park. Then 1 more dog joins them. How many dogs are in the park now?

| 7 | 1 |

_____

$$7 + 1 = \underline{\quad}$$

2. Some birds are sitting in the tree. Four more birds sit in the tree. Then there are 9 birds. How many birds were in the tree before?

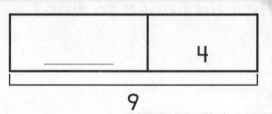

$$\underline{\quad} + 4 = 9$$

3. There are 4 horses in the field. Some more horses run to the field. Then there were 10 horses in the field. How many horses run to the field?

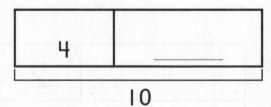

$$4 + \underline{\quad} = 10$$

Math Talk
How does a model help you solve Exercise 1? Explain.

MATHEMATICAL PRACTICES

© Houghton Mifflin Harcourt Publishing Company

Share and Show

Read the problem. Use the bar model to solve.
Complete the model and the number sentence.

✓4. Luis has 12 crayons.
5 of the crayons are red.
The rest are blue. How
many crayons are blue?

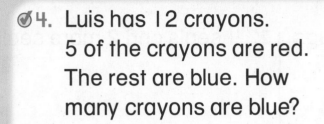

5	_____

12

$5 + \underline{\quad} = 12$

✓5. 8 bugs are flying.
2 more bugs fly with
them. How many bugs
are flying now?

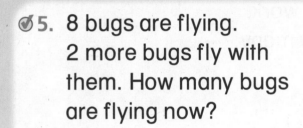

8	2

$8 + 2 = \underline{\quad}$

6. **H.O.T.** Some ducks are
swimming in a pond. 3 more
ducks swim in the pond.
Then there are 6 ducks in
the pond. How many ducks
were in the pond before?

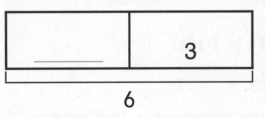

_____	3

6

$\underline{\quad} + 3 = 6$

TAKE HOME ACTIVITY • Have your child describe each of the
parts of a bar model using the number sentence $7 + 3 = 10$.

FOR MORE PRACTICE:
Standards Practice Book, pp. P9–P10

Mid-Chapter Checkpoint

Concepts and Skills

Use ▣ to show adding to.
Draw the ▣. Write the sum. (CC.1.OA.1)

1. 3 ladybugs and 4 more ladybugs	2. 4 seals and 2 more seals

$$3 + 4 = \rule{1cm}{0.15mm}$$

$$4 + 2 = \rule{1cm}{0.15mm}$$

Use ● to solve. Draw to show your work.
Write the number sentence and how many. (CC.1.OA.1)

3. There are 5 red marbles and
4 blue marbles. How many
marbles are there?

_____ marbles

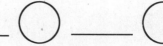

⭐ Test Prep

Solve. (CC.1.OA.1)

4. 6 bunnies sit in the grass.
2 more bunnies join them.
How many bunnies are
in the grass now?

3	4	8	9
○	○	○	○

Name _____

Algebra • Add Zero

Essential Question What happens when you add 0 to a number?

COMMON CORE STANDARD CC.1.OA.3
Understand and apply properties of operations and the relationship between addition and subtraction.

Listen and Draw REAL WORLD

Use ⬤ to model the problem.
Draw the ⬤ you use.

FOR THE TEACHER • Read the following problem. Scott has 4 marbles. Jennifer has no marbles. How many marbles do they have?

Math Talk
Explain your drawing.

MATHEMATICAL PRACTICES

© Houghton Mifflin Harcourt Publishing Company

Chapter 1

What happens when **zero** is added to a number?

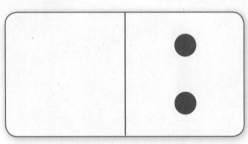

What happens when a number is added to zero?

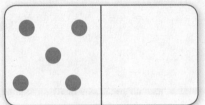

$$\underline{}5\phantom{\underline{5}} + \underline{}0\phantom{\underline{0}} = \underline{}5\phantom{\underline{5}}$$
sum

$$\underline{}0\phantom{\underline{0}} + \underline{}3\phantom{\underline{3}} = \underline{}3\phantom{\underline{3}}$$
sum

Share and Show

Use the picture to write each part. Write the sum.

1.

____ + ____ = ____

2.

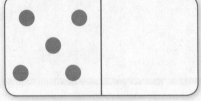

____ + ____ = ____

✓ 3.

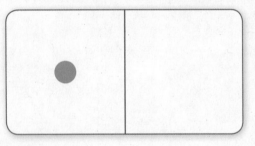

____ + ____ = ____

✓ 4.

____ + ____ = ____

Name _____

On Your Own

Draw circles to show the number.
Write the sum.

5. $2 + 0 =$ ____	**6.** $0 + 1 =$ ____	**7.** $4 + 6 =$ ____
8. $0 + 5 =$ ____	**9.** $3 + 4 =$ ____	**10.** $0 + 6 =$ ____
11. $3 + 0 =$ ____	**12.** $1 + 4 =$ ____	**13.** $4 + 0 =$ ____
14. $5 + 2 =$ ____	**15.** $1 + 3 =$ ____	**16.** $5 + 4 =$ ____

H.O.T. Complete the addition sentence.

17. ____ + ____ = 0

PROBLEM SOLVING REAL WORLD

Write Math

Write the addition sentence to solve.

18. Mike has 7 books.
Cheryl does not have any books.
How many books do they
both have?

___ + ___ = ___

___ books

19. 3 dogs sit.
5 dogs run to them.
How many dogs are there now?

___ + ___ = ___

___ dogs

20. **H.O.T.** There are 5 birds.
How many birds are inside?

___ birds

21. ⭐ **Test Prep** What is the sum for 0 + 6?

0	5	6	7
○	○	○	○

TAKE HOME ACTIVITY · Write the numbers 0 to 9 on small squares of paper. Shuffle and place the cards facedown. Have your child turn the top card and add zero to that number. Say the sum. Repeat the activity for each card.

FOR MORE PRACTICE:
Standards Practice Book, pp. P11–P12

Algebra • Add in Any Order

Essential Question Why can you add addends in any order?

COMMON CORE STANDARD **CC.1.OA.3**
Understand and apply properties of operations and the relationship between addition and subtraction.

Listen and Draw

Use ▨▨ to model the addition sentence.
Draw to show your work.

Math Talk
How is 2 + 3 = 5 the same as 3 + 2 = 5? **Explain** how it is different.

MATHEMATICAL PRACTICES

FOR THE TEACHER • Direct children to do the following. Use connecting cubes to show 2 + 3 and then 3 + 2.

Model and Draw

The **order** of the **addends** changes.
What do you notice about the sum?

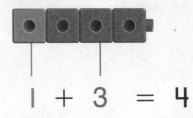   

$$1 + 3 = 4$$

addends   sum

Share and Show

Use  to add. Color to match. Write the sum.	Change the order of the addends. Color to match. Write the addition sentence.

1.

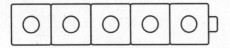   

$$2 + 3 = \underline{}$$ $$\underline{} \bigcirc \underline{} \bigcirc \underline{}$$

2.

   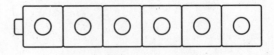

$$2 + 4 = \underline{}$$ $$\underline{} \bigcirc \underline{} \bigcirc \underline{}$$

3.

   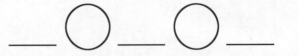

$$4 + 1 = \underline{}$$ $$\underline{} \bigcirc \underline{} \bigcirc \underline{}$$

On Your Own

Use . Write the sum.
Circle the addition sentences
in each row that have the same
addends in a different order.

4.

1 + 2 = ___   1 + 3 = ___   2 + 1 = ___

5.

1 + 5 = ___   4 + 2 = ___   2 + 4 = ___

6.

3 + 7 = ___   7 + 3 = ___   3 + 3 = ___

7.

3 + 6 = ___   4 + 5 = ___   5 + 4 = ___

8.

0 + 6 = ___   6 + 0 = ___   5 + 1 = ___

9. **H.O.T.** Write two addition sentences that
tell about the picture.

PROBLEM SOLVING REAL WORLD

Write Math

Draw pictures to match the addition sentences.
Write the sum.

10. $2 + 6 =$ ___

     $6 + 2 =$ ___

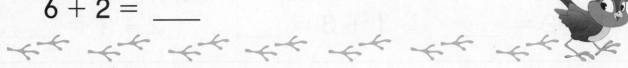

11. $1 + 5 =$ ___

     $5 + 1 =$ ___

12. **H.O.T.** Choose addends to complete the
addition sentence. Change the order.
Write the numbers.

   ___ + ___ = 10 | ___ + ___ = ___

13. ⭐ **Test Prep** Which shows the same
addends in a different order?

$$2 + 3 = 5$$

$2 + 5 = 7$ $3 + 2 = 5$ $3 + 5 = 8$ $4 + 2 = 6$

   ○   ○   ○   ○

TAKE HOME ACTIVITY · Ask your child to use small objects of
the same kind to show 2 + 4 and 4 + 2 and then explain to you
why the sums are the same. Repeat with other addition sentences.

FOR MORE PRACTICE:
Standards Practice Book, pp. P13–P14

Name _____

Algebra • Put Together Numbers to 10

Essential Question How can you show all the ways to make a number?

COMMON CORE STANDARD CC.1.OA.1
Represent and solve problems involving addition and subtraction.

Listen and Draw

Use to show all the ways to make 5.
Color to show your work.

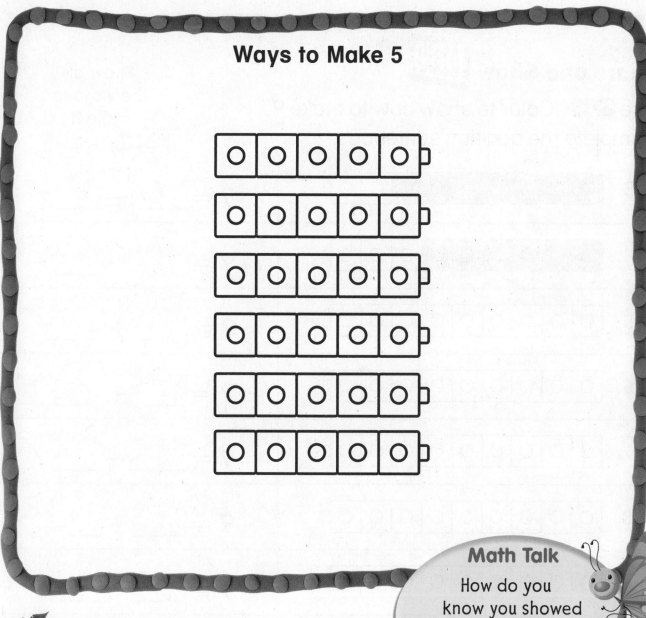

Ways to Make 5

Math Talk
How do you know you showed all the ways? **Explain.**

MATHEMATICAL PRACTICES

FOR THE TEACHER • Read the following problem and have children show all the ways to solve the problem. Grandma has 5 flowers. How many can she put in her red vase and how many in her blue vase?

Model and Draw

Now Grandma has 9 flowers. How many can she put in her red vase and how many in her blue vase?

Complete the addition sentences.

1. $9 = \underline{9} + \underline{0}$

2. $9 = \underline{8} + \underline{1}$

Share and Show

Use ▪▫. Color to show how to make 9. Complete the addition sentences.

Show all the ways to make 9.

3. $9 = \underline{7} + \underline{\quad}$

4. $9 = \underline{\quad} + \underline{\quad}$

5. $9 = \underline{\quad} + \underline{\quad}$

6. $9 = \underline{\quad} + \underline{\quad}$

7. $9 = \underline{\quad} + \underline{\quad}$

8. $9 = \underline{\quad} + \underline{\quad}$

9. $9 = \underline{\quad} + \underline{\quad}$

10. $9 = \underline{\quad} + \underline{\quad}$

Name _____

On Your Own

Use ▣▣. Color to show how to make 10.
Complete the addition sentences.

Show all
the ways to
make 10.

11. ○○○○○○○○○○   10 = __10__ + __0__

12. ○○○○○○○○○○   10 = ___ + ___

13. ○○○○○○○○○○   10 = ___ + ___

14. ○○○○○○○○○○   10 = ___ + ___

15. ○○○○○○○○○○   10 = ___ + ___

16. ○○○○○○○○○○   10 = ___ + ___

17. ○○○○○○○○○○   10 = ___ + ___

18. ○○○○○○○○○○   10 = ___ + ___

19. ○○○○○○○○○○   10 = ___ + ___

20. ○○○○○○○○○○   10 = ___ + ___

21. ○○○○○○○○○○   10 = ___ + ___

© Houghton Mifflin Harcourt Publishing Company

PROBLEM SOLVING REAL WORLD

Write Math

22. **H.O.T.** I have 8 marbles.
Some are red.
Some are blue.

How many of each could I have?
Find and write as many ways
as you can.

Red	Blue	Sum

23. ⭐ **Test Prep** Which shows a way to make 7?

○   ○   ○   ○

TAKE HOME ACTIVITY • Write 6 = 6 + 0. Model the problem with
pennies. Ask your child to make 6 another way. Take turns until
you and your child model all of the ways to make 6.

FOR MORE PRACTICE:
Standards Practice Book, pp. P15–P16

Name _____

Addition to 10

Essential Question Why are some addition facts easy to add?

COMMON CORE STANDARD CC.1.OA.6
Add and subtract within 20.

Listen and Draw REAL WORLD

Draw a picture to show the problem.
Then write the addends and the sum in two ways.

 ___ + ___ = ___   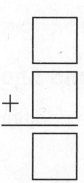 +

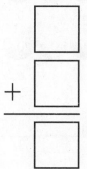 ___ + ___ = ___   +

FOR THE TEACHER • Read the following for the top of the page. There are 2 children in line for the slide. 4 more children get in line. How many children are in line for the slide? Read the following for the bottom of the page. Christy has 3 stickers. Mike gives her 2 more stickers. How many stickers does Christy have now?

Math Talk
Why is the sum the same when you add across or down? **Explain.**

MATHEMATICAL PRACTICES

Chapter 1

forty-one **41**

Write the addition problem.

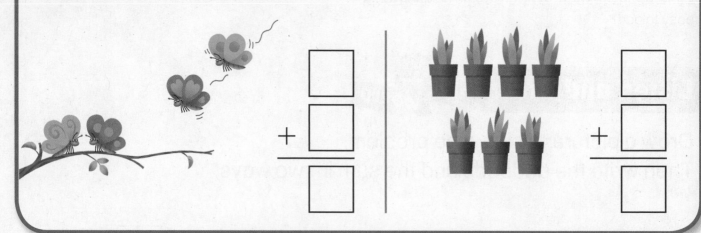

$+$

$+$

Share and Show

Write the addition problem.

1.

$+$

2.

$+$

3.

$+$

4.

$+$

Name _____

On Your Own

Write the sum.

5.	6.	7.	8.	9.	10.
1 +2	2 +2	0 +3	1 +1	4 +2	8 +1

11.	12.	13.	14.	15.	16.
0 +4	2 +5	4 +4	9 +1	6 +3	4 +3

17.	18.	19.	20.	21.	22.
1 +6	4 +6	7 +3	6 +2	3 +3	3 +5

23. **Explain** Sam showed how he added 4 + 2. Tell how Sam could find the correct sum.

$$\begin{array}{r} 4 \\ +2 \\ \hline 7 \end{array}$$

_____

_____

_____

_____

_____

© Houghton Mifflin Harcourt Publishing Company

PROBLEM SOLVING REAL WORLD

Write Math

24. Add. Write the sum. Use the sum and the key to color the flower.

KEY

7 — YELLOW
8 — RED
9 — PURPLE
10 — PINK

$3 + 7 =$ _____

$0 + 9 =$ _____

$\begin{array}{r} 2 \\ +7 \\ \hline \end{array}$

$\begin{array}{r} 5 \\ +5 \\ \hline \end{array}$

$5 + 2 =$ _____

$6 + 4 =$ _____

$7 + 1 =$ _____

$\begin{array}{r} 7 \\ +0 \\ \hline \end{array}$

$\begin{array}{r} 4 \\ +5 \\ \hline \end{array}$

$3 + 5 =$ _____

$\begin{array}{r} 2 \\ +6 \\ \hline \end{array}$

$3 + 4 =$ _____

25. **H.O.T.** How many flowers are yellow or purple?

_____ ◯ _____ ◯ _____

26. ⭐ **Test Prep** What is the sum?

1   9   10   11

$\begin{array}{r} 5 \\ +4 \\ \hline \end{array}$

◯   ◯   ◯   ◯

TAKE HOME ACTIVITY • Write addition sentences to add across. Then write addition sentences to add down. Have your child find the sum for each.

44 forty-four

© Houghton Mifflin Harcourt Publishing Company

FOR MORE PRACTICE:
Standards Practice Book, pp. P17–P18

Name _____

Vocabulary

Circle the **addends**. (p. 34)
Underline the **sum**. (p. 18)

1. $3 + 2 = 5$

Concepts and Skills

Write how many.

2. How many bears? (CC.1.OA.1)

2 bears   and   I more bear   ____ bears

Use 🎲 to show adding to.
Draw the 🎲. Write the sum. (CC.1.OA.1)

3. 2 ducks and 3 more ducks | 4. 5 lions and 2 more lions

$2 + 3 =$ ____ $5 + 2 =$ ____

5. What is the sum of
1 and 5? (CC.1.OA.1)

          3   6   7   8
          ○   ○   ○   ○

6. There are 3 red
cubes and 3 green
cubes. How many
cubes are there? (CC.1.OA.1)

          6   5   4   0
          ○   ○   ○   ○

7. There are 2 people in the house.
Some more people go in the
house. Then there were 6 people
in the house. How many people
go in the house? (CC.1.OA.1)

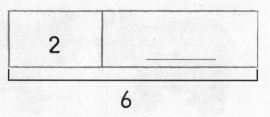

6

$$2 + \_\_\_ = 6$$

  8   6   5   4
  ○   ○   ○   ○

8. 3 birds are in the tree.
No birds join them.
How many birds are
there now? (CC.1.OA.3)

$$3 + 0 = 3 \quad 3 + 2 = 5 \quad 0 + 2 = 2 \quad 3 + 1 = 4$$
    ○   ○   ○   ○

Name _____

9. Which shows the same addends
in a different order? (CC.1.OA.3)

$$3 + 1 = 4$$

$2 + 2 = 4$	$1 + 3 = 4$	$4 + 1 = 5$	$3 + 2 = 5$
○	○	○	○

10. What is the sum? (CC.1.OA.3)

$$3 + 2 = 5 \qquad 2 + 3 = \boxed{}$$

2	3	5	7
○	○	○	○

11. Which is a way to make 8? (CC.1.OA.1)

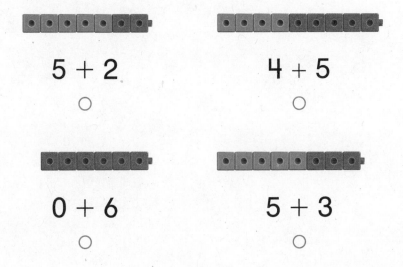

5 + 2   4 + 5
  ○   ○

0 + 6   5 + 3
  ○   ○

12. What is the sum? (CC.1.OA.6)

$$\begin{array}{r} 6 \\ +3 \\ \hline \end{array}$$

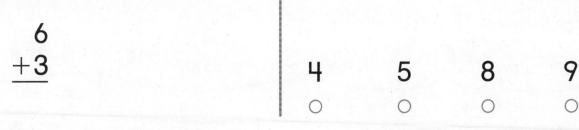

4	5	8	9
○	○	○	○

Performance Task (CC.1.OA.1, CC.1.OA.3)

Katie is drawing dot cards and writing addition sentences with a sum of 8. How many different dot cards can Katie draw?

- Draw the dot cards.
- Write the addition sentence for each dot card.
- Show all the ways to make 8.

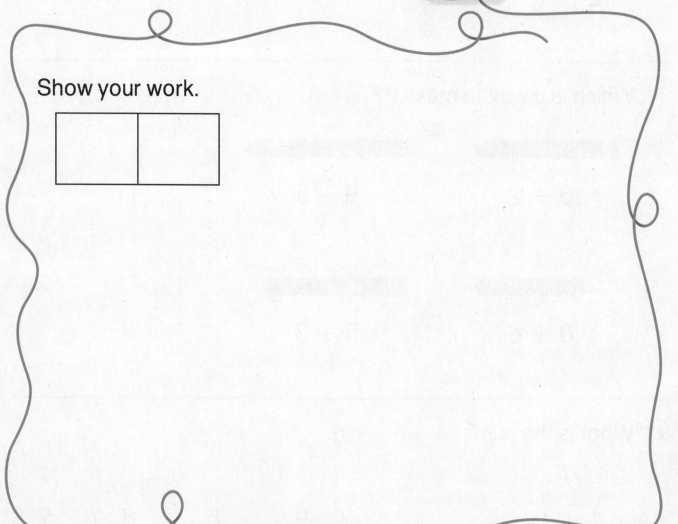

Show your work.

Curious About Math with
Curious George

Look at the picture.
Make up a subtraction
story problem.

Name _____

Explore Numbers 1 to 4

Show the number with 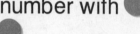.
Draw the 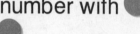.

1.

4

2.

2

Numbers 1 to 10

How many objects are in each set?

3.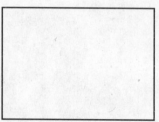

____ butterflies

4.

____ cat

5.

____ leaves

Use Pictures to Subtract

How many are left?

6.

5 − 4 = ____

7.

4 − 2 = ____

Family note: This page checks your child's understanding of important skills needed for success in Chapter 2.

 GO Online   Assessment Options
Soar to Success Math

Vocabulary Builder

Visualize It

Sort the review words from the box.

Subtraction   **Addition**

_____   _____

_____   _____

Understand Vocabulary

Circle the part you take from the group. Then cross it out.

1.

   5 oranges   2 are eaten

2.

   4 balloons   3 fly away

3.

   3 toy cars   I rolls away

Game Subtraction Slide

Materials • 5 ⬤

• 5 ⬤ • 8 ▪

Play with a partner.
Take turns.

1 Toss the .

2 Take away that number
from 8. Use ▪ to find
what is left.

3 If you see the answer on your
slide, cover it with a ⬤.

4 If the answer is not on your
slide, your turn is over.

5 The first player to cover a
whole slide wins.

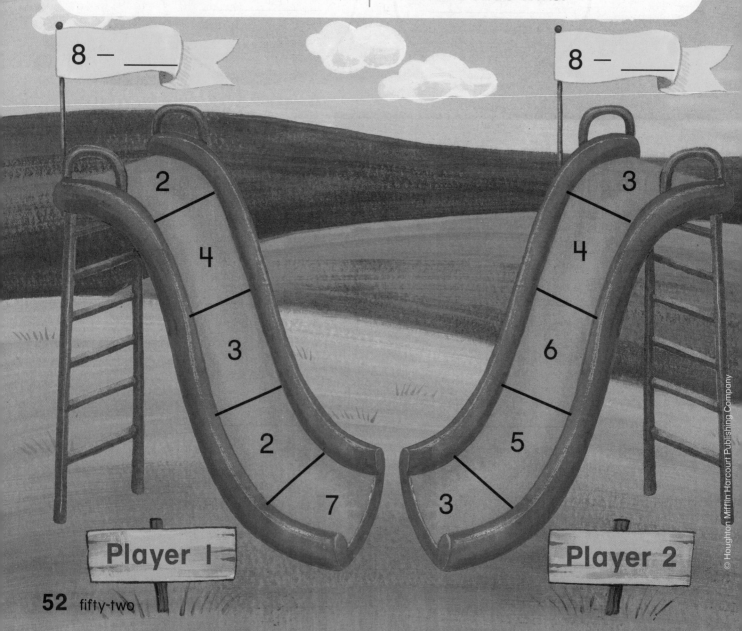

8 – _____

8 – _____

Player 1

2
4
3
2
7

Player 2

3
4
6
5
3

Name _____

Use Pictures to Show Taking From

Essential Question How can you show taking from with pictures?

COMMON CORE STANDARD CC.1.OA.1
Represent and solve problems involving addition and subtraction.

Listen and Draw REAL WORLD

Draw to show taking from.
Write how many there are now.

____ children now

 FOR THE TEACHER • Read the following problem. Have children draw a picture to show the problem. There are 5 children in the sandbox. 2 walk away. How many children are in the sandbox now?

Math Talk
How did you find how many are in the sandbox now? **Explain.**
MATHEMATICAL PRACTICES

Chapter 2

Model and Draw

There are 4 cats in the whole group.

4 cats   I cat walks away.   __3__ cats now

Share and Show

Math Board

Circle the part you are taking from the group.
Then cross it out. Write how many there are now.

☑ 1.

6 bugs   2 bugs fly away.   ____ bugs now

☑ 2.

3 dogs   I dog walks away.   ____ dogs now

Name _____

On Your Own

Circle the part you are taking from the group.
Then cross it out. Write how many there are now.

3.

7 chicks   2 chicks walk away.   _____ chicks now

4.

6 ducks   3 ducks walk away.   _____ ducks now

5.

10 fish   6 fish swim away.   _____ fish now

6. **H.O.T.** Choose numbers to complete the story.
Write the numbers. Draw to show the problem.

_____ worms   _____ worms wiggle away.   3 worms now

PROBLEM SOLVING REAL WORLD

Write Math

Solve.

7. There are 6 cats.
1 cat runs away.
How many cats
are there now?

____ cats

8. There are 5 birds.
3 birds fly away.
How many birds
are there now?

____ birds

9. H.O.T. Use the picture.
Write the numbers.

8 birds   ____ birds fly away.   ____ birds now

10. ★ Test Prep There are 7 whales.
2 whales swim away. How many
whales are there now?

2   3   5   9
○   ○   ○   ○

TAKE HOME ACTIVITY · Have your child draw and solve the
subtraction problem: There are 6 cows. 3 cows walk away.
How many cows are there now?

56 fifty-six

FOR MORE PRACTICE:
Standards Practice Book, pp. P23–P24

Name _____

Model Taking From

Essential Question How do you model taking from a group?

COMMON CORE STANDARD CC.1.OA.1
Represent and solve problems involving addition and subtraction.

Listen and Draw REAL WORLD

Use ▣ to show taking from.
Draw to show your work.

FOR THE TEACHER • Read the following problem. Have children use connecting cubes to model the problem and draw to show their work. There are 9 butterflies. 2 butterflies fly away. How many butterflies are there now?

Math Talk
Are there more than or fewer than 9 butterflies now? **Explain.**

MATHEMATICAL PRACTICES

4 bunnies   3 bunnies hop away.

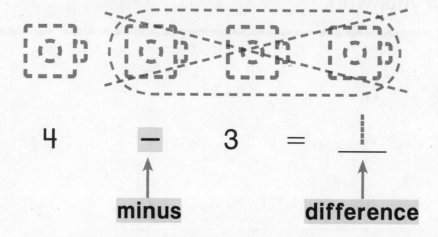

4   —   3   = |

↑ **minus**   ↑ **difference**

4 − 3 = 1 is a **subtraction sentence**.

Share and Show

Use 🔲 to show taking from. Draw the 🔲.
Circle the part you take away from the group.
Then cross it out. Write the difference.

☑ 1. 8 dogs   3 dogs run away.   ☑ 2. 6 frogs   4 frogs hop away.

8 − 3 = ___   6 − 4 = ___

Name _____

On Your Own

Use  to show taking from. Draw the ▣.
Circle the part you take away from the group.
Then cross it out. Write the difference.

3. 5 seals   4 seals swim away.

$5 - 4 =$ ___

4. 9 bears   6 bears run away.

$9 - 6 =$ ___

5. 7 owls   I owl flies away.

$7 - 1 =$ ___

6. 8 snails   6 snails crawl away.

$8 - 6 =$ ___

7. ☀H.O.T.☀ Use the picture. Circle a part to take
from the group. Then cross it out. Write the
subtraction sentence.

___ ◯ ___ ◯ ___

PROBLEM SOLVING REAL WORLD

Write Math

Draw to solve. Complete the subtraction sentence.

8. There are 5 boys.
3 boys go home.
How many are
there now?

___ − ___ = ___

____ boys

9. There are 8 bunnies.
2 bunnies hop away.
How many bunnies
are there now?

___ − ___ = ___

____ bunnies

10. **H.O.T.** Draw a picture to show a
subtraction sentence. Write the
subtraction sentence.

___ − ___ = ___

11. ⭐**Test Prep** What is the difference?

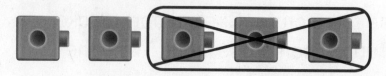

2   3   5   8
○   ○   ○   ○

TAKE HOME ACTIVITY · Use pennies or other small objects of
the same kind to model a subtraction situation for numbers
within 10. Ask your child to write the subtraction sentence for it.
Then switch roles and repeat the activity.

FOR MORE PRACTICE:
Standards Practice Book, pp. P25–P26

Name _____

Model Taking Apart

Essential Question How do you model taking apart?

COMMON CORE STANDARD CC.1.OA.1
Represent and solve problems involving addition and subtraction.

Listen and Draw

Use ⬤ to model the problem. Draw and color to show your model. Write the numbers and a subtraction sentence.

_____ red apples   _____ yellow apples

$$\underline{}\;5\; \underline{} \;\ominus\; \underline{}\;3\;\underline{} \;\text{⊜}\; \underline{}$$

Jeff has _____ yellow apples.

FOR THE TEACHER • Have children model the problem using counters. Jeff has 5 apples. 3 apples are red. The rest are yellow. How many apples are yellow?

Math Talk
How did you solve this problem? **Explain.**

MATHEMATICAL PRACTICES

Subtract to find how many small cups there are.

Mary has 6 cups. 2 cups are big. The rest are small. How many cups are small?

_____ small cups

 **Share and Show** Math Board

Use ● to solve. Draw to show your work.
Write the number sentence and how many.

1. There are 7 folders. 6 folders are red. The rest are yellow. How many folders are yellow?

____ yellow folder

2. There are 8 pencils. 3 pencils are short. The rest are long. How many pencils are long?

____ long pencils

Name _____

On Your Own

Use  to solve. Draw to show your work.
Write the number sentence and how many.

3. There are 9 fish. 5 fish have
   spots. The rest have stripes.
   How many fish have stripes?

   _____ striped fish   ___ ◯ ___ ◯ ___

4. There are 7 ants. 4 ants are
   big. The rest are small.
   How many ants are small?

   _____ small ants   ___ ◯ ___ ◯ ___

5. There are 8 hats. 2 hats
   are small. The rest are big.
   How many hats are big?

   _____ big hats   ___ ◯ ___ ◯ ___

6. There are 5 trees. I tree
   is short. The rest are tall.
   How many trees are tall?

   _____ tall trees   ___ ◯ ___ ◯ ___

PROBLEM SOLVING

Write Math

Solve. Draw a model to explain.

7. There are 6 bears. 4 are big. The rest are small. How many bears are small?

_____ small bears

8. There are 7 bears. 5 bears walk away. How many bears are there now?

_____ bears

9. **H.O.T.** There are 4 bears. Some are black and some are brown. There are fewer than 2 black bears. How many bears are brown?

_____ brown bears

10. ⭐ **Test Prep** Which number sentence solves the problem? There are 4 buckets. 3 buckets are red. The rest are blue. How many buckets are blue?

$4 + 3 = 7$ ○ $4 - 3 = 1$ ○ $4 - 2 = 2$ ○ $3 + 4 = 7$ ○

TAKE HOME ACTIVITY • Have your child collect a group of up to 10 small objects of the same kind and use them to make up subtraction stories.

FOR MORE PRACTICE:
Standards Practice Book, pp. P27–P28

Name _____

Problem Solving • Model Subtraction

Essential Question How do you solve
subtraction problems by making a model?

COMMON CORE STANDARD CC.1.OA.1
Represent and solve problems involving
addition and subtraction.

Tom has 6 crayons in a box.
He takes 2 crayons out of the box.
How many crayons are in the box now?
How can you use a model to find out?

Unlock the Problem REAL WORLD

What do I need to find?

_____

how many __crayons__ in

the box now

What information do I need to use?

__6__ crayons in a box

__2__ crayons taken out

Show how to solve the problem.

2	4

6

6 − 2 = _____

HOME CONNECTION • Your child used a bar model to help him or her
understand and solve the subtraction problems.

Try Another Problem

Read the problem. Use the model to solve. Complete the model and the number sentence.

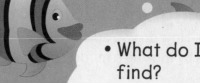

- What do I need to find?
- What information do I need to use?

1. There are 10 stickers. 7 stickers are orange. The rest are brown. How many stickers are brown?

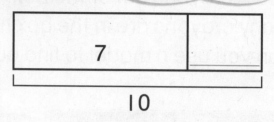

7	

10

$$10 - 7 = \underline{\quad}$$

2. Some birds were in the tree. 2 birds flew away. Then there were 6 birds. How many birds were in the tree before?

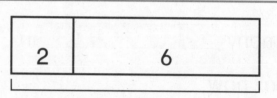

2	6

___

$$\underline{\quad} - 2 = 6$$

3. There were 5 cars. Some cars drove away. Then there was 1 car. How many cars drove away?

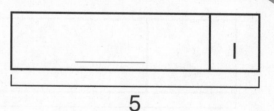

	1

5

$$5 - \underline{\quad} = 1$$

Math Talk
What does each part of the model show?
Explain.

MATHEMATICAL PRACTICES

Name _____

Read the problem. Use the model to solve.
Complete the model and the number sentence.

4. Some goats were in the field. 3 goats ran away. Then there were 4 goats. How many goats were in the field before?

3	4

_____

$$\underline{\quad} - 3 = 4$$

---

5. There are 8 sleds. Some sleds slide down the hill. Then there were 4 sleds. How many sleds slide down the hill?

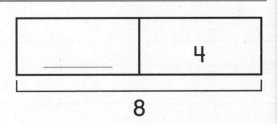

8

$$8 - \underline{\quad} = 4$$

---

6. There are 10 buttons. 3 buttons are small. The rest are big. How many buttons are big?

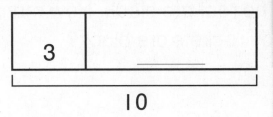

10

$$10 - 3 = \underline{\quad}$$

On Your Own

Solve.

7. There were 8 spiders in the grass. Some spiders crawled away. Then there were 3 spiders. How many spiders crawled away?

____ spiders

8. **H.O.T.** Write your own story problem using the bar model.

	7	2

9

_____

_ _

_____

_ _

_____

9. ⭐ **Test Prep** There are 7 toy rockets. 4 toy rockets are red. The rest are black. How many toy rockets are black?

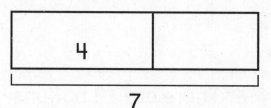

4	

7

2   3   4   7
○   ○   ○   ○

TAKE HOME ACTIVITY • Ask your child to describe what the bottom part of a bar model means when subtracting.

© Houghton Mifflin Harcourt Publishing Company

FOR MORE PRACTICE:
Standards Practice Book, pp. P29–P30

Use Pictures and Subtraction to Compare

Essential Question How can you use pictures to compare and subtract?

COMMON CORE STANDARD CC.1.OA.8
Work with addition and subtraction equations.

Listen and Draw  REAL WORLD

Draw bowls to show the problems.
Draw lines to match.

 FOR THE TEACHER • Read the problem. There are 9 brown dogs. There are 5 bowls. How many more dogs need a bowl? There are 7 white dogs. There are 8 bowls. How many more bowls are not needed?

Math Talk
Explain how many more dogs or bowls there are.

MATHEMATICAL PRACTICES

Model and Draw

Compare the groups.
Subtract to find how many
fewer or how many **more**.

$10 - 7 =$ _____ 3 _____

_____ 3 _____ fewer

$6 - 4 =$ _____

_____ more

Share and Show

Draw lines to match.
Subtract to compare.

1.

$8 - 5 =$ _____

_____ fewer

70 seventy

© Houghton Mifflin Harcourt Publishing Company

Name _____

On Your Own

Draw lines to match. Subtract to compare.

2.

$9 - 3 =$ _____   _____ more

3.

$10 - 6 =$ _____   _____ fewer

4.

$9 - 7 =$ _____   _____ fewer

5.

_____ more

$7 - 2 =$ _____   _____ fewer

PROBLEM SOLVING REAL WORLD

Write Math

Draw a picture to show the problem. Write a subtraction sentence to match your picture.

6. Sam has 5 baseball bats and 3 baseballs. How many fewer baseballs does Sam have?

____ − ____ = ____   ____ fewer

7. **H.O.T.** If Jill has 2 more cats than dogs, how many fewer dogs does Jill have? Draw a picture to explain.

Jill has ____ fewer dogs.

8. ⭐ **Test Prep** How many fewer 🍂 are there?

8 − 5 = ____

2 fewer   3 fewer   5 fewer   8 fewer 🍂
○   ○   ○   ○

 TAKE HOME ACTIVITY · Show your child two groups of up to 10 pennies. Have your child match them to see how many more or how many fewer and then write a subtraction sentence to show the problem.

FOR MORE PRACTICE: Standards Practice Book, pp. P31–P32

Name _____

Subtract to Compare

Essential Question How can you use models to compare and subtract?

COMMON CORE STANDARD CC.1.OA.1
Represent and solve problems involving addition and subtraction.

Listen and Draw REAL WORLD

Use ● to show the problem. Draw the ●.
Model the problem using the bar model.

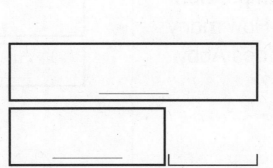

Math Talk
Explain how you find how many more puzzle pieces Mindy has than David.

MATHEMATICAL PRACTICES

FOR THE TEACHER • Read the problem. Mindy has 8 puzzle pieces. David has 5 puzzle pieces. How many more puzzle pieces does Mindy have than David?

Chapter 2

Model and Draw

James has 4 stones. Heather has 7 stones. How many fewer stones does James have than Heather?

```
┌─────────────────┐
│        _____    │
├─────────────┬───┤
│    _____    │   │
└─────────────┴───┘
         _____
```

_____ fewer stones

◯ _____ ◯ _____ _____

Share and Show Math Board

Read the problem. Use the bar model to solve. Write the number sentence. Then write how many.

1. Abby has 8 stamps. Ben has 6 stamps. How many more stamps does Abby have than Ben?

```
┌──────────────────────┐
│        _____         │
├──────────────────┬───┤
│     _____        │   │
└──────────────────┴───┘
               _____
```

_____ more stamps

_____ ◯ _____ ◯ _____

2. Tanner has 3 books. Vicky has 6 books. How many fewer books does Tanner have than Vicky?

```
┌──────────────────────┐
│        _____         │
├──────────┬───────────┤
│  _____   │           │
└──────────┴───────────┘
                 _____
```

_____ fewer books

_____ ◯ _____ ◯ _____

© Houghton Mifflin Harcourt Publishing Company

On Your Own

Read the problem. Use the bar model to solve.
Write the number sentence. Then write how many.

3. Pam has 4 marbles. Rick
has 10 marbles. How many
fewer marbles does Pam
have than Rick?

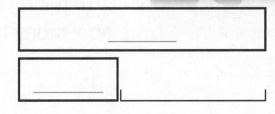

____ fewer marbles

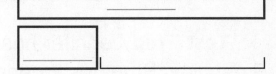

4. Sally has 5 feathers. James
has 2 feathers. How many
more feathers does Sally
have than James?

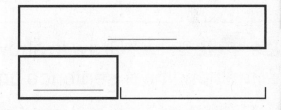

____ more feathers

5.  Kyle has 6 keys.
Kyle has 4 more keys than
Lee. How many keys does
Lee have?

____ keys

TAKE HOME ACTIVITY • Have your child explain how he or she solved
exercise 3 using the bar model.

FOR MORE PRACTICE:
Standards Practice Book, pp. P33–P34

✓ Mid-Chapter Checkpoint

Concepts and Skills

Circle the part you are taking from the group. Then
cross it out. Write how many there are now. (CC.1.OA.1)

1.

7 birds   3 birds fly away.   _____ birds now

Use ⬤ to solve. Draw to show your work.
Write the number sentence and how many. (CC.1.OA.1)

2. There are 4 cans. 1 can is red.
    The rest are yellow. How many
    cans are yellow?

_____ yellow cans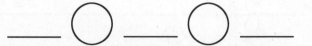

---

3. ⭐ **Test Prep** Jennifer has
    3 pennies. Brad has 9 pennies.
    How many fewer pennies does
    Jennifer have than Brad? (CC.1.OA.1)

	9
3	

3   5   6   9
○   ○   ○   ○

Name _____

Subtract All or Zero

Essential Question What happens when you subtract 0 from a number?

COMMON CORE STANDARD CC.1.OA.8
Work with addition and subtraction equations.

Listen and Draw  REAL WORLD

Use ● to show the problem. Draw the ●.
Write the numbers.

_____ – _____ = _____

_____ – _____ = _____

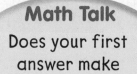

Math Talk
Does your first answer make sense? **Explain.**

MATHEMATICAL PRACTICES

FOR THE TEACHER • Read the following problem. 4 toys are on the shelf. 0 toys are taken off. How many toys are on the shelf? Then read the following problem. 4 toys are on the shelf. 4 toys are taken off. How many toys are there now?

When you subtract zero,
how many are left?

$$\underline{5} - 0 = \underline{5}$$

When you subtract all,
how many are left?

$$\underline{5} - \underline{5} = 0$$

Share and Show

Use the picture to complete the
subtraction sentence.

1.

$$\underline{} - 0 = \underline{}$$

2.

$$\underline{} - \underline{} = 0$$

3.

$$\underline{} - \underline{} = 0$$

4.

$$\underline{} - 0 = \underline{}$$

5.

$$\underline{} - 0 = \underline{}$$

6.

$$\underline{} - \underline{} = 0$$

Name _____

On Your Own

Complete the subtraction sentence.

7.

1 − 0 = ___

8.

___ = 6 − 6

9.

0 = ___ − 3

10.

1 − 1 = ___

11.

3 − 0 = ___

12.

___ = 8 − 0

13.

7 − ___ = 7

14.

8 − 8 = ___

15.

5 − 5 = ___

16.

___ = 0 − 0

H.O.T. Choose numbers to complete the subtraction sentence.

17. ___ − ___ = 0

18. ___ − ___ = 0

PROBLEM SOLVING REAL WORLD

Write Math

Write the number sentence and tell how many.

19. There are 6 bookmarks on the table. 4 are blue and the rest are yellow. How many bookmarks are yellow?

___ ◯ ___ ◯ ___

____ yellow bookmarks

20. Jared has 8 pictures. He gave some to Wendy. Jared has 2 pictures now. How many pictures did Jared give to Wendy?

___ ◯ ___ ◯ ___

____ pictures

21. **H.O.T.** Kevin has 3 fewer leaves than Sandy. Sandy has 3 leaves. How many leaves does Kevin have?

___ ◯ ___ ◯ ___

____ leaves

22. ⭐ **Test Prep** What is the difference for 5 − 0?

  0   1   5   6
  ◯   ◯   ◯   ◯

TAKE HOME ACTIVITY • Have your child explain how 4 − 4 and 4 − 0 are different.

FOR MORE PRACTICE:
Standards Practice Book, pp. P35–P36

Name _____

Algebra • Take Apart Numbers

Essential Question How can you show
all the ways to take apart a number?

COMMON CORE STANDARD CC.1.OA.1
Represent and solve problems involving
addition and subtraction.

Listen and Draw  REAL WORLD

Use ▣ to show all the ways to take apart 5.
Color and draw to show your work.

Take Apart 5

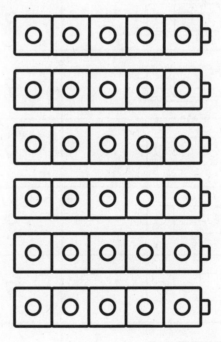

FOR THE TEACHER • Read the following problem
and have children show all the ways to solve the
problem. Jenny has 5 pennies. What are all the
ways she can share the pennies with her sister?

Math Talk
How do you know
you showed all
the ways?
Explain.

MATHEMATICAL
PRACTICES

Model and Draw

Now Jenny has 9 pennies. What are all the ways she can share the pennies with her sister?

> Complete the number sentence.

1. $9 - \underline{0} = \underline{9}$

2. $9 - \underline{1} = \underline{8}$

Share and Show

Use ▣. Color and draw to show how to take apart 9. Complete the subtraction sentence.

> Show all the ways to take apart 9.

3. $9 - \underline{} = \underline{}$

4. $9 - \underline{} = \underline{}$

5. $9 - \underline{} = \underline{}$

6. $9 - \underline{} = \underline{}$

7. $9 - \underline{} = \underline{}$

8. $9 - \underline{} = \underline{}$

9. $9 - \underline{} = \underline{}$

10. $9 - \underline{} = \underline{}$

Name _____

On Your Own

Use ▣. Color and draw to show how to take apart 10. Complete the subtraction sentence.

Show all the ways to take apart 10.

11. ◻◻◻◻◻◻◻◻◻◻ $10 - \underline{} = \underline{}$

12. ◻◻◻◻◻◻◻◻◻◻ $10 - \underline{} = \underline{}$

13. ◻◻◻◻◻◻◻◻◻◻ $10 - \underline{} = \underline{}$

14. ◻◻◻◻◻◻◻◻◻◻ $10 - \underline{} = \underline{}$

15. ◻◻◻◻◻◻◻◻◻◻ $10 - \underline{} = \underline{}$

16. ◻◻◻◻◻◻◻◻◻◻ $10 - \underline{} = \underline{}$

17. ◻◻◻◻◻◻◻◻◻◻ $10 - \underline{} = \underline{}$

18. ◻◻◻◻◻◻◻◻◻◻ $10 - \underline{} = \underline{}$

19. ◻◻◻◻◻◻◻◻◻◻ $10 - \underline{} = \underline{}$

20. ◻◻◻◻◻◻◻◻◻◻ $10 - \underline{} = \underline{}$

21. ◻◻◻◻◻◻◻◻◻◻ $10 - \underline{} = \underline{}$

PROBLEM SOLVING REAL WORLD

Write Math

22. **H.O.T.** I use 6 marbles to play a game.
I lose marbles 1 at a time.
Now I have 0 marbles.

How many marbles do I have left
each time? Write the numbers.

Start	Lose	Difference

23. ⭐ **Test Prep** Which shows a way
to take apart 9?

$10 - 1 = 9$	$10 - 9 = 1$	$9 + 9 = 18$	$9 - 1 = 8$
○	○	○	○

TAKE HOME ACTIVITY • Write $5 - 0 = 5$ and $5 - 1 = 4$.
Ask your child to subtract from 5 another way. Take turns
to show all the ways to subtract from 5.

FOR MORE PRACTICE:
Standards Practice Book, pp. P37–P38

Name _____

Subtraction from 10 or Less

Essential Question Why are some subtraction facts easy to subtract?

COMMON CORE STANDARD CC.1.OA.6
Add and subtract within 20.

Listen and Draw REAL WORLD

Draw a picture to show the problem. Then write the subtraction problem two different ways.

___ − ___ = ___

$$\boxed{} \\ -\,\boxed{} \\ \boxed{}$$

___ − ___ = ___

$$\boxed{} \\ -\,\boxed{} \\ \boxed{}$$

FOR THE TEACHER • Read the following problem for the top section. There are 5 birds in a tree. 2 birds flew away. How many birds are still in the tree? Read the following problem for the bottom section. Steve has 6 crayons. He gives 4 to Matt. How many crayons does Steve have now?

Math Talk
Look at the top problem. **Explain** why the difference is the same.
MATHEMATICAL PRACTICES

Write the subtraction problem.

 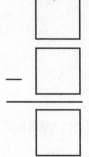

$$\begin{array}{r} \square \\ -\ \square \\ \hline \square \end{array}$$

 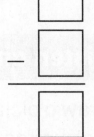

$$\begin{array}{r} \square \\ -\ \square \\ \hline \square \end{array}$$

Share and Show

Write the subtraction problem.

1.

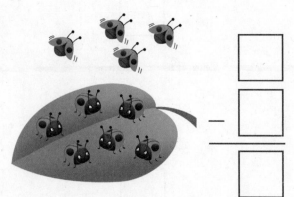

$$\begin{array}{r} \square \\ -\ \square \\ \hline \square \end{array}$$

2.

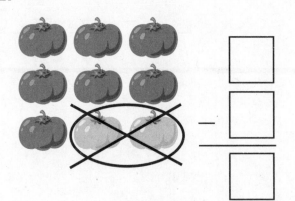

$$\begin{array}{r} \square \\ -\ \square \\ \hline \square \end{array}$$

☑ 3.

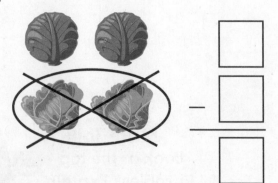

$$\begin{array}{r} \square \\ -\ \square \\ \hline \square \end{array}$$

☑ 4.

$$\begin{array}{r} \square \\ -\ \square \\ \hline \square \end{array}$$

Name _____

On Your Own

Write the difference.

5. 2
   − 1
   ___

6. 3
   − 3
   ___

7. 5
   − 4
   ___

8. 7
   − 3
   ___

9. 6
   − 2
   ___

10. 10
   − 7
   ___

11. 9
   − 9
   ___

12. 8
   − 2
   ___

13. 7
   − 4
   ___

14. 6
   − 3
   ___

15. 8
   − 0
   ___

16. 9
   − 4
   ___

17. 8
   − 7
   ___

18. 7
   − 5
   ___

19. 8
   − 6
   ___

20. 10
   − 1
   ___

21. 6
   − 5
   ___

22. 9
   − 7
   ___

23. **Explain** how the picture shows subtraction.

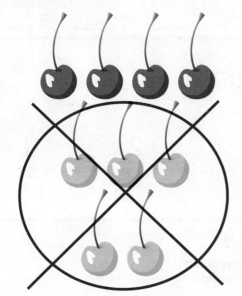

_____

_____

_____

_____

PROBLEM SOLVING REAL WORLD

Write Math

24. **H.O.T.** Draw a picture to show subtraction. Write the subtraction problem to match the picture.

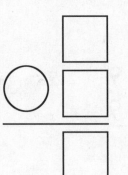

25. Write the number sentence.

I0 ducks are at the pond.
All the ducks fly away.
How many ducks are
still at the pond?

_____ − _____ = _____

26. ⭐ **Test Prep** What is the difference?

$$\begin{array}{r} 7 \\ -3 \\ \hline \end{array}$$

4   3   2   1
○   ○   ○   ○

TAKE HOME ACTIVITY • Tell your child a subtraction problem. Have your child write the problem to subtract two different ways. Then have your child find the difference.

FOR MORE PRACTICE:
Standards Practice Book, pp. P39–P40

 **Chapter 2 Review/Test**

Vocabulary

Circle the **minus** sign. (p. 58)
Underline the **difference**. (p. 58)

1. $5 - 2 = 3$

Concepts and Skills

Circle the part you are taking from the group.
Then cross it out. Write how many there are now. (CC.1.OA.1)

2.

5 zebras   3 zebras walk away.   ____ zebras now

Use  to show taking from. Draw the ■.
Circle the part you take away from the group.
Then cross it out. Write the difference. (CC.1.OA.1)

3. 6 cats   3 cats run away.   4. 5 dogs   4 dogs run away.

$6 - 3 =$ ___ $5 - 4 =$ ___

5. **What is the difference?** (CC.1.OA.1)

$$5 - 2 = \underline{}$$

1	2	3	4
○	○	○	○

6. Which number sentence solves the problem?
There are 6 toy cars. 4 toy cars are big.
The rest are small. How many toy cars
are small? (CC.1.OA.1)

$6 - 4 = 2$	$4 + 4 = 8$	$3 + 3 = 6$	$6 + 4 = 10$
○	○	○	○

7. There are 9 flowers. 5 flowers are
pink. The rest are yellow. How
many flowers are yellow? (CC.1.OA.1)

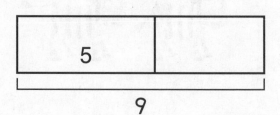

2	3	4	9
○	○	○	○

8. How many fewer bats are there? (CC.1.OA.8)

$$10 - 3 = \underline{}$$

10 fewer	7 fewer	4 fewer	3 fewer
○	○	○	○

9. Mandy has 2 rocks.
   Peter has 8 rocks.
   How many more rocks
   does Peter have
   than Mandy? (CC.1.OA.1)

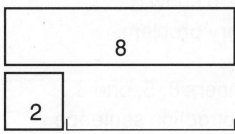

2   6   7   8
○   ○   ○   ○

----

10. What number completes the
    subtraction sentence?

    (CC.1.OA.8)

    4 – ___ = 4

    0   1   2   4
    ○   ○   ○   ○

----

11. Which shows a way
    to take apart 7? (CC.1.OA.1)

    7 + 7 = 14 | 8 – 1 = 7 | 7 – 2 = 5 | 9 – 7 = 2
    ○   ○   ○   ○

----

12. What is the difference?

    (CC.1.OA.6)

    $\begin{array}{r} 9 \\ -5 \\ \hline \end{array}$

    2   3   4   5
    ○   ○   ○   ○

Performance Task (CC.1.OA.1)

Draw a picture to show a
subtraction story problem.

- Use the numbers 8, 5, and 3.
- Write the subtraction sentence.
- Tell or write your story problem.

Show your work.

Curious About Math with
Curious George

There are 4 fish in the tank. If you doubled the number of fish, how many would there be?

Name _____

Show What You Know ✓

Model Addition

Use to show each number. Draw the cubes.
Write how many in all.

1.

$$2 \qquad + \qquad 3$$

_ _ _ _ _ _ _

Use Symbols to Add

Use the picture. Write the addition sentence.

2.

___ ◯ ___ ◯ ___

3.

___ ◯ ___ ◯ ___

Add in Any Order

Use and to add. Color to match.
Write each sum.

4.
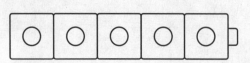

$$1 + 4 = \text{\_\_\_}$$

5.
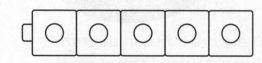

$$4 + 1 = \text{\_\_\_}$$

Family note: This page checks your child's understanding
of important skills needed for success in Chapter 3.

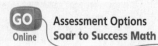

GO
Online   Assessment Options
          Soar to Success Math

© Houghton Mifflin Harcourt Publishing Company

Name _____

Vocabulary Builder

Review Words
add
addends
addition
   sentence
sum

Visualize It

Write the addends and the sum for
the addition sentence.

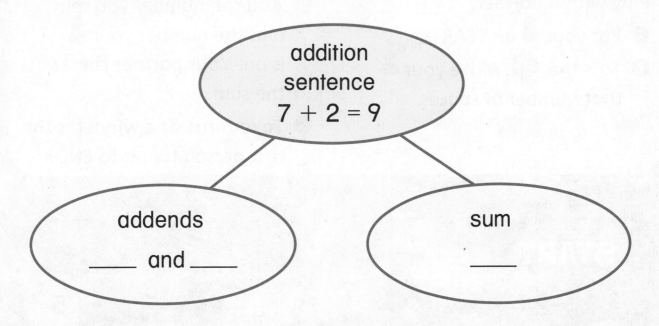

addition
sentence
7 + 2 = 9

addends

____ and ____

sum

____

Understand Vocabulary

Use a review word to complete the sentence.

1. 4 and 3 in 4 + 3 = 7 are _____.

2. 4 + 3 = 7 is an _____.

3. 4 cubes and 3 cubes are put together to

_____ the groups.

Game Ducky Sums

Materials • • ✏️ • 📎
• 👥 •

Play with a partner.

1 Put your ♟ on START.

2 Toss the . Move your ♟ that number of spaces.

3 Use a ⊕, a 📎, and a ✏️ to make the spinner. Spin.

4 Add the number you spin and the number your ♟ is on. Your partner checks the sum.

5 Take turns. The winner is the first person to get to END.

START

8 9 4 6 5

7 6 9 5 8 3 7

4

8

3 6 5 7 9

END

Name _____

Algebra • Add in Any Order

Essential Question What happens if you change the order of the addends when you add?

COMMON CORE STANDARD CC.1.OA.3
Understand and apply properties of operations and the relationship between addition and subtraction.

Listen and Draw REAL WORLD

Use and _____. Color to model the problem.
Write the addition sentence.

_____ + _____ = _____

Use _____ and _____. Color to change the order.
Write the addition sentence.

_____ + _____ = _____

FOR THE TEACHER • Read the problem. George sees 7 blue birds and 8 red birds. How many birds does he see? Help children work through changing the order of the addends.

Math Talk
Explain how knowing the fact 7 + 8 helps you find 8 + 7.

MATHEMATICAL PRACTICES

Chapter 3

Model and Draw

If you use the same addends, what other fact can you write?

$$5$$
$$+6$$

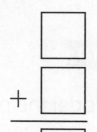

$+$ ☐ ☐ / ☐

Share and Show

Add. Change the order of the addends. Add again.

1.

$$8$$
$$+9$$

$+$ ☐ ☐ / ☐

2.

$$6$$
$$+7$$

$+$ ☐ ☐ / ☐

3.

$$7$$
$$+5$$

$+$ ☐ ☐ / ☐

4.

$$2$$
$$+8$$

$+$ ☐ ☐ / ☐

✔ 5.

$$9$$
$$+2$$

$+$ ☐ ☐ / ☐

✔ 6.

$$8$$
$$+4$$

$+$ ☐ ☐ / ☐

Name _____

On Your Own

Add. Change the order of
the addends. Add again.

7.

$$\begin{array}{r} 9 \\ +6 \\ \hline \end{array}$$ ☐
+ ☐
☐

8.

$$\begin{array}{r} 0 \\ +6 \\ \hline \end{array}$$ ☐
+ ☐
☐

9.

$$\begin{array}{r} 8 \\ +3 \\ \hline \end{array}$$ ☐
+ ☐
☐

10.

$$\begin{array}{r} 5 \\ +9 \\ \hline \end{array}$$ ☐
+ ☐
☐

11.

$$\begin{array}{r} 4 \\ +5 \\ \hline \end{array}$$ ☐
+ ☐
☐

12.

$$\begin{array}{r} 8 \\ +5 \\ \hline \end{array}$$ ☐
+ ☐
☐

13.

$$\begin{array}{r} 9 \\ +1 \\ \hline \end{array}$$ ☐
+ ☐
☐

14.

$$\begin{array}{r} 7 \\ +9 \\ \hline \end{array}$$ ☐
+ ☐
☐

15.

$$\begin{array}{r} 4 \\ +6 \\ \hline \end{array}$$ ☐
+ ☐
☐

16. **Explain** If Adam knows $4 + 7 = 11$,
what other addition fact does he know?
Write the new fact in the box. Tell how
Adam knows the new fact.

_____

_____

PROBLEM SOLVING REAL WORLD

Write Math

Write two addition sentences you can use to solve the problem. Write the answer.

17. Roy sees 4 big fish and 9 small fish. How many fish does Roy see?

___ fish

___ + ___ = ___

___ + ___ = ___

18. Justin has 6 dimes. He gets 8 more dimes. How many dimes does he have now?

___ dimes

___ + ___ = ___

___ + ___ = ___

19. H.O.T. Anna has two groups of pennies. She has 10 pennies in all. When she changes the order of the addends, the addition sentence is the same. What sentence can Anna write?

___ = ___ + ___

20. ★ Test Prep Which shows the same addends in a different order?

$$9 + 3 = 12$$

$6 + 3 = 9$ | $3 + 9 = 12$ | $4 + 8 = 12$ | $3 + 8 = 11$

○ | ○ | ○ | ○

TAKE HOME ACTIVITY · Ask your child to explain what happens to the sum when you change the order of the addends.

FOR MORE PRACTICE:
Standards Practice Book, pp. P45–P46

Count On

Essential Question How do you count on 1, 2, or 3?

COMMON CORE STANDARD **CC.1.OA.5**
Add and subtract within 20.

Start at 9. How can you count on to add?

Add 1.

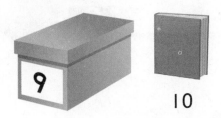

10

$9 + 1 =$ ___

Add 2.

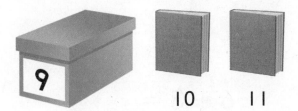

10   11

$9 + 2 =$ ___

Add 3.

10   11   12

$9 + 3 =$ ___

FOR THE TEACHER • Read the problem and use the top workspace to solve. Sam has 9 books in a box. He gets 1 more. How many books does he have? Repeat for the other two workspaces, saying, *He gets 2 more.* and *He gets 3 more.*

Math Talk
How is counting on 2 like adding 2? **Explain.**

MATHEMATICAL PRACTICES

Chapter 3

one hundred one **101**

You can **count on** to add 1, 2, or 3.
Start with the greater addend.

6   7   8

3 + ⑤ = 8

Start with 5.
Count on 3.

Share and Show

Circle the greater addend. Draw   to
count on 1, 2, or 3. Write the sum.

1.

2 + ⑥ = 8

2.

6 + 3 = ___

3.

___ = 1 + 6

4.

___ = 7 + 1

☑5.

2 + 7 = ___

☑6.

___ = 7 + 3

Name _____

On Your Own

Circle the greater addend.
Count on to find the sum.

7. 1
    + 9
    ____

8. 8
    + 3
    ____

9. 1
    + 8
    ____

10. 1
    + 6
    ____

11. 9
    + 3
    ____

12. 7
    + 2
    ____

13. 2
    + 6
    ____

14. 5
    + 3
    ____

15. 7
    + 1
    ____

16. 3
    + 7
    ____

17. 9
    + 2
    ____

18. 3
    + 4
    ____

19. 4
    + 1
    ____

20. 2
    + 8
    ____

21. 2
    + 4
    ____

22. 5
    + 2
    ____

23. 3
    + 6
    ____

24. 5
    + 1
    ____

25. 9
    + 3
    ____

26. 2
    + 7
    ____

27. 6
    + 2
    ____

28. 3
    + 4
    ____

29. 8
    + 1
    ____

30. 3
    + 5
    ____

31. **Explain** Terry added 3 and 7.
    He got a sum of 9. His answer
    is **not** correct. Describe how
    Terry can find the correct sum.

_____

_ _

_____

_ _

PROBLEM SOLVING REAL WORLD

Write Math

Draw to solve. Write the addition sentence.

32. Cindy and Joe pick 8 oranges.
Then they pick 3 more oranges.
How many oranges do they pick?

_____ + _____ = _____ oranges

Which three numbers can you use
to complete the problem?

33. H.O.T. Jennifer has _____ stamps.

She gets _____ more stamps.
How many stamps does she have now?

_____ + _____ = _____ stamps

34. ⭐ Test Prep Count on to solve 3 + 8.

10	11	12	13
○	○	○	○

TAKE HOME ACTIVITY • Have your child tell you how to
count on to find the sum for 6 + 3.

104 one hundred four

FOR MORE PRACTICE:
Standards Practice Book, pp. P47–P48

Name _____

Add Doubles

Essential Question What are doubles facts?

Listen and Draw REAL WORLD

Use . Draw to solve.
Write the addition sentence.

___ + ___ = ___

Math Talk
Describe how your model shows a doubles fact.
MATHEMATICAL PRACTICES

FOR THE TEACHER • Read the following problem. Sal built two towers. Each tower has 4 cubes. How many cubes does Sal use to build both towers?

© Houghton Mifflin Harcourt Publishing Company

Model and Draw

Why are these **doubles** facts?

$$\begin{array}{r} 1 \\ + 1 \\ \hline 2 \end{array}$$

$$\begin{array}{r} 2 \\ + 2 \\ \hline \end{array}$$

Share and Show

Use ◾. Draw ◾ to show your work.
Write the sum.

1.
$$\begin{array}{r} 3 \\ + 3 \\ \hline \end{array}$$

2.
$$\begin{array}{r} 4 \\ + 4 \\ \hline \end{array}$$

☑ 3.
$$\begin{array}{r} 5 \\ + 5 \\ \hline \end{array}$$

☑ 4.
$$\begin{array}{r} 6 \\ + 6 \\ \hline \end{array}$$

Name _____

On Your Own

Use ▪. Draw ▪ to show your work.
Write the sum.

5.   7
    + 7
    _____

6.   8
    + 8
    _____

7. ☀H.O.T.☀ Look back at Exercises 1–6.
Write the fact that would be next in the
pattern. Draw ▪ to show your work.

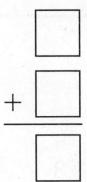

Add.

8. 5	9. 7	10. 6	11. 10	12. 4	13. 8
+ 5	+ 7	+ 6	+ 10	+ 4	+ 8

PROBLEM SOLVING REAL WORLD

Write Math

Write a doubles fact to solve.

14. Meg and Paul each put 8 apples into a basket. How many apples are in the basket?

_____ + _____ = _____

15. **H.O.T.** There are 18 people at the party. Some are boys and some are girls. The number of boys is the same as the number of girls.

_____ = _____ + _____

16. ⭐ **Test Prep** Which is a doubles fact?

7	6	5	4
+1	+0	+5	+3
8	6	10	7
○	○	○	○

TAKE HOME ACTIVITY • Have your child choose a number from 1 to 10 and use that number in a doubles fact. Repeat with other numbers.

FOR MORE PRACTICE:
Standards Practice Book, pp. P49–P50

Use Doubles to Add

Essential Question How can you use doubles to help you add?

COMMON CORE STANDARD **CC.1.OA.6**
Add and subtract within 20.

Listen and Draw REAL WORLD

Draw to show the problem.
Write the number of fish.

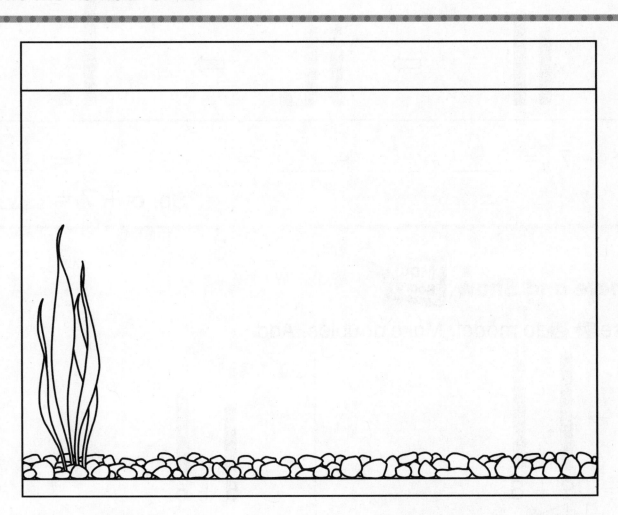

There are ____ fish.

Math Talk
How does knowing
3 + 3 help you
solve the problem?
Explain.

MATHEMATICAL
PRACTICES

FOR THE TEACHER • Read the following problem.
There are 3 orange fish, 3 striped fish, and 1 white
fish in the class fish tank. How many fish are in the
fish tank?

Chapter 3

one hundred nine **109**

Model and Draw

How can a doubles fact help you solve 6 + 7?

> Break apart the 7.
> 7 is the same
> as 6 + 1.

⇨

> Solve the
> doubles fact,
> 6 + 6.

⇨

> **THINK**
> What is one more
> than 12?

 ⇨ ⇨

$$6 + 7 = \underline{6} + \underline{6} + \underline{1} = \underline{12} + \underline{1} = \underline{13}$$

So, 6 + 7 = _____.

Share and Show

Math Board

Use  to model. Make doubles. Add.

✓ 1.

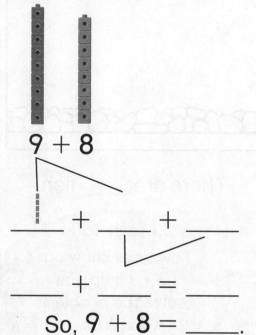

9 + 8

_____ + _____ + _____

_____ + _____ = _____

So, 9 + 8 = _____.

✓ 2.

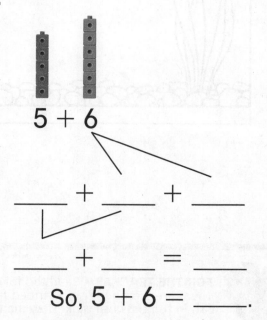

5 + 6

_____ + _____ + _____

_____ + _____ = _____

So, 5 + 6 = _____.

Name _____

On Your Own

Use . Make doubles. Add.

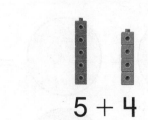

3.

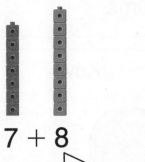

$$7 + 8$$

____ + ____ + ____

So, $7 + 8 = $ ____ .

4.

$$5 + 4$$

____ + ____ + ____

So, $5 + 4 = $ ____ .

Use doubles to help you add.

5. $8 + 9 = $ ____	6. $4 + 5 = $ ____	7. $6 + 7 = $ ____
8. $7 + 6 = $ ____	9. $6 + 5 = $ ____	10. $9 + 8 = $ ____

Explain Would you use count on
or doubles to solve? Why?

11. $3 + 4$

_____
_____
_____
_____

12. $3 + 9$

_____
_____
_____
_____

PROBLEM SOLVING

Write Math

13. H.O.T. Use what you know about doubles to complete the Key. Write the missing sums.

◯ + ◯ = 4

◯ + ● = ____

● + ● = 6

● + ◐ = ____

◐ + ◐ = 8

Key

◯ = ____

● = ____

◐ = ____

14. ⭐ Test Prep Which has the same sum as 9 + 8 ?

○ 6 + 6 + 1

○ 6 + 6 + 2

○ 1 + 8 + 8

○ 2 + 8 + 8

TAKE HOME ACTIVITY • Ask your child to show you how to use what he or she knows about doubles to help solve 6 + 5.

FOR MORE PRACTICE:
Standards Practice Book, pp. P51–P52

© Houghton Mifflin Harcourt Publishing Company

Name _____

Doubles Plus 1 and Doubles Minus 1

Essential Question How can you use what you know
about doubles to find other sums?

COMMON CORE STANDARD CC.1.OA.6
Add and subtract within 20.

Listen and Draw

How can you use the doubles fact, 4 + 4,
to solve each problem? Draw to show how.
Complete the addition sentence.

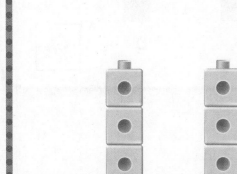

$$4 + \underline{} = 9$$

$$4 + \underline{} = 7$$

FOR THE TEACHER • Read the problems.
Look at the doubles fact, 4 + 4. Draw to
show 1 more in the first workspace. Draw to
show 1 less in the second workspace.

Math Talk
Explain what happens
to the doubles fact when
you increase one addend
by one or decrease one
addend by one.

MATHEMATICAL
PRACTICES

© Houghton Mifflin Harcourt Publishing Company

Model and Draw

Use the doubles fact 5 + 5 to add.

Use **doubles plus one**.
Add 1 to the
doubles fact 5 + 5.

Use **doubles minus one**.
Subtract 1 from the
doubles fact 5 + 5.

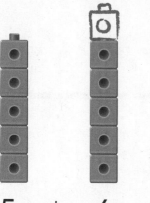

$$5 + 6 = \boxed{11}$$

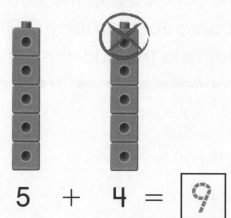

$$5 + 4 = \boxed{9}$$

Share and Show

Use 🔲🔲 to add. Solve the doubles fact.
Then use doubles plus one or doubles minus one.
Circle + or − to show how you solved each one.

1. $2 + 2 = \boxed{}$ $2 + 3 = \boxed{}$ $2 + 1 = \boxed{}$

   doubles $^+_-$ one   doubles $^+_-$ one

2. $3 + 3 = \boxed{}$ $3 + 4 = \boxed{}$ $3 + 2 = \boxed{}$

   doubles $^+_-$ one   doubles $^+_-$ one

3. $4 + 4 = \boxed{}$ $4 + 5 = \boxed{}$ $4 + 3 = \boxed{}$

   doubles $^+_-$ one   doubles $^+_-$ one

On Your Own

Add. Write the doubles fact
you used to solve the problem.

4.　　　$8 + 9 = $ ___
　　○　　　○
___ ○ ___ ○ ___

5.　　　$2 + 3 = $ ___
　　○　　　○
___ ○ ___ ○ ___

6.　　　$7 + 6 = $ ___
　　○　　　○
___ ○ ___ ○ ___

7.　　　$6 + 5 = $ ___
　　○　　　○
___ ○ ___ ○ ___

8.　　　$3 + 4 = $ ___
　　○　　　○
___ ○ ___ ○ ___

9.　　　$4 + 5 = $ ___
　　○　　　○
___ ○ ___ ○ ___

10.　　　$8 + 7 = $ ___
　　○　　　○
___ ○ ___ ○ ___

11.　　　$6 + 7 = $ ___
　　○　　　○
___ ○ ___ ○ ___

12.　　　$9 + 8 = $ ___
　　○　　　○
___ ○ ___ ○ ___

13.　　　$7 + 8 = $ ___
　　○　　　○
___ ○ ___ ○ ___

H.O.T. Add. Write the doubles plus one fact.
Write the doubles minus one fact.

14.　　　$\begin{array}{r} 6 \\ + 6 \\ \hline \end{array}$

doubles plus one	doubles minus one

PROBLEM SOLVING REAL WORLD

Write Math

15. **H.O.T.** Grace wants to write the sums for the doubles plus one and doubles minus one facts. She has started writing sums. Help her find the rest of the sums.

+	0	1	2	3	4	5	6	7	8	9
0	0	1								
1	1	2	3							
2		3	4	5						
3			5	6	7					
4				7	8					
5						10	11			
6						11	12			
7								14	15	
8								15	16	
9										18

16. ⭐ **Test Prep** Which doubles fact helps you solve 6 + 7 = 13?

$5 + 5 = 10$ | $6 + 6 = 12$ | $8 + 8 = 16$ | $9 + 9 = 18$
○   ○   ○   ○

TAKE HOME ACTIVITY • Have your child explain how to use a doubles fact to solve the doubles plus one fact 4 + 5 and the doubles minus one fact 4 + 3.

FOR MORE PRACTICE:
Standards Practice Book, pp. P53–P54

Practice the Strategies

Essential Question What strategies can you use to solve addition fact problems?

COMMON CORE STANDARD CC.1.OA.6
Add and subtract within 20.

Listen and Draw

Think of different addition strategies. Write or draw two ways you can solve $4 + 3$.

$4 + 3 = $ ___	
Way 1	**Way 2**

Math Talk

Explain why the sum is the same when you use different strategies.

MATHEMATICAL PRACTICES

FOR THE TEACHER • Encourage children to use different strategies to show two ways they can solve $4 + 3$. Have children share answers and discuss all strategies.

Model and Draw

These are the ways you have learned to find sums.

 You can count on.

$9 + 1 = \underline{10}$

$9 + 2 = \underline{}$

$9 + 3 = \underline{}$

$5 + 5 = \underline{10}$

$5 + 6 = \underline{}$

$5 + 4 = \underline{}$

You can use doubles, doubles plus 1, and doubles minus 1.

Share and Show

1.

Count On 1
$4 + 1 = \underline{}$
$5 + 1 = \underline{}$
$6 + 1 = \underline{}$
$7 + 1 = \underline{}$

2.

Count On 2
$5 + 2 = \underline{}$
$6 + 2 = \underline{}$
$7 + 2 = \underline{}$
$8 + 2 = \underline{}$

✓ 3.

Count On 3
$6 + 3 = \underline{}$
$7 + 3 = \underline{}$
$8 + 3 = \underline{}$
$9 + 3 = \underline{}$

4.

Doubles
$7 + 7 = \underline{}$
$8 + 8 = \underline{}$
$9 + 9 = \underline{}$
$10 + 10 = \underline{}$

✓ 5.

Doubles Plus One
$5 + 6 = \underline{}$
$6 + 7 = \underline{}$

Doubles Minus One
$8 + 7 = \underline{}$
$9 + 8 = \underline{}$

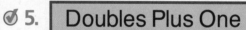

Name _____

On Your Own

Add. Color doubles facts ▬. Color count on facts ▬.
Color doubles plus one or doubles minus one facts ▬.

6.	7.	8.
$9 + 9 =$ ___	$7 + 1 =$ ___	$5 + 3 =$ ___
9.	10.	11.
$2 + 9 =$ ___	$7 + 3 =$ ___	$7 + 7 =$ ___
12.	13.	14.
$6 + 5 =$ ___	$2 + 8 =$ ___	$8 + 8 =$ ___
15.	16.	17.
$8 + 9 =$ ___	$9 + 3 =$ ___	$7 + 8 =$ ___
18.	19.	20.
$3 + 8 =$ ___	$6 + 6 =$ ___	$1 + 9 =$ ___

H.O.T. Make a counting on problem.
Write the missing numbers.

21. _____ birds were in a tree.
 _____ more birds flew there.
 How many birds are in the tree now?

 _____ birds

TAKE HOME ACTIVITY • Have your child point out a doubles fact,
a doubles plus one fact, a doubles minus one fact, and a fact
he or she solved by counting on. Have him or her describe
how each strategy works.

Mid-Chapter Checkpoint

Concepts and Skills

Add. Change the order of
the addends. Add again. (CC.1.OA.3)

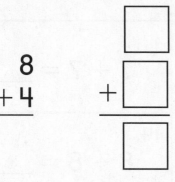

1.

$$\begin{array}{r} 8 \\ +4 \\ \hline \end{array}$$
$$+ \boxed{}$$

2.

$$\begin{array}{r} 7 \\ +9 \\ \hline \end{array}$$
$$+ \boxed{}$$

Circle the greater addend. Count on to find the sum. (CC.1.OA.5)

3. $\begin{array}{r} 1 \\ +8 \\ \hline \end{array}$ | 4. $\begin{array}{r} 3 \\ +7 \\ \hline \end{array}$ | 5. $\begin{array}{r} 9 \\ +2 \\ \hline \end{array}$ | 6. $\begin{array}{r} 6 \\ +3 \\ \hline \end{array}$ | 7. $\begin{array}{r} 7 \\ +1 \\ \hline \end{array}$ | 8. $\begin{array}{r} 2 \\ +8 \\ \hline \end{array}$

Use doubles to help you add. (CC.1.OA.6)

9. $7 + 8 =$ _____ | 10. $6 + 7 =$ _____ | 11. $9 + 8 =$ _____

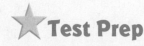 Test Prep

12. Which is the doubles plus one fact for $6 + 6$? (CC.1.OA.6)

| $6 + 6 = 12$ | $6 + 7 = 13$ | $6 + 5 = 11$ | $5 + 7 = 12$ |

○   ○   ○   ○

Name _____

Add 10 and More

Essential Question How can you use
a ten frame to add 10 and some more?

COMMON CORE STANDARD CC.1.OA.6
Add and subtract within 20.

Listen and Draw REAL WORLD

What is 10 + 5? Use ⬤ ⬤ and the ten frame.
Model and draw to solve.

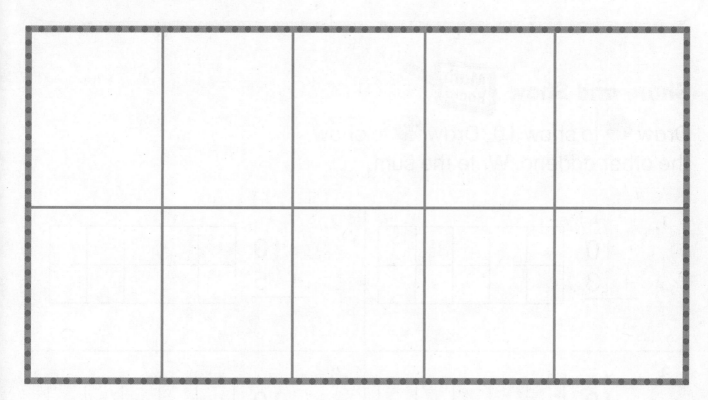

 FOR THE TEACHER • Read the following problem.
Ali has 10 red apples in a bag. She has 5 yellow
apples next to the bag. How many apples
does Ali have?

Math Talk
Explain how
your model
shows 10 + 5.

MATHEMATICAL
PRACTICES

Model and Draw

You can use a ten frame to add $10 + 6$.

$$\begin{array}{r} 10 \\ + \ 6 \\ \hline 16 \end{array}$$

Color the counters to show 10 red. Color the counters to show 6 yellow.

Share and Show 🖊 Math Board

Draw ● to show 10. Draw ○ to show the other addend. Write the sum.

1.
$$\begin{array}{r} 10 \\ + \ 3 \end{array}$$
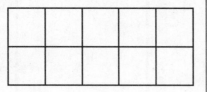

2.
$$\begin{array}{r} 10 \\ + \ 5 \end{array}$$
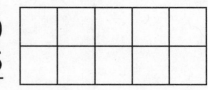

3.
$$\begin{array}{r} 10 \\ + \ 1 \end{array}$$

4.
$$\begin{array}{r} 10 \\ + \ 2 \end{array}$$
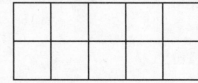

☑ 5.
$$\begin{array}{r} 10 \\ + \ 4 \end{array}$$
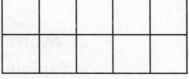

☑ 6.
$$\begin{array}{r} 10 \\ + \ 7 \end{array}$$
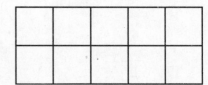

Name _____

On Your Own

Draw 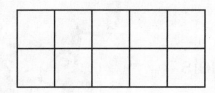 to show 10. Draw ⬤ to show
the other addend. Write the sum.

7. 10
   + 8
   [ten frame grid]

8. 10
   + 2
   [ten frame grid]

9. 10
   + 6
   [ten frame grid]

10. 10
   + 9
   [ten frame grid]

Add.

11. 10
    + 1

12.   4
    +10

13.   5
    +10

14. 10
    + 3

15.   0
    +10

16. 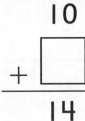 **H.O.T.** Draw ⬤ to show 10. Draw ⬤
    to show the missing addend. Write
    the missing addend.

     10
    +☐
    ―――
     14

    [ten frame grid]

PROBLEM SOLVING

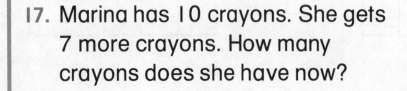

H.O.T. Draw 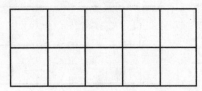 to solve.
Write the addition sentence.
Write to explain your model.

17. Marina has 10 crayons. She gets
7 more crayons. How many
crayons does she have now?

_____ + _____ = _____

_____

_____

_____

_____

18. ⭐ **Test Prep** What number sentence
does this model show?

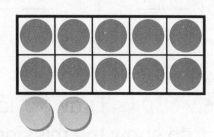

$10 - 2 = 8$ | $10 + 2 = 12$ | $5 + 2 = 7$ | $5 + 1 = 6$

  ○   ○   ○   ○

TAKE HOME ACTIVITY • Have your child choose a number between 1 and 10
and then find the sum of 10 and that number. Repeat using other numbers.

FOR MORE PRACTICE:
Standards Practice Book, pp. P57–P58

Make a 10 to Add

Essential Question How do you use the make a ten strategy to add?

COMMON CORE STANDARD CC.1.OA.6
Add and subtract within 20.

Listen and Draw

What is 9 + 6? Use 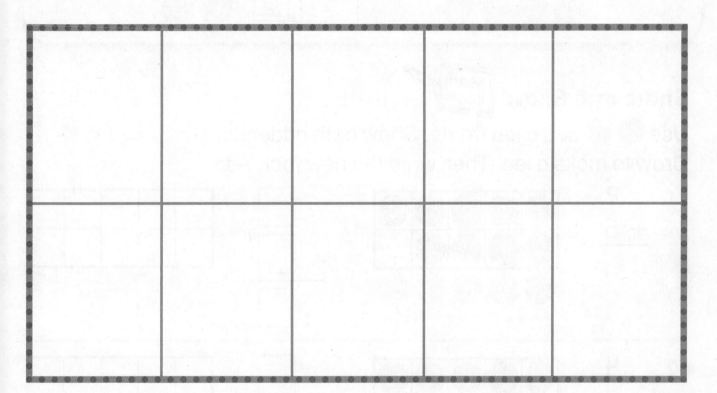 and the ten frame.
Model and draw to solve.

FOR THE TEACHER • Ask children: What is 9 + 6?
Have children use red and yellow counters to model.
Then move one counter from the 6 to make a ten.

Math Talk
Explain why you start by putting 9 counters in the ten frame.
MATHEMATICAL PRACTICES

Chapter 3

Model and Draw

Why do you show 8 in the ten frame to find $4 + 8$?

Put 8 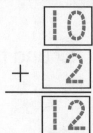 in the ten frame.
Then show 4 .

$$\begin{array}{r} 4 \\ +8 \\ \hline \end{array}$$

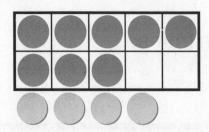

Draw to **make a ten**.
Then write the new fact.

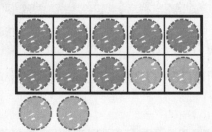

Share and Show

Use and a ten frame. Show both addends.
Draw to make a ten. Then write the new fact. Add.

1.
$$\begin{array}{r} 9 \\ +5 \\ \hline \end{array}$$

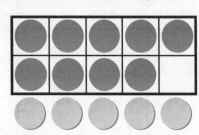

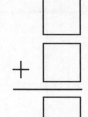

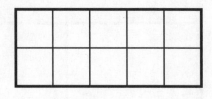

2.
$$\begin{array}{r} 4 \\ +7 \\ \hline \end{array}$$

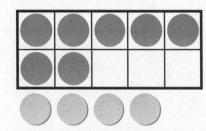

3.
$$\begin{array}{r} 9 \\ +8 \\ \hline \end{array}$$

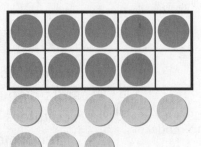

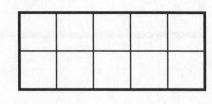

Name _____

Start with the greater addend.

REMEMBER
Start with the greater addend.

On Your Own

Use 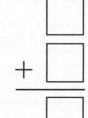 and a ten frame. Show both addends.
Draw to make a ten. Then write the new fact. Add.

4.   5
   + 8

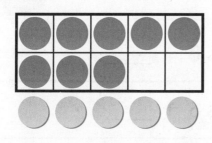   + ☐
             ☐   ☐
                         ☐

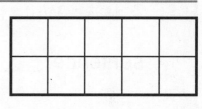

5.   9
   + 6

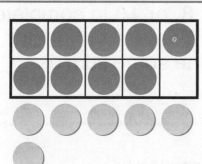   ☐
             + ☐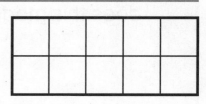
                ☐

6.   7
   + 9

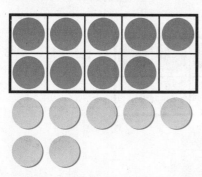   ☐
             + ☐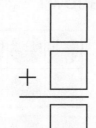
                ☐

7. **Explain** What strategy would you
   choose to solve 7 + 8? Why?

_____

_ _ _ _ _ _ _ _ _ _ _ _ _ _ _ _ _ _ _ _

_____

_ _ _ _ _ _ _ _ _ _ _ _ _ _ _ _ _ _ _ _

_____

PROBLEM SOLVING

Write Math

Solve.

8. 10 + 8 has the same sum as 9 + ____.

9. 10 + 7 has the same sum as 8 + ____.

10. 10 + 5 has the same sum as 6 + ____.

11. **H.O.T.** Write the numbers **6, 8,** or **10** to complete the

sentence. ____ + ____ has the same sum as ____ + 8.

12. ⭐**Test Prep** What number sentence
does this model show?

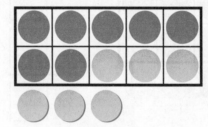

10 − 3 = 7 ○   7 + 2 = 9 ○

10 + 2 = 12 ○   10 + 3 = 13 ○

 TAKE HOME ACTIVITY • Cut off 2 cups from an egg carton
or draw a 5-by-2 grid on a sheet of paper to create a ten
frame. Have your child use small objects to show how to
make a ten to solve 8 + 3, 7 + 6, and 9 + 9.

FOR MORE PRACTICE:
Standards Practice Book, pp. P59–P60

Name _____

Use Make a 10 to Add

Essential Question How can you make a ten
to help you add?

COMMON CORE STANDARD CC.1.OA.6
Add and subtract within 20.

Listen and Draw REAL WORLD

Draw to show the addends. Then draw to show
how to make a ten. Write the sum.

$$\begin{array}{r} 6 \\ + 7 \\ \hline \end{array}$$

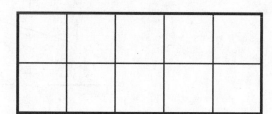

Math Talk
Describe how
the drawings show
how to make a ten
to solve 6 + 7.

MATHEMATICAL
PRACTICES

FOR THE TEACHER • Read the following problem.
Sean has 6 big paper clips and 7 small paper clips.
How many paper clips does he have? Ask children
to draw counters in the ten frames to show how
to solve by making a ten.

Chapter 3

one hundred twenty-nine **129**

Model and Draw

What is 9 + 6?

Start with the greater addend.

Make a ten.

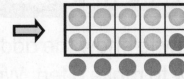

Find the sum.

$$\frac{9}{\;} + \frac{1}{\;} + 5$$

$$\frac{10}{\;} + \frac{5}{\;} = \underline{\quad}$$

So, 6 + 9 = _____.

Share and Show

Write to show how you make a ten. Then add.

1. What is 8 + 4?

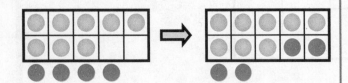

$$\underline{\quad} + \underline{\quad} + 2$$

$$\underline{\quad} + \underline{\quad} = \underline{\quad}$$

So, 8 + 4 = _____.

2. What is 5 + 7?

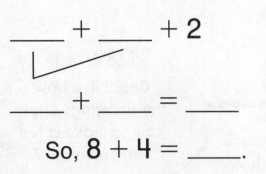

$$\underline{\quad} + \underline{\quad} + 2$$

$$\underline{\quad} + \underline{\quad} = \underline{\quad}$$

So, 5 + 7 = _____.

On Your Own

Write to show how you make a ten. Then add.

3. What is 7 + 8?

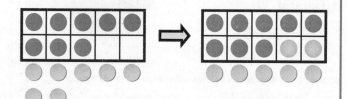

___ + ___ + ___

___ + ___ = ___

So, 7 + 8 = ___.

4. What is 9 + 8?

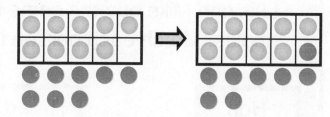

___ + ___ + ___

___ + ___ = ___

So, 9 + 8 = ___.

H.O.T. Use the model. Write to show how you make a ten. Then add.

5.

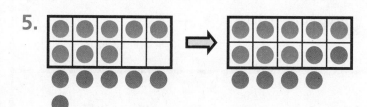

___ + ___ + ___

___ + ___ = ___

So, ___ + ___ = ___.

PROBLEM SOLVING REAL WORLD

Write Math

Use the clues to solve. Draw lines to match.

6. Han, Luis, and Mike buy apples. Mike buys 10 red apples and 4 green apples. Luis and Mike buy the same number of apples. Match each person to his apples.

| Han |
| Luis |
| Mike |

| 10 red apples and 4 green apples |
| 6 red apples and 8 green apples |
| 8 red apples and 7 green apples |

7. **H.O.T.** Look at Exercise 6. Han eats one apple. Now he has the same number of apples as Luis and Mike. How many red and green apples could he have?

_____ red apples and _____ green apples

8. ⭐ **Test Prep** Which way shows how to make a ten to solve 9 + 7?

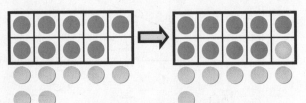

- 5 + 4 + 5
- 7 + 3 + 9
- 9 + 1 + 6
- 9 + 1 + 7

TAKE HOME ACTIVITY • Have your child show you how to make a ten to solve 8 + 7.

FOR MORE PRACTICE:
Standards Practice Book, pp. P61–P62

© Houghton Mifflin Harcourt Publishing Company

Name _____

Algebra • Add 3 Numbers

Essential Question How can you add
three addends?

COMMON CORE STANDARD CC.1.OA.3
Understand and apply properties of
operations and the relationship
between addition and subtraction.

Listen and Draw REAL WORLD

Use ▪ to model the problem.
Draw to show your work.

_____ birds

Math Talk
Which two addends
did you add first?
Explain.

MATHEMATICAL
PRACTICES

FOR THE TEACHER • Read the following problem.
Kelly sees 7 birds. Bill sees 2 birds. Joe sees 3 birds.
How many birds do they see?

Chapter 3

one hundred thirty-three **133**

Model and Draw

$2 + 3 + 1 = \underline{}$

You can change which two addends you add first. The sum stays the same.

Add 2 and 3. Then add 1.

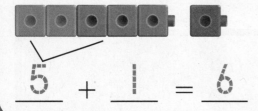

$\underline{5} + \underline{1} = \underline{6}$

Add 3 and 1. Then add 2.

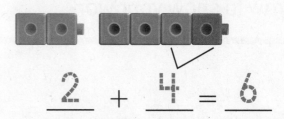

$\underline{2} + \underline{4} = \underline{6}$

Share and Show

Use ▪ ▪ ▪ to change which two addends you add first. Complete the addition sentences.

1. $5 + 2 + 3 = \underline{}$

$\underline{} + \underline{} = \underline{}$

$\underline{} + \underline{} = \underline{}$

2. $3 + 4 + 6 = \underline{}$

$\underline{} + \underline{} = \underline{}$

$\underline{} + \underline{} = \underline{}$

On Your Own

Look at the . Complete the addition sentences showing two ways to find the sum.

3. $7 + 3 + 1 =$ ___

___ + ___ = ___   ___ + ___ = ___

4. $3 + 6 + 3 =$ ___

___ + ___ = ___   ___ + ___ = ___

Solve both ways.

5. $2 + 3 + 7 =$ ___ $2 + 3 + 7 =$ ___

___ + ___ = ___   ___ + ___ = ___

6. **H.O.T.** I used  to model 3 addends. Use my model. Write the 3 addends.

> My Model

___ + ___ + ___ = 7

PROBLEM SOLVING

Write Math

7. **H.O.T.** Choose three numbers from 1 to 6.
Write the numbers in an addition sentence.
Show two ways to find the sum.

8. ⭐ **Test Prep** What is the sum for $2 + 2 + 8$?

10	11	12	20
○	○	○	○

TAKE HOME ACTIVITY • Have your child draw to show
two ways to add the numbers 2, 4, and 6.

FOR MORE PRACTICE:
Standards Practice Book, pp. P63–P64

© Houghton Mifflin Harcourt Publishing Company

Name _____

Algebra • Add 3 Numbers

Essential Question How can you group numbers to add three addends?

COMMON CORE STANDARD CC.1.OA.3
Understand and apply properties of operations and the relationship between addition and subtraction.

Listen and Draw REAL WORLD

Listen to the problem. Show two ways to group and add the numbers.

3	6	3

FOR THE TEACHER • Read the following problem. There are 3 children at one table. There are 6 children at another table. There are 3 children in line. How many children are there?

Math Talk
Describe the two ways you grouped the numbers to add.

MATHEMATICAL PRACTICES

Model and Draw

You can group the addends in any order and in different ways to find the sum.

Add 8 and 2 to use the strategy make a ten. Then add 10 and 6.

Add 6 and 2 to use the strategy count on. Then add doubles 8 and 8.

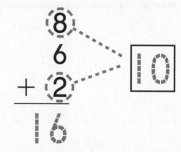

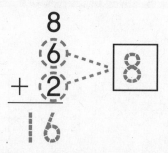

Share and Show

Choose a strategy. Circle two addends to add first. Write the sum. Then find the total sum. Then use a different strategy and add again.

THINK
Use count on, doubles, doubles plus one, doubles minus one, or make a ten to add.

1.
```
  6          6
  4   []     4   []
+ 2        + 2
```

2.
```
  3          3
  4   []     4   []
+ 4        + 4
```

3.
```
  2          2
  5   []     5   []
+ 0        + 0
```

4.
```
  5          5
  4   []     4   []
+ 5        + 5
```

Name _____

On Your Own

Choose a strategy. Circle two addends
to add first. Write the sum.

5.	6.	7.	8.
8 2 + 2	6 0 + 8	3 4 + 6	2 3 + 7

9.	10.	11.	12.
7 7 + 2	1 9 + 1	5 4 + 4	5 5 + 5

13.	14.	15.	16.
3 5 + 2	2 6 + 4	9 9 + 1	1 2 + 8

 Write the missing addends. Add.

17.

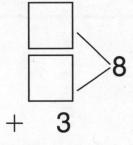

+   3

18.

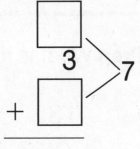

PROBLEM SOLVING REAL WORLD

Write Math

Draw a picture. Write the number sentence.

19. Maria has 3 cats. Jim has 2 cats. Cheryl has 5 cats. How many cats do they have?

_____ + _____ + _____ = _____ cats

_____

20. Tony sees 5 small turtles.
He sees 0 medium turtles.
He sees 4 big turtles.
How many turtles does he see?

_____ + _____ + _____ = _____ turtles

_____

21. H.O.T. Kathy sees 13 fish in the tank. 6 fish are gold. The rest are blue or red. How many of each could she see?

_____ + _____ + 6 = 13 fish

22. ★ **Test Prep** What is the sum of 7 + 4 + 3?

7	13	14	15
○	○	○	○

TAKE HOME ACTIVITY · Have your child look at Exercise 21. Have your child tell you how he or she decided which numbers to use. Have him or her tell you two new numbers that would work.

© Houghton Mifflin Harcourt Publishing Company

FOR MORE PRACTICE:
Standards Practice Book, pp. P65–P66

Name _____

Problem Solving • Use Addition Strategies

Essential Question How do you solve addition word problems by drawing a picture?

COMMON CORE STANDARD **CC.1.OA.2**
Represent and solve problems involving addition and subtraction.

Megan put 8 fish in the tank. Tess put in 2 more fish. Then Bob put in 3 more fish. How many fish are in the tank now?

🔑 Unlock the Problem   REAL WORLD

What do I need to find?

how many _____ fish _____ are in the tank

What information do I need to use?

Megan put in __8__ fish.

Tess put in __2__ fish.

Bob put in __3__ fish.

Show how to solve the problem.

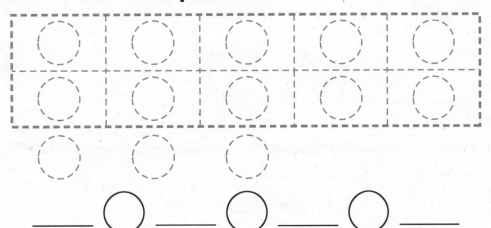

_____ fish

HOME CONNECTION • Your child will continue to use this chart throughout the year to help him or her unlock the problem. In this lesson, your child used the strategy draw a picture to solve problems.

Try Another Problem

Draw a picture to solve.

- What do I need to find?
- What information do I need to use?

I. Mark has 9 green toy cars.
He has 1 yellow toy car.
He also has 5 blue toy cars.
How many toy cars does he have?

____ ◯ ____ ◯ ____ ◯ ____

____ toy cars

Math Talk

Explain how make a ten helps you solve the problem.

MATHEMATICAL PRACTICES

Name _____

Share and Show

Draw a picture to solve.

---

2. Ken put 5 pennies in a jar. Lou put in
   0 pennies. Mae put in 5 pennies. How
   many pennies did they put in the jar?

___ ◯ ___ ◯ ___ ◯ ___   ___ pennies

---

3. Ava has 3 kites. Lexi has 3 kites.
   Fred has 5 kites. How many kites
   do they have?

___ ◯ ___ ◯ ___ ◯ ___   ___ kites

---

4. Al got 8 books at the library. Ryan
   got 7 books. Dee got 1 book. How
   many books do they have?

___ ◯ ___ ◯ ___ ◯ ___   ___ books

---

5. Haley has 6 pencils. Mac has
   4 pencils. Sid has 4 pencils.
   How many pencils do they have?

___ ◯ ___ ◯ ___ ◯ ___   ___ pencils

On Your Own

Solve. Draw or write to show your work.

Model • Reason • Make Sense

6. Kevin has 15 baseball cards. He gives away 8 baseball cards. How many baseball cards does he have?

_____ baseball cards

7. Pete sends 4 letters. Then he sends 3 more letters. Then he sends 2 more letters. How many letters did Pete send?

Dear Jane, I am going to Mexico. I will fly on a plane.

_____ letters

8. H.O.T. 12 marbles are in a bag. Shelly takes 3 marbles. Dan puts in 4. How many marbles are in the bag now?

_____ marbles

9. ★ Test Prep Brooke has 7 pink shells, 8 white shells, and 3 brown shells. How many shells does she have?

10 shells ○   11 shells ○   15 shells ○   18 shells ○

 TAKE HOME ACTIVITY • Ask your child to look at Exercise 8 and tell how he or she found the answer.

144 one hundred forty-four

FOR MORE PRACTICE:
Standards Practice Book, pp. P67–P68

© Houghton Mifflin Harcourt Publishing Company

✓ Chapter 3 Review/Test

Vocabulary

Match each fact to a strategy you would use to solve.

1. $5 + 5 = 10$ •
2. $5 + 2 = 7$ •
3. $5 + 4 = 9$ •
4. $5 + 6 = 11$ •

• **count on** (p. 102)
• **doubles** (p. 106)
• **doubles plus one** (p. 114)
• **doubles minus one** (p. 114)

Concepts and Skills

Use ⬤ ◯ and a ten frame. Show both addends.
Draw to make a ten. Then write the new fact. Add. (CC.1.OA.6)

5.

$$\begin{array}{r} 8 \\ + 7 \\ \hline \end{array}$$

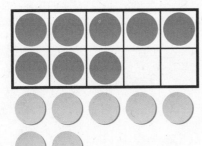 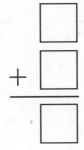 

Look at the . Complete the addition sentences
showing two ways to find the sum. (CC.1.OA.3)

6. $3 + 4 + 5 = $ ___

___ + ___ = ___   ___ + ___ = ___

7. Rick has 10 shells.
He finds 4 more shells.
How many shells does
Rick have now? (CC.1.OA.6)

5 shells   6 shells   10 shells   14 shells
○   ○   ○   ○

---

8. Which number sentence
matches the model? (CC.1.OA.5)

8 + 3 = 11   8 + 4 = 12
○   ○

12 − 3 = 9   11 − 4 = 7
○   ○

---

9. What is the
sum? (CC.1.OA.5)

$\begin{array}{r} 2 \\ + 9 \\ \hline \end{array}$

9   10   11   12
○   ○   ○   ○

---

10. Which doubles fact does
the model show? (CC.1.OA.6)

2 + 2 = 4   3 + 3 = 6
○   ○

4 + 4 = 8   5 + 5 = 10
○   ○

11. What is the sum of the doubles minus one fact? (CC.1.OA.6)

$$\begin{array}{r} 8 \\ + 7 \\ \hline \end{array}$$

13   14   15   16

○   ○   ○   ○

12. What is the missing sum? (CC.1.OA.6)

Count On 3
$6 + 3 = 9$
$7 + 3 = 10$
$8 + 3 = $ ___

13   12   11   10

○   ○   ○   ○

13. Which shows the same addends in a different order? (CC.1.OA.3)

$$\begin{array}{r} 8 \\ + 5 \\ \hline 13 \end{array}$$

$$\begin{array}{r} 8 \\ - 5 \\ \hline 3 \end{array} \qquad \begin{array}{r} 13 \\ - 5 \\ \hline 8 \end{array} \qquad \begin{array}{r} 8 \\ + 5 \\ \hline 13 \end{array} \qquad \begin{array}{r} 5 \\ + 8 \\ \hline 13 \end{array}$$

○   ○   ○   ○

14. Which shows how to use doubles to solve $9 + 8$?

(CC.1.OA.6)

$8 + 8 + 8$ $1 + 8 + 8$

○   ○

$8 + 8 + 9$ $8 + 1 + 9$

○   ○

Performance Task (CC.1.OA.3, CC.1.OA.6)

Ben chooses 3 addends and finds the sum.
He uses the following strategies.

- Add 3 numbers.
- Add doubles.
- Make a 10 to add.
- Add in any order.

Show 3 addends Ben may choose. Solve.
Use numbers, pictures, or words to explain.

Show your work.

Subtraction Strategies

Curious About Math with
Curious George

Six little chicks are on the fence. Two chicks hop away. How many are there now?

Name _____

Show What You Know

Model Subtraction

Use  to show each number.
Take away. Write how many are left.

1.

    5 take away 2   _____

2. 3 take away 1   _____

Use Symbols to Subtract

Use the picture. Write the subtraction sentence.

3.

   ___ ◯ ___ ◯ ___

4.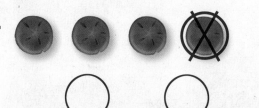

   ___ ◯ ___ ◯ ___

Subtract All or Zero

Write how many are left.

5.

   3 − 0 = ___

6.

   4 − 4 = ___

Family note: This page checks your child's understanding
of important skills needed for success in Chapter 4.

 Online   Assessment Options
Soar to Success Math

© Houghton Mifflin Harcourt Publishing Company

Vocabulary Builder

Visualize It

Complete the chart.
Mark each row with a ✔.

Word	I Know	Sounds Familiar	I Do Not Know
difference			
subtract			
subtraction sentence			
take away			

Understand Vocabulary

Complete the sentences with review words.

1. 3 is the _____ for $5 - 2 = 3$.

2. $7 - 4 = 3$ is a _____.

3. You _____ to solve $5 - 1$.

4. You can _____ 2 ⬤ from 6 ⬤.

Game Under the Sea

Materials • • 12

Play with a partner. Take turns.
1. Put your on START.
2. Spin the . Move that number of spaces.
3. Spin again. Subtract that number from the number on the game board space.
4. Use to check your answer. If you are not correct, lose a turn.
5. The first player to get to END wins.

START
4
6
8
5
10
9
8
Move ahead 1 space.
9
Go back 1 space.
7
10
Move ahead 2 spaces.
7
5
10
Go back 1 space.
9
5
Move ahead 1 space.
4
6
8
END
Go back 1 space.
4
5
Go back 1 space.
4
5

Name _____

Count Back

Essential Question How can you count back 1, 2, or 3?

COMMON CORE STANDARD CC.1.OA.5
Add and subtract within 20.

Listen and Draw

Start at 9. Count back to find the difference.

8 9

$$9 - 1 = \underline{\quad}$$

7 8 9

$$9 - 2 = \underline{\quad}$$

6 7 8 9

$$9 - 3 = \underline{\quad}$$

Math Talk
Explain why you count backward to find the difference.

MATHEMATICAL PRACTICES

HOME CONNECTION • Your child counted back to find the difference. Counting back is a strategy that can be used to help learn subtraction facts.

Model and Draw

You can **count back**
to subtract.

Use 8 ●.

Count back 1 ●.

The difference is 7.

7   8

$8 - 1 = \underline{7}$

Share and Show

Use ●.

Count back 1, 2, or 3 to subtract.
Write the difference.

1. $5 - 1 = \underline{}$	2. $\underline{} = 5 - 2$
3. $6 - 1 = \underline{}$	4. $\underline{} = 6 - 3$
5. $7 - 2 = \underline{}$	6. $\underline{} = 7 - 3$
7. $10 - 1 = \underline{}$	8. $\underline{} = 10 - 2$
9. $12 - 3 = \underline{}$	10. $\underline{} = 8 - 2$
✓11. $4 - 3 = \underline{}$	✓12. $\underline{} = 9 - 1$

Name _____

On Your Own

Count back 1, 2, or 3.
Write the difference.

13. 9 – 3 = ___	14. ___ = 5 – 3	15. 6 – 3 = ___
16. 7 – 2 = ___	17. ___ = 10 – 1	18. 8 – 1 = ___
19. 5 – 2 = ___	20. ___ = 8 – 3	21. 11 – 3 = ___
22. 7 – 1 = ___	23. ___ = 9 – 1	24. 6 – 2 = ___
25. 4 – 1 = ___	26. ___ = 7 – 2	27. 3 – 1 = ___
28. 12 – 3 = ___	29. ___ = 11 – 2	30. 10 – 2 = ___
31. 3 – 2 = ___	32. ___ = 4 – 2	33. 9 – 2 = ___
34. 8 – 2 = ___	35. ___ = 10 – 3	36. 7 – 3 = ___

37. **H.O.T.** Alex subtracts 3 from 10. What is a subtraction sentence he could write?

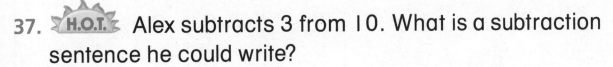

PROBLEM SOLVING REAL WORLD

Write a subtraction sentence to solve.

38. Paco has 11 train cars.
He puts 2 train cars on the track.
How many train cars are off
the track?

____ − ____ = ____ train cars

39. **H.O.T.** Paco puts 1 more train car on
the track. How many train cars are off
the track now?

Look back at
Exercise 38 for
information to
solve.

____ − ____ = ____ train cars

40. ⭐ **Test Prep** Josh had 9 toy cars. He
gave some of them to Paul. Now Josh
has 7 toy cars. How many did he give
to Paul? Which subtraction sentence
answers the problem?

$7 - 2 = 5$ ○ | $8 - 1 = 7$ ○ | $9 - 1 = 8$ ○ | $9 - 2 = 7$ ○

TAKE HOME ACTIVITY · Have your child show how to use the count back
strategy to find the difference for 7 − 2. Repeat with other problems to
count back 1, 2, or 3 from 12 or less.

156 one hundred fifty-six

Name _____

Think Addition to Subtract

Essential Question How can you use an addition fact to find the answer to a subtraction fact?

COMMON CORE STANDARD CC.1.OA.4
Understand and apply properties of operations and the relationship between addition and subtraction.

Listen and Draw

Use 🔲🔲 to model the problem.

Draw 🔲🔲 to show your work.

What is
12 − 5?

5 + ___ = 12

12 − 5 = ___

Math Talk
Explain how
5 + 7 = 12 can help
you find
12 − 5.
MATHEMATICAL
PRACTICES

FOR THE TEACHER • Read the following problems. Joey had 5 cubes. Sarah gave him more cubes. Now Joey has 12 cubes. How many cubes did Sarah give him? Children use the top workspace to solve. Then have children solve this problem: Joey had 12 cubes. He gave Sarah 5 cubes. How many cubes does Joey have now?

Chapter 4

© Houghton Mifflin Harcourt Publishing Company

Model and Draw

What is $9 - 4$?

Think

$$4 + \underline{\ ?\ } = 9$$

Think $4 + \underline{\ 5\ } = 9$ So $9 - 4 = \underline{\ 5\ }$

Share and Show

Math Board

Use to add and to subtract.

1. What is $8 - 6$?

Think $6 + \underline{\ \ \ } = 8$

So $8 - 6 = \underline{\ \ \ }$

2. What is $8 - 4$?

Think $4 + \underline{\ \ \ } = 8$

So $8 - 4 = \underline{\ \ \ }$

3. What is $10 - 4$?

Think $4 + \underline{\ \ \ } = 10$

So $10 - 4 = \underline{\ \ \ }$

4. What is $12 - 6$?

Think $6 + \underline{\ \ \ } = 12$

So $12 - 6 = \underline{\ \ \ }$

Name _____

On Your Own

Use  to add and to subtract.

5. 8
   − 3
   ———
    ?

Think
  3
+ □
———
  8

So
  8
− 3

6. 9
   − 5
   ———
    ?

Think
  5
+ □
———
  9

So
  9
− 5

7. 12
   − 7
   ———
    ?

Think
  7
+ □
———
  12

So
  12
− 7

 Solve.

8. Carol can use an addition sentence to write a subtraction sentence. Write a subtraction sentence she can solve using 6 + 8 = 14.

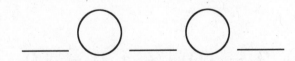

9. Write an addition sentence Carol can use to help her solve 13 − 9.

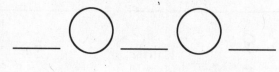

PROBLEM SOLVING REAL WORLD

Write Math

Write a number sentence to solve.

10. There are 14 cats. 7 are black. The rest are yellow. How many yellow cats are there?

___ ◯ ___ ◯ ___

___ yellow cats

11. I had some pencils. I gave 4 pencils away. Now I have 2 pencils. How many pencils did I start with?

___ ◯ ___ ◯ ___

___ pencils

12. **H.O.T.** Sarah has 8 fewer flowers than Ann. Ann has 16 flowers. How many flowers does Sarah have?

___ ◯ ___ ◯ ___

___ flowers

13. ⭐ **Test Prep** Which addition sentence helps you solve $10 - 7$?

$3 + 4 = 7$ | $5 + 5 = 10$ | $7 + 3 = 10$ | $6 + 4 = 10$
○ | ○ | ○ | ○

TAKE HOME ACTIVITY • Write $5 + 4 =$ ___ and ask your child to write the sum. Have him or her explain how to use $5 + 4 = 9$ to solve ___ $- 4 = 5$ and then write the answer.

FOR MORE PRACTICE:
Standards Practice Book, pp. P75–P76

Name _____

Use Think Addition to Subtract

Essential Question How can you use addition to help you find the answer to a subtraction fact?

COMMON CORE STANDARD CC.1.OA.4
Understand and apply properties of operations and the relationship between addition and subtraction.

Listen and Draw

Use . Draw to show your work.
Write the number sentences.

What is
10 − 3?

FOR THE TEACHER • Read the problem. Maria has 7 games. She gets 3 more. How many games does she have? Children use the top workspace to solve. Then have children solve this problem: Maria has 10 games. She gives 3 of them to her friends. How many games are there now?

Math Talk
Do your answers make sense? Explain.

MATHEMATICAL PRACTICES

Model and Draw

An addition fact can help you subtract.

What is 8 − 6?

Use   <u>6</u> + ___ = 8

So   8 − 6 = ___

Share and Show

Think of an addition fact to help you subtract.

1. What is 9 − 6?

Use  <u>6</u> + ___ = 9

So   9 − 6 = ___

2. What is 11 − 5?

Use   ___ + ___ = 11

So   11 − 5 = ___

☑3. What is 10 − 8?

Use   ___ + ___ = 10

So   10 − 8 = ___

☑4. What is 7 − 4?

Use   ___ + ___ = 7

So   7 − 4 = ___

Name _____

On Your Own

Think of an addition fact to help you subtract.

5. 16
  − 8

8
+ ■
16

6. 10
  − 6

6
+ ■
10

7. 7
  − 5

8. 10
  − 5

9. 8
  − 5

10. 11
   − 6

11. 13
   − 7

12. 11
   − 4

13. 14
   − 7

14. 9
   − 3

15. 11
   − 7

16. 12
   − 7

17. H.O.T. Emil has 13 pencils in a cup.
He takes some pencils out.
There are 6 pencils left in the cup.
How many pencils does he take out?

What addition fact can you use to solve
this problem?

____ + ____ = ____

So, Emil takes out ____ pencils.

TAKE HOME ACTIVITY · Ask your child to explain how the
addition fact 8 + 6 = 14 can help him or her to find 14 − 6.

FOR MORE PRACTICE:
Standards Practice Book, pp. P77–P78

Mid-Chapter Checkpoint

Concepts and Skills

Count back 1, 2, or 3 to subtract.
Write the difference. (CC.1.OA.5)

1. $7 - 1 = $ _____

2. _____ $= 7 - 2$

3. $12 - 3 = $ _____

4. $9 - 3 = $ _____

5. $6 - 2 = $ _____

6. $8 - 3 = $ _____

7. _____ $= 11 - 3$

8. $5 - 2 = $ _____

Use ▮▮ to add and to subtract. (CC.1.OA.4)

9. $\begin{array}{r} 11 \\ -\ 5 \\ \hline ? \end{array}$

Think
$\begin{array}{r} 5 \\ +\ \boxed{} \\ \hline 11 \end{array}$

So
$\begin{array}{r} 11 \\ -\ 5 \\ \hline \end{array}$

10. $\begin{array}{r} 14 \\ -\ 7 \\ \hline ? \end{array}$

Think
$\begin{array}{r} 7 \\ +\ \boxed{} \\ \hline 14 \end{array}$

So
$\begin{array}{r} 14 \\ -\ 7 \\ \hline \end{array}$

★ Test Prep

11. Which subtraction sentence can you
    solve by using $3 + 9 = 12$? (CC.1.OA.4)

$9 - 3 = $ _____ ○

$10 - 3 = $ _____ ○

$12 - 6 = $ _____ ○

$12 - 3 = $ _____ ○

Name _____

Use 10 to Subtract

Essential Question How can you make a ten to help you subtract?

COMMON CORE STANDARD CC.1.OA.6
Add and subtract within 20.

Listen and Draw REAL WORLD

Use ⚫ to show the problem.
Draw to show your work.

Math Talk
Explain how your drawing can help you solve 15 – 9.

MATHEMATICAL PRACTICES

FOR THE TEACHER • Read the following problem.
Austin puts 9 red counters in the first ten frame.
Then he puts 1 yellow counter in the ten frame.
How many more yellow counters does Austin need
to make 15?

You can make a ten to help you subtract.

$13 - 9 = $ <u>?</u>

Start at 9.

Count up I
to make 10.

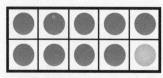

Count up 3
more to 13.

You counted up 4.

$13 - 9 = $ ___

$17 - 8 = $ <u>?</u>

Start at 8.

Count up _2_
to make 10.

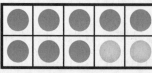

Count up _7_
more to 17.

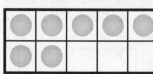

You counted up _9_.

$17 - 8 = $ ___

Share and Show

Use ⬤ and ten frames. Make a ten to subtract.
Draw to show your work.

I. $12 - 8 = $ <u>?</u>

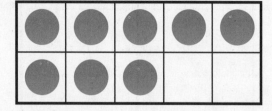

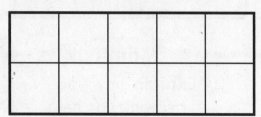

$12 - 8 = $ ___

✔2. $11 - 9 = $ <u>?</u>

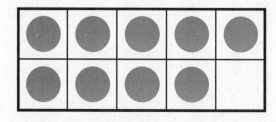

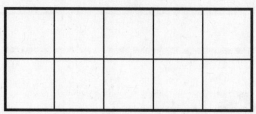

$11 - 9 = $ ___

On Your Own

Use and ten frames. Make a ten to subtract. Draw to show your work.

3. $14 - 9 =$ _?_

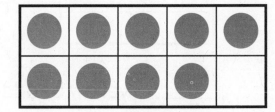

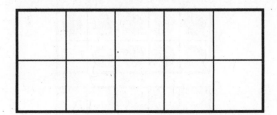

$14 - 9 =$ ___

4. $11 - 8 =$ _?_

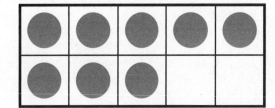

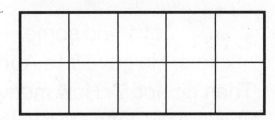

$11 - 8 =$ ___

5. $15 - 8 =$ _?_

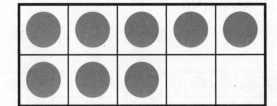

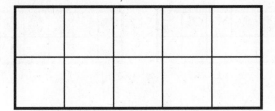

$15 - 8 =$ ___

6. $17 - 9 =$ _?_

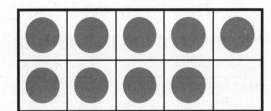

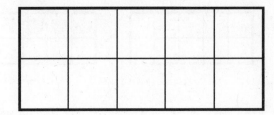

$17 - 9 =$ ___

PROBLEM SOLVING

REAL WORLD

Write Math

Solve. Use the ten frames to make a ten to help you subtract.

7. Alice has 18 beads. 9 are red and the rest are yellow. How many beads are yellow?

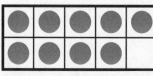

_____ yellow beads

8. **H.O.T.** John had some stickers. He gave 9 to April. Then he had 7. How many stickers did John start with?

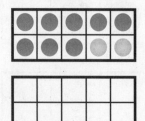

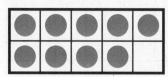

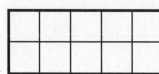

_____ stickers

9. ⭐ **Test Prep** Which shows a way to make a ten to subtract?

$15 - 8 = \underline{\ ?\ }$

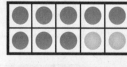

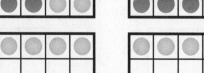

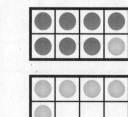

○   ○   ○   ○

TAKE HOME ACTIVITY • Ask your child to explain how he or she solved Exercise 7.

FOR MORE PRACTICE:
Standards Practice Book, pp. P79–P80

Name _____

Break Apart to Subtract

Essential Question How do you break apart
a number to subtract?

COMMON CORE STANDARD CC.1.OA.6
Add and subtract within 20.

Listen and Draw REAL WORLD

Use ⬤ to solve each problem.
Draw to show your work.

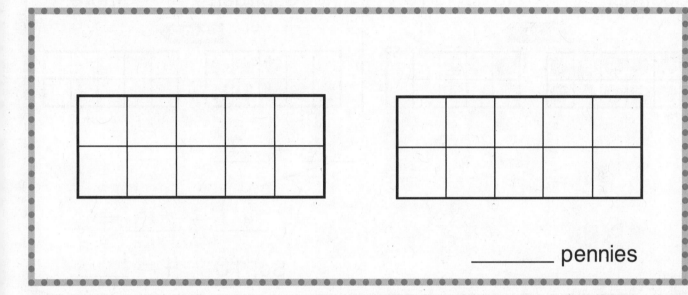

_____ pennies

_____ pennies

FOR THE TEACHER • Read the following
problem. Tom had 14 pennies. He gave 4
pennies to his sister. How many pennies does
Tom have now? Have children use the top
workspace to solve. Then read this part of
the problem: Then Tom gave 2 pennies to
his brother. How many pennies does Tom
have now?

Math Talk
How many pennies
did Tom give away?
Explain.

MATHEMATICAL
PRACTICES

Chapter 4

one hundred sixty-nine **169**

Model and Draw

Think about ten to find 13 − 4.
Place 13 counters in two ten frames.

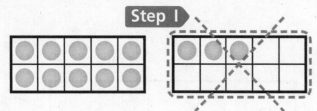
How many do you
subtract to get to 10?

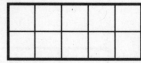
How many more
to subtract 4?

Subtract _3_ to get to 10.

Then subtract _1_ more.

Step 1

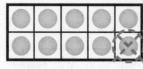

Step 2

13 − 3 − 1

10 − 1 = ___

So, 13 − 4 = ___.

Share and Show

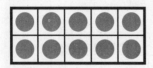 Math Board

Subtract.

THINK
What is the best way
to break apart the 7?

 1. What is 15 − 7?

Step 1

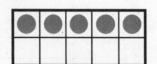

Step 2

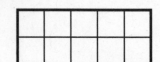

___ − ___ − ___

___ − ___ = ___

So, 15 − 7 = ___.

On Your Own

Subtract.

2. What is 14 − 6?

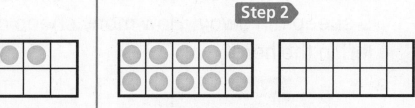

Step 1 | Step 2

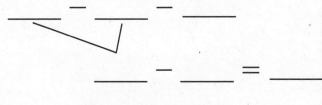

$$\_\_ - \_\_ - \_\_$$

$$\_\_ - \_\_ = \_\_$$

So, 14 − 6 = ____.

---

3. What is 16 − 7?

Step 1 | Step 2

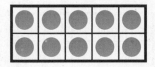 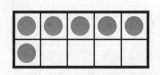 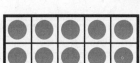 

$$\_\_ - \_\_ - \_\_$$

$$\_\_ - \_\_ = \_\_$$

So, ____ − ____ = ____.

PROBLEM SOLVING REAL WORLD

Use the ten frames.
Write a number sentence to solve.

4. **H.O.T.** There are 14 sheep in the herd.
5 sheep run away. How many sheep are
left in the herd?

Step 1

 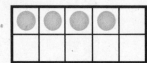

Step 2

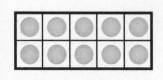 

_____ ◯ _____ ◯ _____

_____ sheep

5. ⭐ **Test Prep** Which way shows how to
make a ten to solve 15 − 6?

Step 1

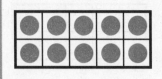 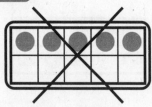

Step 2

 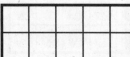

15 − 5   15 − 5 − 1
  ○   ○

10 − 5   10 − 5 − 1
  ○   ○

TAKE HOME ACTIVITY · Ask your child to explain
how they solved Exercise 4.

FOR MORE PRACTICE:
Standards Practice Book, pp. P81–P82

Name _____

Problem Solving • Use Subtraction Strategies

Essential Question How can acting out a problem help you solve the problem?

COMMON CORE STANDARD CC.1.OA.1
Represent and solve problems involving addition and subtraction.

Kyle had 13 hats. He gave 5 hats to Jake. How many hats does Kyle have now?

🔑 Unlock the Problem REAL WORLD

What do I need to find?	What information do I need to use?
how many <u>hats</u> Kyle has now	Kyle had __13__ hats. Kyle gave __5__ to Jake.

Show how to solve the problem.

Step 1

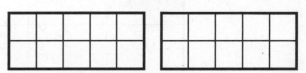

Step 2

Kyle has __8__ hats now.

HOME CONNECTION • Your child used counters to act out the subtraction story. The graphic organizer helps your child analyze the information given in the problem.

Try Another Problem

Act it out to solve. Draw to show your work.

• What do I need to find?
• What information do I need to use?

1. Heather has 14 crackers. Some crackers are broken. 8 crackers are not broken. How many crackers are broken?

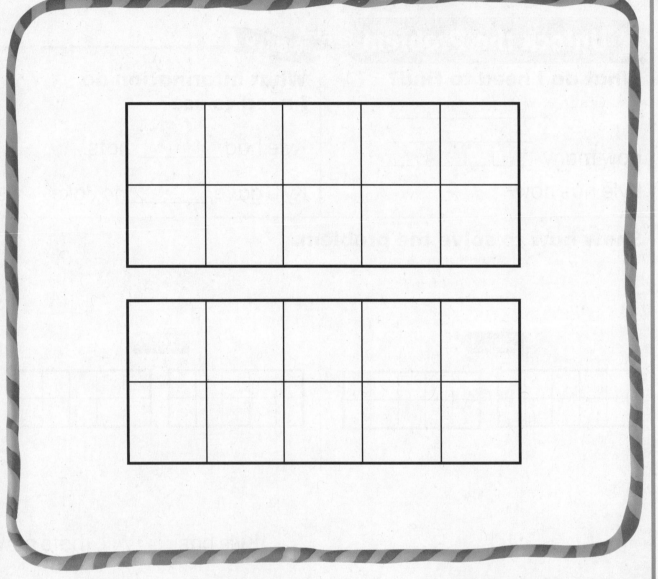

$14 - \boxed{} = 8$

_____ crackers are broken.

Math Talk
Explain how you can show how many crackers are broken.

MATHEMATICAL PRACTICES

Name _____

Share and Show

Act it out to solve. Draw to show your work.

---

2. Phil had some stickers.
   He lost 7 stickers.
   Now he has 9 stickers.
   How many stickers
   did Phil start with?

   $\boxed{} - 7 = 9$

   Phil started with _____ stickers.

---

3. Hillary has 9 dolls.
   Abby has 15 dolls.
   How many fewer
   dolls does Hillary
   have than Abby?

   $15 - 9 = \boxed{}$

   Hillary has _____ fewer dolls.

☑ 4. Sid had 12 pennies.
   He tossed some into a
   fountain. He has 5 left.
   How many pennies did he
   toss in the fountain?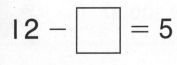

   $12 - \boxed{} = 5$

   Sid tossed _____ pennies.

☑ 5. Cami has 13 apples.
   Some are green and
   some are red. She
   has 8 red apples.
   How many apples
   are green?

   $13 - \boxed{} = 8$

   _____ apples are green.

On Your Own

Choose a way to solve. Draw or write to explain.

6. 10 frogs are in the tree. 3 more frogs jump into the tree. Then 4 frogs jump out of the tree. How many frogs are in the tree now?

_____ frogs

7. There are 9 more turtles in the water than on a log. 13 turtles are in the water. How many turtles are on a log?

_____ turtles

8. H.O.T. Choose a number to fill in the blank. Solve.

10 dogs are at the park.

_____ dogs are brown. The rest have black spots. How many dogs have black spots?

_____ dogs

9. ⭐ **Test Prep**   Cheryl has 14 flowers. She gives some away. She has 8 left. How many flowers does she give away?

9   8   7   6
○   ○   ○   ○

TAKE HOME ACTIVITY • Tell your child a subtraction story. Ask your child to use small objects to act out the problem to solve it.

FOR MORE PRACTICE:
Standards Practice Book, pp. P83–P84

Chapter 4 Review/Test

Vocabulary

1. Which fact do you use **count back** to solve? Circle it. (p.154)

$$8 - 2 = \underline{\qquad}$$

$$1 + 7 = \underline{\qquad}$$

Concepts and Skills

Use ⬤ to solve.
Draw to show your work. (CC.1.OA.5)

2. What is $12 - 3 = \underline{\qquad}$?

$$12 - 3 = \underline{\qquad}$$

Count back 1, 2, or 3 to subtract.
Write the difference. (CC.1.OA.5)

3. $\underline{\qquad} = 7 - 3$

4. $10 - 2 = \underline{\qquad}$

5. $10 - 1 = \underline{\qquad}$

6. $\underline{\qquad} = 8 - 2$

7. $\underline{\qquad} = 9 - 2$

8. $11 - 3 = \underline{\qquad}$

9. $6 - 2 = \underline{\qquad}$

10. $\underline{\qquad} = 4 - 1$

11. What is 11 − 5? (CC.1.OA.4)

> Think 5 + ___ = 11

> So 11 − 5 = ___

3   4   5   6
○   ○   ○   ○

12. Which addition fact helps solve this subtraction fact?

(CC.1.OA.4)

14
− 6

6	7	8	8
+ 6	+ 7	+ 6	+ 9
12	14	14	17
○	○	○	○

13. What subtraction sentence does the model show? (CC.1.OA.6)

Step 1   Step 2

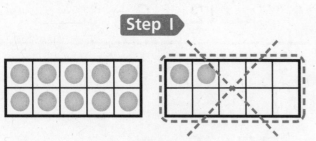   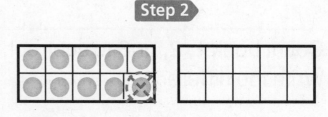

12 − 3 = 9   10 − 1 = 9
○   ○

10 − 3 = 7   12 − 2 = 10
○   ○

178 one hundred seventy-eight

TEST PREP

14. Which shows a way to make a ten to subtract? (CC.1.OA.6)

$$13 - 9 = \underline{\ \ ?\ \ }$$

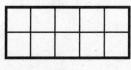
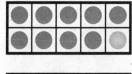
○

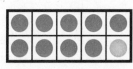
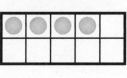
○

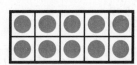
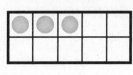
○

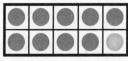
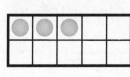
○

15. Adam had 12 crackers. He ate some. He has 5 left. Which shows a way to find how many crackers Adam ate? (CC.1.OA.1)

○ $12 - \boxed{} = 5$

○ $12 - 2 = \boxed{}$

○ $10 - 5 = \boxed{}$

○ $2 + \boxed{} = 5$

16. Elsa had some marbles. She gave 9 marbles away. Now she has 9 marbles. How many marbles did Elsa start with? (CC.1.OA.1)

```
   0      9     18     19
   ○      ○      ○      ○
```

Performance Task (CC.1.OA.1, CC.1.OA.5, CC.1.OA.6)

Shantel solves a subtraction problem.
She uses the following clues.

- The difference is 4.
- You can count back 1, 2, or 3.
- Use addition to help you subtract.
- Complete the subtraction sentence
  _____ − _____ = 4.

Show a subtraction problem
Shantel may solve.
Use numbers, pictures, or words.

Show your work.

Addition and Subtraction Relationships

Curious About Math with

Curious George

Children tap the Liberty Bell
4 times. Then they tap it
9 more times. How many
times do the children
tap the bell?

Show What You Know

Add in Any Order

Use 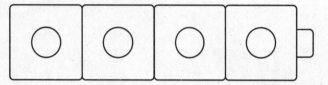. Color to match.
Write each sum.

1.

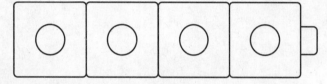

$1 + 3 =$ _____

$3 + 1 =$ _____

Count On

Use the number line to add. Write each sum.

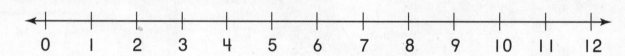

2. $6 + 3 =$ ___   3. $7 + 1 =$ ___   4. $8 + 2 =$ ___

Count Back

Use the number line to subtract. Write each difference.

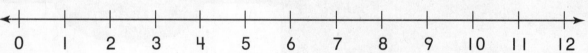

5. $11 - 2 =$ ___   6. $8 - 3 =$ ___   7. $9 - 1 =$ ___

Family note: This page checks your child's understanding
of important skills needed for success in Chapter 5.

GO Online

Assessment Options
Soar to Success Math

© Houghton Mifflin Harcourt Publishing Company

Vocabulary Builder

Review Words
add
addition fact
difference
subtract
subtraction fact
sum

Visualize It

Sort the review words from the box.

Addition Words   Subtraction Words

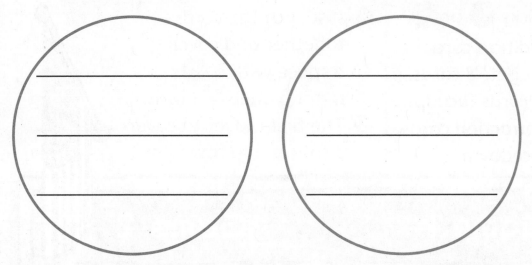

Understand Vocabulary

Follow the directions.

1. Write an addition fact.

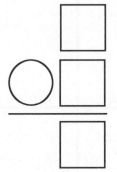

2. What is the sum?

_____

3. Write a subtraction fact.

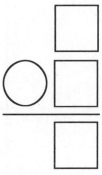

4. What is the difference?

_____

Game · Add to Subtract Bingo

Materials · 16 | 5 + 3 |

· 16 | 8 − 3 | · 18 ●

Play with a partner.
Each player picks ● or ●.

1. Mix the addition cards. Each player gets 8 cards. Show your cards faceup.

2. Put the subtraction cards in a pile facedown.

3. Take a subtraction card. Do you have the addition fact that helps you subtract?

4. If so, put the cards together and cover a space with a ●. If not, you lose a turn.

5. The first player to cover 3 spaces in a row wins.

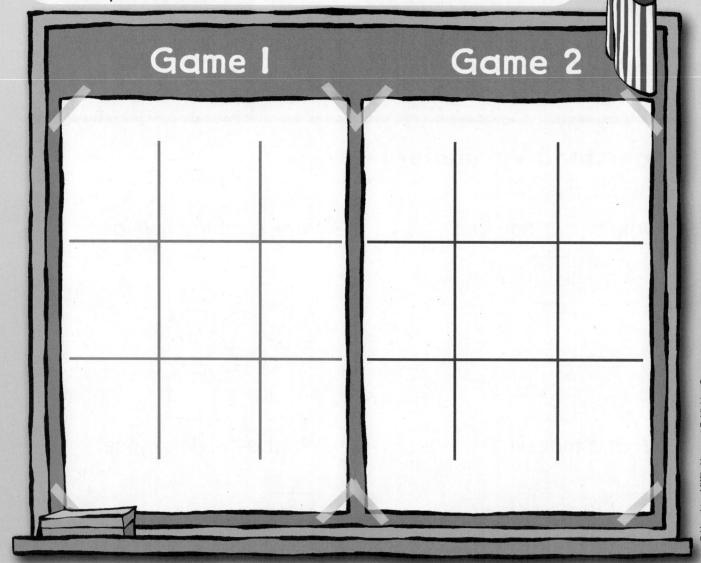

Game 1   Game 2

Problem Solving • Add or Subtract

Essential Question How can making
a model help you solve a problem?

COMMON CORE STANDARD CC.1.OA.1
Represent and solve problems involving
addition and subtraction.

Nicole sees 16 turtles on the beach.
Some turtles swim away. There are
9 turtles still on the beach. How many
turtles swim away?

Unlock the Problem REAL WORLD

What do I need to find?

how many ~~turtles~~
swim away

What information do I need
to use?

16 turtles

? swim away

9 turtles still on the beach

Show how to solve the problem.

	9
___	

16

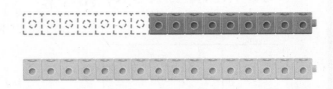

16 turtles _____ swim away 9 turtles still on the beach

HOME CONNECTION • Your child made a model to visualize the problem.
The model helps your child see what part of the problem to find.

Try Another Problem

Make a model to solve.

Use 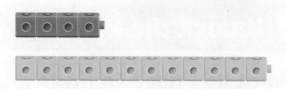 to help you.

- What do I need to find?
- What information do I need to use?

1. There are 4 rabbits in the field. Some more rabbits come. Now there are 12 rabbits. How many rabbits come to the field?

4	

12

4 rabbits   ____ rabbits come   12 rabbits in the field

2. There are 14 birds in a tree. Some birds fly away. There are 9 birds still in the tree. How many birds fly away?

	9

14

14 birds   ____ birds fly away   9 birds still in the tree

Math Talk

Explain how to find the missing number.

MATHEMATICAL PRACTICES

© Houghton Mifflin Harcourt Publishing Company

Name _____

Share and Show

Make a model to solve.

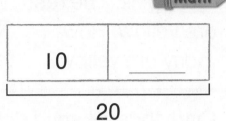

3. There are 20 ducks in the pond. Then 10 ducks swim away. How many ducks are still in the pond?

10	
20	

20 ducks   10 swim away   ____ ducks still in the pond

4. 3 eagles land in the trees. Now 12 eagles are in the trees. How many eagles were in the trees to start?

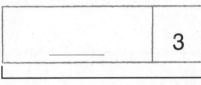

	3
12	

____ eagles   3 eagles land   12 eagles in the tree

5. 8 squirrels are in the park. Some more squirrels come. Now there are 16 squirrels. How many squirrels come to the park?

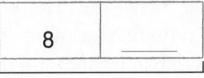

8	
16	

8 squirrels   ____ squirrels come   16 squirrels in the park

On Your Own

Solve. Draw or write to show your work.

6. Liz picks 15 flowers. 7 are pink. The rest are yellow. How many are yellow?

_____ yellow flowers

7. Cindy has 14 sand dollars. She has the same number of large and small sand dollars. Write a number sentence about the sand dollars.

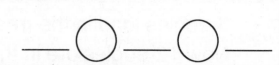

8. **H.O.T.** Sam has three more books than Ed. Sam has 8 books. How many books does Ed have?

_____ books

9. ⭐ **Test Prep** There are 13 fish in the tank. Some fish swim behind the rock. There are 8 fish in front of the rock. How many fish are behind the rock?

| 4 | 5 | 6 | 7 |
| ○ | ○ | ○ | ○ |

TAKE HOME ACTIVITY • Ask your child to look at Exercise 7 and use the number 18 as the total number. Then have your child write a number sentence.

188 one hundred eighty-eight

Name _____

Record Related Facts

Essential Question How do related facts help you find missing numbers?

Listen and Draw  REAL WORLD

Listen to the problem.
Model with ▪▪ ▪▪. Draw ▪▪ ▪▪.
Write the number sentence.

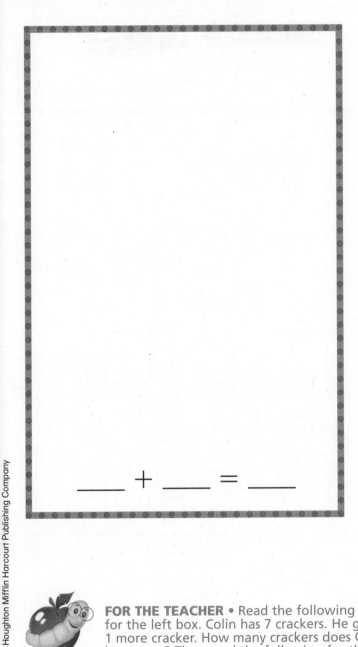

___ + ___ = ___

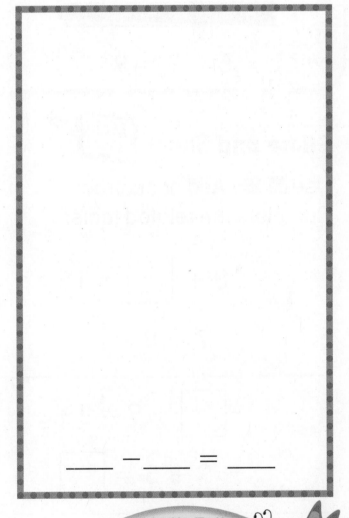

___ − ___ = ___

FOR THE TEACHER • Read the following problem for the left box. Colin has 7 crackers. He gets 1 more cracker. How many crackers does Colin have now? Then read the following for the right box. Colin has 8 crackers. He gives one to Jacob. How many crackers does Colin have now?

Math Talk
Explain how your model helps you write your number sentence.

MATHEMATICAL PRACTICES

Chapter 5

one hundred eighty-nine **189**

How can one model help you write four **related facts**?

$$4 + 5 = 9$$

$$9 - 5 = 4$$

$$5 + 4 = 9$$

$$9 - 4 = 5$$

Share and Show

Use . Add or subtract.
Complete the related facts.

1.

$$8 + \boxed{} = 15 \qquad 15 - 7 = \boxed{}$$

$$7 + 8 = \boxed{} \qquad \boxed{} - \boxed{} = \boxed{}$$

2.

$$\boxed{} + 9 = 14 \qquad 14 - \boxed{} = 5$$

$$9 + 5 = \boxed{} \qquad \boxed{} - \boxed{} = \boxed{}$$

3.

$$7 + \boxed{} = 13 \qquad 13 - 6 = \boxed{}$$

$$6 + 7 = \boxed{} \qquad \boxed{} - \boxed{} = \boxed{}$$

Name _____

On Your Own

Use ▣▪▣▪. Add or subtract.
Complete the related facts.

4.
$\boxed{} + 8 = 13$ $13 - \boxed{} = 5$

$8 + 5 = \boxed{}$ $\boxed{} - \boxed{} = \boxed{}$

5.
$\boxed{} + 8 = 17$ $17 - \boxed{} = 9$

$8 + 9 = \boxed{}$ $\boxed{} - \boxed{} = \boxed{}$

6.
$9 + \boxed{} = 15$ $\boxed{} - 6 = 9$

$6 + \boxed{} = 15$ $\boxed{} - \boxed{} = \boxed{}$

7. **H.O.T.** Circle the number sentence that has a mistake.
Correct it to complete the related facts.

$7 + 9 = 16$

$16 + 9 = 7$

$9 + 7 = 16$

$16 - 7 = 9$

___ ◯ ___ ◯ ___

© Houghton Mifflin Harcourt Publishing Company

Chapter 5 • Lesson 2

PROBLEM SOLVING

8. H.O.T. Choose three numbers to make related facts. Choose numbers between 0 and 18. Write your numbers. Write the related facts.

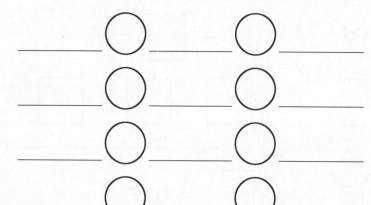

9. ⭐ **Test Prep** Which completes the related facts?

$$9 + 8 = 17 \qquad 17 - 8 = 9$$
$$8 + 9 = 17$$

○ $9 - 6 = 3$ ○ $17 - 8 = 9$

○ $9 + 9 = 18$ ○ $17 - 9 = 8$

 TAKE HOME ACTIVITY • Write an addition fact. Ask your child to write three other related facts.

FOR MORE PRACTICE: Standards Practice Book, pp. P91–P92

Name _____

Identify Related Facts

Essential Question How do you know if addition and subtraction facts are related?

COMMON CORE STANDARD CC.1.OA.6
Add and subtract within 20.

Listen and Draw

Use ▣▣ to show $4 + 9 = 13$.
Draw ▣▣ to show a related subtraction fact.
Write the subtraction sentence.

_____ ◯ _____ ◯ _____

Math Talk
Explain why your subtraction sentence is related to $4 + 9 = 13$.

MATHEMATICAL PRACTICES

HOME CONNECTION • Your child has been learning how addition and subtraction facts are related. Have your child tell you the two related facts on this page.

Use the pictures. What two facts can you write?

$$3 \oplus 9 \ominus 12$$

$$12 \ominus 9 \ominus 3$$

These are related facts. If you know one of these facts, you also know the other fact.

Share and Show

Add and subtract.
Circle the related facts.

1. $6 + 4 = $ ___	2. ___ $= 9 + 8$	3. $9 + 5 = $ ___
$10 - 4 = $ ___	___ $= 17 - 8$	$9 - 5 = $ ___
4. $8 + 7 = $ ___	5. ___ $= 9 + 2$	6. $6 + 3 = $ ___
$15 - 7 = $ ___	___ $= 9 - 2$	$12 - 3 = $ ___
7. $4 + 8 = $ ___	⊘8. ___ $= 7 + 6$	⊘9. $9 + 9 = $ ___
$12 - 8 = $ ___	___ $= 13 - 6$	$18 - 9 = $ ___

On Your Own

10. Add and subtract. Color the leaves that have related facts.

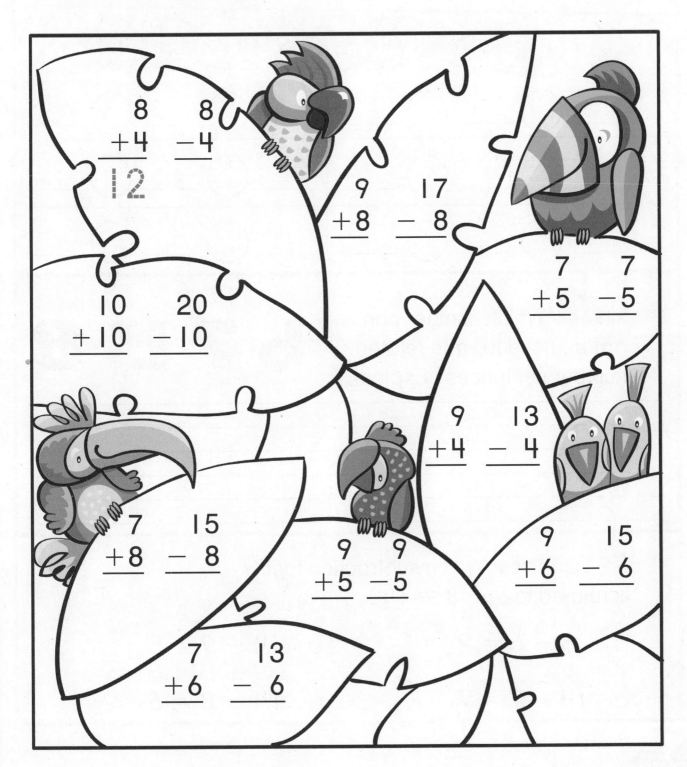

$$8 \atop +4 \over 12 \qquad 8 \atop -4$$

$$9 \atop +8 \qquad 17 \atop -8$$

$$7 \atop +5 \qquad 7 \atop -5$$

$$10 \atop +10 \qquad 20 \atop -10$$

$$9 \atop +4 \qquad 13 \atop -4$$

$$7 \atop +8 \qquad 15 \atop -8$$

$$9 \atop +5 \qquad 9 \atop -5$$

$$9 \atop +6 \qquad 15 \atop -6$$

$$7 \atop +6 \qquad 13 \atop -6$$

PROBLEM SOLVING

Write Math

Use the numbers to write related addition and subtraction sentences.

4   5   6   7   8   9   12   13   14

11. ___ ___ ◯ ___ ___ ◯ ___ | ___ ___ ◯ ___ ___ ◯ ___

12. ___ ___ ◯ ___ ___ ◯ ___ | ___ ___ ◯ ___ ___ ◯ ___

13. ___ ___ ◯ ___ ___ ◯ ___ | ___ ___ ◯ ___ ___ ◯ ___

14. **H.O.T.** Which number can **not** be used to write related number sentences? Explain.

 6 7 15 8

_____

_____

_____

_____

15. ⭐ **Test Prep** Which subtraction fact is related to 6 + 8 = 14?

○ $8 - 6 = 2$ ○ $14 - 9 = 5$

○ $14 - 7 = 7$ ○ $14 - 8 = 6$

 TAKE HOME ACTIVITY • Write 7, 9, 16, +, −, and = on separate slips of paper. Have your child use the slips of paper to show related facts.

FOR MORE PRACTICE:
Standards Practice Book, pp. P93–P94

Name _____

Use Addition to Check Subtraction

Essential Question How can you use addition to check subtraction?

COMMON CORE STANDARD CC.1.OA.6
Add and subtract within 20.

Listen and Draw REAL WORLD

Draw and write to solve the problem.

____ ◯ ____ ◯ ____

____ ◯ ____ ◯ ____

FOR THE TEACHER • Read the problem. Erin has 11 books. I borrow 4 of them. How many books does Erin still have? Allow children time to solve, using the top workspace. Then read this part of the problem: I give 4 books back to Erin. How many books does Erin have now?

Math Talk
Does Erin get all her books back? Use the number sentences to **explain** how you know.

MATHEMATICAL PRACTICES

Chapter 5

one hundred ninety-seven **197**

Why can you use addition
to check subtraction?

You subtract
one part from
the whole. The
difference is the
other part.

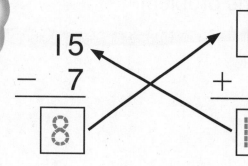

$$\begin{array}{r} 15 \\ -\ \ 7 \\ \hline \boxed{8} \end{array} \qquad \begin{array}{r} \boxed{8} \\ +\ \ 7 \\ \hline \boxed{15} \end{array}$$

When you add
the parts, you
get the same
whole.

Share and Show

Subtract. Then add to check your answer.

1.
$$\begin{array}{r} 13 \\ -\ \ 7 \\ \hline \boxed{} \end{array} \qquad \begin{array}{r} \boxed{} \\ +\ \ 7 \\ \hline \boxed{} \end{array}$$

2.
$$\begin{array}{r} 14 \\ -\ \ 5 \\ \hline \boxed{} \end{array} \qquad \begin{array}{r} \boxed{} \\ +\ \ 5 \\ \hline \boxed{} \end{array}$$

✓ 3.
$$\begin{array}{r} 12 \\ -\ \ 5 \\ \hline \boxed{} \end{array} \qquad \begin{array}{r} \boxed{} \\ +\ \ 5 \\ \hline \boxed{} \end{array}$$

✓ 4.
$$\begin{array}{r} 17 \\ -\ \ 9 \\ \hline \boxed{} \end{array} \qquad \begin{array}{r} \boxed{} \\ +\ \ 9 \\ \hline \boxed{} \end{array}$$

Name _____

On Your Own

Subtract. Then add to check your answer.

5. $11 - 3 = \square$

$\square + 3 = \square$

6. $13 - 9 = \square$

$\square + 9 = \square$

7. $16 - 7 = \square$

$\square + 7 = \square$

8. $14 - 8 = \square$

$\square + 8 = \square$

9. $\square = 13 - 8$

$\square = \square + 8$

10. $\square = 12 - 4$

$\square = \square + 4$

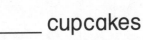 Subtract to solve. Then add to check your answer.

11. Liam brings 15 cupcakes to the party. His friends eat all but 6 of them. How many cupcakes did they eat?

____ cupcakes

$$\square - \square \qquad \square + \square$$

TAKE HOME ACTIVITY • Write $11 - 7 = \square$ on a sheet of paper. Ask your child to find the difference and then write an addition sentence he or she can use to check the subtraction.

Chapter 5 • Lesson 4

FOR MORE PRACTICE: Standards Practice Book, pp. P95–P96

one hundred ninety-nine 199

Name _____

☑ Mid-Chapter Checkpoint

Concepts and Skills

Use . Add or subtract.
Complete the related facts. (CC.1.OA.6)

1. $\boxed{} + 8 = 14$ $\qquad$ $14 - \boxed{} = 6$

$8 + 6 = \boxed{}$ $\qquad$ $\boxed{} - \boxed{} = \boxed{}$

2. $7 + \boxed{} = 13$ $\qquad$ $\boxed{} - 6 = 7$

$6 + \boxed{} = 13$ $\qquad$ $\boxed{} - \boxed{} = \boxed{}$

Add and subtract. Circle the related facts. (CC.1.OA.6)

3. $9 + 3 =$ ___ $\qquad$ 4. $7 + 8 =$ ___ $\qquad$ 5. ___ $= 6 + 5$

$9 - 3 =$ ___ $\qquad$ $15 - 8 =$ ___ $\qquad$ ___ $= 6 - 5$

⭐ Test Prep

6. Which addition sentence
can you use to check
the subtraction? (CC.1.OA.6)

$11 - 2 = \boxed{}$

$9 + 2 = 11$ $\qquad$ $6 + 2 = 8$
○ $\qquad\qquad\qquad$ ○

$2 + 7 = 9$ $\qquad$ $2 + 2 = 4$
○ $\qquad\qquad\qquad$ ○

© Houghton Mifflin Harcourt Publishing Company

Name _____

Algebra • Missing Numbers

Essential Question How can you use
a related fact to find a missing number?

COMMON CORE STANDARD CC.1.OA.8
Work with addition and subtraction
equations.

Listen and Draw REAL WORLD

Listen to the problem. Use ▪-▪ to show
the story. Draw to show your work.

Math Talk
How many toy cars
are blue? **Explain**
how you got
your answer.

MATHEMATICAL
PRACTICES

FOR THE TEACHER • Read the problem. Calvin
has 7 toy cars that are red. He has some blue
toy cars. He has 10 toy cars. How many blue toy
cars does Calvin have?

Chapter 5

What are the missing numbers?

$8 + \boxed{3} = 11$

$11 - 8 = \boxed{3}$

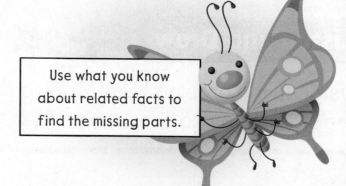

Use what you know about related facts to find the missing parts.

Share and Show Math Board

Use ▪▪ ▪▪ to find the missing numbers.
Write the numbers.

1. $8 + \boxed{} = 15$

$15 - 8 = \boxed{}$

2. $13 = 9 + \boxed{}$

$\boxed{} = 13 - 9$

3. $5 + \boxed{} = 14$

$14 - 5 = \boxed{}$

4. $14 = 6 + \boxed{}$

$\boxed{} = 14 - 6$

5. $9 + \boxed{} = 16$

$16 - 9 = \boxed{}$

6. $17 = 8 + \boxed{}$

$\boxed{} = 17 - 8$

Name _____

On Your Own

HINT
Use a related fact to help you.

Write the missing numbers.
Use  if you need to.

7. $7 + \boxed{} = 15$

$15 - 7 = \boxed{}$

8. $5 + \boxed{} = 11$

$11 - 5 = \boxed{}$

9. $\boxed{} + 10 = 20$

$20 - 10 = \boxed{}$

10. $\boxed{} + 9 = 16$

$16 - 9 = \boxed{}$

11. $\boxed{} = 9 + 9$

$9 = \boxed{} - 9$

12. $\boxed{} = 5 + 8$

$5 = \boxed{} - 8$

H.O.T. Solve.

13. Rick has 10 party hats.
He needs 19 hats for his
party. How many more
party hats does Rick need?

_____ party hats

PROBLEM SOLVING REAL WORLD

Use cubes or draw a picture to solve.

14. Todd has 12 bunnies. He gives 4 bunnies to his sister. How many bunnies does Todd have now?

_____ bunnies

---

15. Brad has 11 trucks. Some are small trucks. 4 are big trucks. How many small trucks does he have?

	4

11

_____ small trucks

---

16. **H.O.T.** There are 15 children at the park. 6 of the children go home. Then 4 more children come to the park. How many children are in the park now?

_____ children

---

17. ⭐ **Test Prep**

What is the missing number?

$9 + \boxed{} = 18$

8   9   10   11

○   ○   ○   ○

TAKE HOME ACTIVITY • Have your child explain how using subtraction can help him or her find the missing number in $7 + \square = 16$.

© Houghton Mifflin Harcourt Publishing Company

FOR MORE PRACTICE:
Standards Practice Book, pp. P97-P98

Algebra • Use Related Facts

Essential Question How can you use
a related fact to find a missing number?

COMMON CORE STANDARD CC.1.OA.8
Work with addition and subtraction
equations.

Listen and Draw

What number can you add to 8 to get 10?
Draw a picture to solve. Write the missing number.

$$8 + \boxed{} = 10$$

Math Talk
Describe how to
solve this problem
using cubes.
MATHEMATICAL
PRACTICES

HOME CONNECTION • Your child has been learning
how to find missing numbers in number sentences
using related addition or subtraction facts.

Model and Draw

You can use an addition fact to find a related subtraction fact.

Find $10 - 3$.

I know that
$3 + 7 = 10$, so
$10 - 3 = 7$.

$3 + \underline{}7 = 10$

$10 - 3 = \underline{}7$

Share and Show

 Math Board

Write the missing numbers.

1. Find $14 - 8$.

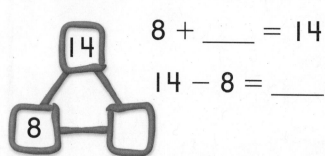

$8 + \underline{} = 14$

$14 - 8 = \underline{}$

2. Find $17 - 8$.

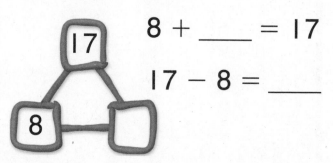

$8 + \underline{} = 17$

$17 - 8 = \underline{}$

3. Find $11 - 6$.

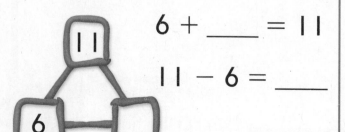

$6 + \underline{} = 11$

$11 - 6 = \underline{}$

4. Find $15 - 9$.

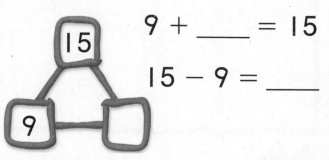

$9 + \underline{} = 15$

$15 - 9 = \underline{}$

On Your Own

Write the missing numbers.

5. Find 20 − 10.

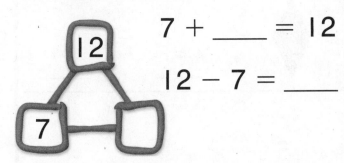

10 + ____ = 20

20 − 10 = ____

6. Find 13 − 4.

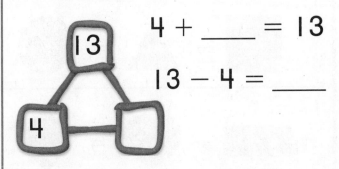

4 + ____ = 13

13 − 4 = ____

7. Find 12 − 7.

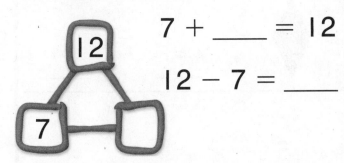

7 + ____ = 12

12 − 7 = ____

8. Find 15 − 8.

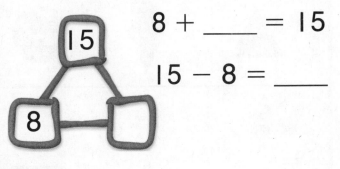

8 + ____ = 15

15 − 8 = ____

H.O.T. Write an addition sentence to help you find the difference. Then write the related subtraction sentence to solve.

9. Find 11 − 5.

____ + ____ = ____

____ − ____ = ____

10. Find 13 − 6.

____ = ____ + ____

____ = ____ − ____

PROBLEM SOLVING

Look at the shapes in the addition sentence.
Draw shapes to show a related subtraction fact.

11. ■ + ▲ = ● 　　 ● − △ = ■

12. ▬ + ♥ = ◆ 　　 ◆ − ♥ = ___ ___

13. ▲ = ◆ + ● 　　 ◆ = ___ − ___

H.O.T.

14.  + ★ = ■ 　　 ■ − ___ = ___

15. + ⬡ = ▲ 　　 ___ = ___ − ___

16. ★ **Test Prep**   Which addition fact helps you solve 17 − 8?

○ 8 + 7 = 15 　　　○ 9 + 8 = 17

○ 8 + 8 = 16 　　　○ 9 + 9 = 18

TAKE HOME ACTIVITY • Give your child 5 small objects, such as paper clips. Then ask your child how many more objects he or she would need to have 12.

FOR MORE PRACTICE:
Standards Practice Book, pp. P99–P100

Name _____

Choose an Operation

Essential Question How do you choose when to add and when to subtract to solve a problem?

COMMON CORE STANDARD CC.1.OA.1
Represent and solve problems involving addition and subtraction.

Listen and Draw REAL WORLD

Listen to the problem. Use ⬤ to solve.
Draw a picture to show your work.

_____ math games

Math Talk

How did you solve this problem? Explain.

MATHEMATICAL PRACTICES

FOR THE TEACHER • Read the following problem. Kira has 16 computer games. There are 8 adventure games. The rest are math games. How many math games does Kira have?

Model and Draw

Mary sees 8 squirrels. Jack sees 9 more squirrels than Mary. How many squirrels does Jack see?

Do you add or subtract to solve?

Explain how you chose to solve the problem.

(add)   **subtract**

____ squirrels

Share and Show

Circle **add** or **subtract**.
Write a number sentence to solve.

1. Hanna has 5 markers. Owen has 9 more markers than Hanna. How many markers does Owen have?

   add   subtract

____ markers

2. Angel has 13 apples. He gives some away. Then there were 5 apples. How many apples does he give away?

   add   subtract

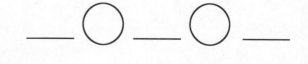

____ apples

3. Deon has 18 blocks. He builds a house with 9 of the blocks. How many blocks does Deon have now?

   add   subtract

____ blocks

Name _____

On Your Own

Circle **add** or **subtract**.
Write a number sentence to solve.

4. Rob sees 5 raccoons. Talia sees 4 more raccoons than Rob. How many raccoons do they see?

   add   **subtract**

   _____

   ____ raccoons

5. Eli has a box with 12 eggs. His other box has no eggs. How many eggs are in both boxes?

   add   **subtract**

   _____

   ____ eggs

6. Leah has a bowl with 16 fish. Some fish have long tails. 7 fish have short tails. How many fish have long tails?

   add   **subtract**

   _____

   ____ fish

7. 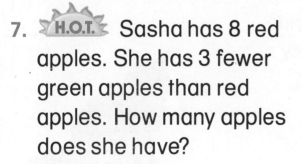 Sasha has 8 red apples. She has 3 fewer green apples than red apples. How many apples does she have?

   add   **subtract**

   _____

    ____ apples

PROBLEM SOLVING

REAL WORLD

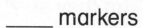

Write Math

Choose a way to solve.
Write or draw to explain.

8. James has 4 big markers
and 7 skinny markers.
How many
markers does
he have?

_____ markers

9. Sam has 9 baseball
cards. She wants to
have 17 cards. How
many more cards
does she need?

_____ more cards

10. H.O.T. Annie gets 15 pennies
on Monday. She gets 1 more
penny each day. How many
pennies does she have
on Friday?

_____ pennies

11. ⭐ **Test Prep** There are 15 kittens.
6 kittens are black. The rest are white.
Which number sentence shows how
to find the number of white kittens?

- $10 + 5 = 15$
- $9 - 6 = 3$
- $15 - 6 = 9$
- $6 + 5 = 11$

TAKE HOME ACTIVITY · Ask your child to write a number sentence
that could be used to solve Exercise 9.

212 two hundred twelve

© Houghton Mifflin Harcourt Publishing Company

FOR MORE PRACTICE:
Standards Practice Book, pp. P101–P102

Name _____

Algebra • Ways to Make Numbers to 20

Essential Question How can you add and subtract in different ways to make the same number?

COMMON CORE STANDARD CC.1.OA.6
Add and subtract within 20.

Listen and Draw

Use 🔲 🔲. Show two ways to make 10.
Draw to show your work.

Way One	Way Two

Math Talk
Explain how your models show two ways to make 10.

MATHEMATICAL
PRACTICES

HOME CONNECTION • Your child worked with making different numbers in various ways. This reinforces number fluency.

Model and Draw

How can you make the
number 12 in different ways?

You can add
or subtract to
make 12.

12
_6_ + _6_
_5_ + _4_ + _3_
_12_ − _0_

Share and Show

Math Board

Use . Write ways to make
the number at the top.

✓1.

13
___ + ___
___ − ___
___ + ___ + ___
___ + ___
___ ◯ ___

✓2.

10
___ − ___
___ + ___
___ − ___
___ + ___ + ___
___ ◯ ___

On Your Own

Use . Write ways to make the number at the top.

3.

17
___ + ___ + ___
___ + ___
___ − ___
___ ◯ ___

4.

14
___ + ___
___ + ___ + ___
___ − ___
___ ◯ ___

5.

16
___ + ___
___ + ___ + ___
___ − ___
___ ◯ ___

6.

18
___ + ___
___ + ___
___ + ___ + ___
___ ◯ ___

H.O.T. Choose a number. Write the number. ☐
Write two ways to make your number.

7.

8.

PROBLEM SOLVING

Write Math

Write numbers to make each line have the same sum.

9.
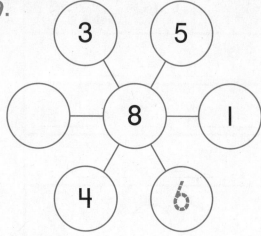

10.
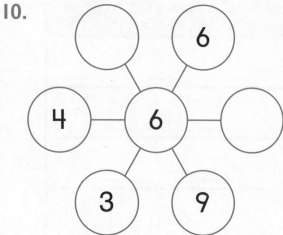

11. H.O.T. Choose a number from 14 to 20 to be the sum. Write numbers to make each line have your sum.

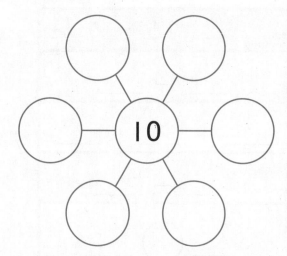

sum for each line ☐

12. ★ Test Prep Which way makes 17?

$8 + 7$ ○ $7 + 8$ ○ $10 - 7$ ○ $10 + 4 + 3$ ○

TAKE HOME ACTIVITY • Have your child explain three different ways to make 15. Encourage him or her to use addition and subtraction, including addition of three numbers.

FOR MORE PRACTICE:
Standards Practice Book, pp. P103–P104

Name _____

Algebra • Equal and Not Equal

Essential Question How can you decide if a number sentence is true or false?

COMMON CORE STANDARD CC.1.OA.7
Work with addition and subtraction equations.

Listen and Draw

Color the cards that make the same number.

$2 + 6$	$12 - 6$	$6 + 1$
$13 - 6$	$3 + 3 + 1$	$10 + 6$
$3 + 4$	$4 + 3$	$5 + 2 + 5$
$3 + 2 + 2$	$11 - 2$	$16 - 9$

Math Talk
Explain why you can use two of the cards you color and an equal sign to make a number sentence.

MATHEMATICAL PRACTICES

FOR THE TEACHER • Have children color the cards that make the same number.

Model and Draw

The equal sign means that both sides are the same.

Write a number to make each true.

$4 + 5 = 5 + 5$ is **not** true. It is false.

$9 = \underline{9}$ $4 + 5 = \underline{}$ $4 + 5 = \underline{} + 4$

Share and Show   Math Board

Which is true? Circle your answer.
Which is false? Cross out your answer.

THINK
Are both sides equal?

1.

$\boxed{7 = 8 - 1}$

$\cancel{1 + 2 = 3 = 2}$

2.

$4 + 1 = 5 + 2$

$6 - 6 = 7 - 7$

3.

$7 + 2 = 6 + 3$

$8 - 2 = 6 + 4$

4.

$5 - 4 = 4 - 3$

$10 = 1 + 0$

Name _____

On Your Own

Which are true? Circle your answers.
Which are false? Cross out your answers.

5.

$1 + 9 = 9 - 1$ | $8 + 1 = 2 + 7$ | $19 = 19$

6.

$8 = 5 + 3$ | $8 + 5 = 5 + 8$ | $6 + 2 = 4 + 4$

7.

$9 + 7 = 16$ | $16 - 9 = 9 + 7$ | $9 - 7 = 7 + 9$

8.

$12 - 3 = 9 - 0$ | $11 = 1 + 5 + 5$ | $10 = 8 - 2$

Write numbers to make sentences that are true.

9.

$2 + 10 = 7 + \underline{\quad}$

10.

$\underline{\quad} = 2 + 3 + 4$

11.

$0 + 9 = \underline{\quad} - 9$

12.

$\underline{\quad} + 7 = 7 + 6$

13.

$\underline{\quad} = \underline{\quad}$

14. H.O.T.

$\underline{\quad} + \underline{\quad} = \underline{\quad} + \underline{\quad}$

PROBLEM SOLVING REAL WORLD

Write Math

15. Which are true? Use 🖍 to color.

$20 = 20$	$9 + 1 + 1 = 11$	$8 - 0 = 8$
$12 = 1 + 2$	$10 + 1 = 1 + 10$	$7 = 14 + 7$

$$6 = 2 + 2 + 2$$

$$11 - 5 = 1 + 5$$

$$1 + 2 + 3 = 4 + 5$$

16. H.O.T. Use the same numbers.
Write a different number sentence
that is true.

$$7 + 8 = 15$$

___ = ___ ◯ ___

17. ⭐ Test Prep Which
makes the sentence true?

$$10 - 3 = 2 + \underline{\quad}$$

5	6	7	8
◯	◯	◯	◯

TAKE HOME ACTIVITY • Write $10 = 7 - 3$ and $10 = 7 + 3$ on a sheet of paper.
Ask your child to explain which is true.

FOR MORE PRACTICE:
Standards Practice Book, pp. P105–P106

Name _____

Basic Facts to 20

Essential Question How can addition and subtraction strategies help you find sums and differences?

COMMON CORE STANDARD CC.1.OA.6
Add and subtract within 20.

Listen and Draw

What is $2 + 8$?
Use 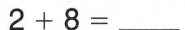. Draw to show a strategy you can use to solve.

$2 + 8 =$ _____

Math Talk

What other strategy could you use to solve the addition fact?

MATHEMATICAL PRACTICES

FOR THE TEACHER • Have children use two-color counters to model a strategy to solve the addition fact. Then have them draw a picture to show the strategy they used.

Sam is reading a story that has 10 pages. He has read 4 pages. How many pages does he have left to read?

THINK
I can use a related addition fact to solve 10 − 4.

What is 10 − 4?

$4 + \boxed{6} = 10$

So, $10 - 4 = \underline{6}$.

Share and Show

Add or subtract.

1. $2 + 5 = \underline{}$

2. $9 - 6 = \underline{}$

3. $\underline{} = 9 + 3$

4. $15 - 7 = \underline{}$

5. $3 - 1 = \underline{}$

6. $\underline{} = 2 + 6$

7. $2 + \boxed{} = 11$

8. $10 - \boxed{} = 2$

9. $8 = 8 + \boxed{}$

10. $12 - 9 = \underline{}$

11. $12 - 4 = \underline{}$

12. $\underline{} = 4 + 9$

13. $\boxed{} + 8 = 13$

14. $\boxed{} - 1 = 6$

15. $9 = \boxed{} + 3$

16. $16 - 7 = \underline{}$

✓17. $11 - 8 = \underline{}$

✓18. $\underline{} = 8 + 7$

Name _____

On Your Own

Add or subtract.

19.
$$\begin{array}{r} 6 \\ + 0 \\ \hline \end{array}$$

20.
$$\begin{array}{r} 17 \\ - 8 \\ \hline \end{array}$$

21.
$$\begin{array}{r} 7 \\ + 4 \\ \hline \end{array}$$

22.
$$\begin{array}{r} 9 \\ - 0 \\ \hline \end{array}$$

23.
$$\begin{array}{r} 17 \\ - 9 \\ \hline \end{array}$$

24.
$$\begin{array}{r} 4 \\ + 6 \\ \hline \end{array}$$

25.
$$\begin{array}{r} 7 \\ + \square \\ \hline 10 \end{array}$$

26.
$$\begin{array}{r} 8 \\ - \square \\ \hline 3 \end{array}$$

27.
$$\begin{array}{r} 8 \\ + \square \\ \hline 11 \end{array}$$

28.
$$\begin{array}{r} 8 \\ - \square \\ \hline 2 \end{array}$$

29.
$$\begin{array}{r} 10 \\ - \square \\ \hline 6 \end{array}$$

30.
$$\begin{array}{r} 9 \\ + \square \\ \hline 17 \end{array}$$

31.
$$\begin{array}{r} 6 \\ + 7 \\ \hline \end{array}$$

32.
$$\begin{array}{r} 4 \\ - \square \\ \hline 0 \end{array}$$

33.
$$\begin{array}{r} 5 \\ + \square \\ \hline 11 \end{array}$$

34.
$$\begin{array}{r} 13 \\ - 6 \\ \hline \end{array}$$

35.
$$\begin{array}{r} 17 \\ - 9 \\ \hline \end{array}$$

36.
$$\begin{array}{r} 8 \\ + \square \\ \hline 16 \end{array}$$

37.
$$\begin{array}{r} 10 \\ + 5 \\ \hline \end{array}$$

38.
$$\begin{array}{r} 13 \\ - 3 \\ \hline \end{array}$$

39.
$$\begin{array}{r} 10 \\ + \square \\ \hline 13 \end{array}$$

40.
$$\begin{array}{r} 20 \\ - 10 \\ \hline \end{array}$$

41.
$$\begin{array}{r} 10 \\ - \square \\ \hline 9 \end{array}$$

42.
$$\begin{array}{r} 9 \\ + \square \\ \hline 19 \end{array}$$

43. **H.O.T.** Use the clues to write the addition fact. The sum is 14. One addend is 2 more than the other.

$$\begin{array}{r} \square \\ + \square \\ \hline \square \end{array}$$

PROBLEM SOLVING REAL WORLD

Write Math

Solve. Write or draw to explain.

44. There are 14 rabbits in the field. Then 7 rabbits hop away. How many rabbits are still in the field?

_____ rabbits

45. There are 11 dogs at the park. 2 dogs are gray. The rest are brown. How many dogs are brown?

_____ brown dogs

46. H.O.T. Fill in the blanks. Solve. Write a number sentence.

There are _____ ladybugs on a leaf. Then _____ more ladybugs come. How many ladybugs are there now?

_____ ladybugs

47. ⭐ Test Prep What is $12 - 4$?

    14   13   11   8

    ○   ○   ○   ○

TAKE HOME ACTIVITY • Have your child draw a picture to solve $7 + 4$. Then have him or her tell a related subtraction fact.

FOR MORE PRACTICE:
Standards Practice Book, pp. P107–P108

Chapter 5 Review/Test

Vocabulary

Write a **related fact** for each number sentence. (p. 190)

1. $8 + 5 = 13$

   ___ ◯ ___ ◯ ___

2. $17 - 8 = 9$

   ___ ◯ ___ ◯ ___

Concepts and Skills

Subtract. Then add to check your answer. (CC.1.OA.6)

3. $14 - 6 = \boxed{}$

   $\boxed{} + 6 = \boxed{}$

4. $11 - 5 = \boxed{}$

   $\boxed{} + 5 = \boxed{}$

5. $20 - 10 = \boxed{}$

   $\boxed{} + 10 = \boxed{}$

6. $13 - 9 = \boxed{}$

   $\boxed{} + 9 = \boxed{}$

Add and subtract.
Circle the related facts. (CC.1.OA.6)

7.

   $5 + 9 = $ ____

   $14 - 5 = $ ____

8.

   $7 + 5 = $ ____

   $7 - 5 = $ ____

9.

   $6 + 4 = $ ____

   $10 - 4 = $ ____

10. Which is a related
    addition fact for
    $15 - 9 = 6$? (CC.1.OA.6)

$15 - 6 = 9$ $9 + 9 = 18$ $6 + 9 = 15$ $6 + 8 = 14$
  ○   ○   ○   ○

---

11. Which is **not** a related fact? (CC.1.OA.6)

$11 - 6 = 5$ $6 - 5 = 1$ $6 + 5 = 11$ $5 + 6 = 11$
  ○   ○   ○   ○

---

12. Which addition sentence
    can you use to check the
    subtraction? (CC.1.OA.6)

    $17 - 9 = \boxed{}$

$4 + 9 = 13$ $6 + 8 = 14$
  ○   ○

$5 + 9 = 14$ $8 + 9 = 17$
  ○   ○

---

13. Pat picks 18 flowers.
    9 are yellow.
    The rest are pink.
    How many are pink? (CC.1.OA.1)

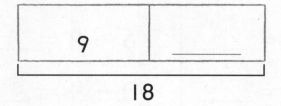

| 9 | _____ |

18

6   7   8   9
○   ○   ○   ○

226 two hundred twenty-six

14. What is the missing number? (CC.1.OA.8)

$$16 = 8 + \boxed{}$$
$$\boxed{} = 16 - 8$$

9	8	7	6
○	○	○	○

15. What is the missing number? (CC.1.OA.8)

$$4 + \underline{} = 10$$

$$10 - 4 = \underline{}$$

4	6	7	10
○	○	○	○

16. Mia scores 8 goals. The team gets 15 goals. Which number sentence shows how many goals are scored by the rest of the team? (CC.1.OA.1)

○ $15 - 9 = 6$ ○ $15 - 8 = 7$

○ $8 + 6 = 14$ ○ $9 + 8 = 17$

17. Which shows a way to make 15? (CC.1.OA.6)

$4 + 5 + 3$	$6 + 8$	$2 + 7 + 6$	$16 - 9$
○	○	○	○

18. Which number makes the sentence true? (CC.1.OA.7)

$$8 + 2 = \underline{}$$

8	10	15	16
○	○	○	○

Performance Task (CC.1.OA.1, CC.1.OA.6)

There are 15 children eating lunch.

_____ children buy lunch.

_____ children do not buy lunch.

- Choose and write numbers to complete the story problem.
- Draw a picture to explain.
- Then write the related facts for your story problem.

Show how to solve the problem.
Use numbers, pictures, or words.

> Show your work.
>
> _____ children buy lunch
> _____ children do not buy lunch
>
>
>
>
>
>
>
>
> ____ + ____ = ____   ____ − ____ = ____
>
> ____ + ____ = ____   ____ − ____ = ____

CRITICAL AREA

Around the Neighborhood

written by **John Hudson**

UNITED STATES POST OFFICE

We Deliver

COLLECTION TIMES

OUT OF TOWN

COMMON CORE

CRITICAL AREA Developing understanding of whole number relationships and place value, including grouping in tens and ones

229

The mail carrier brings letters to
Mr. and Mrs. Jones. How many
letters does she bring?

____ ◯ ____ ◯ ____

© Houghton Mifflin Harcourt Publishing Company

Social Studies

How do mail carriers help us?

The mail carrier brings packages to the fire station. Then she brings more packages. How many packages does she bring?

_____ ◯ _____ ◯ _____

Social Studies

How do firefighters help us?

It is time for lunch. The mail carrier eats in the park. How many boys and girls are playing?

____ ◯ ____ ◯ ____

Social Studies

How do parents help us?

The mail carrier brings 12 packages to the police station. "This person has moved," says the police officer. "You need to take these back." How many packages does the officer keep?

____ ◯ ____ ◯ ____

Social Studies

How do police officers help us?

The mail carrier stops at City Hall.
She brings 8 letters for the mayor.
She brings 4 letters for the city clerk.
How many letters does she bring?

_____ ◯ _____ ◯ _____

Social Studies

How do city workers help us?

Name _____

Write About the Story

One day, Mr. and Mrs. Jones each got the same number of letters. They got 12 letters in all. Draw the two groups of letters.

Mr. Jones

Mrs. Jones

Letters for Mr. Jones

Letters for Mrs. Jones

Write the number sentence. _____ ◯ _____ ◯ _____

 Describe your number sentence. Use a vocabulary word.

_____

_____

_____

_____

© Houghton Mifflin Harcourt Publishing Company

235

How Many Letters?

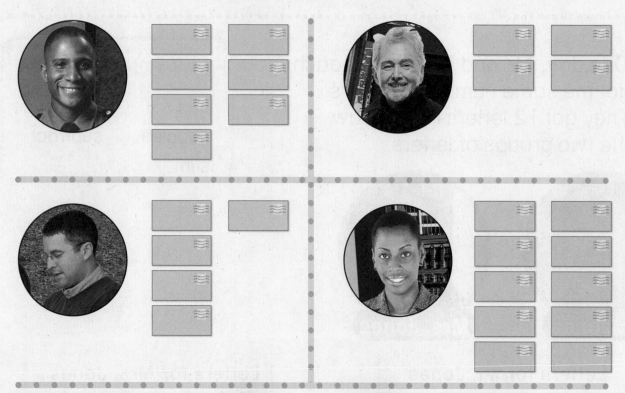

1. How many letters do and have in all?

_____ ◯ _____ ◯ _____

2. How many more letters does have than ?

_____ ◯ _____ ◯ _____

3. Circle the two that have 11 letters in all.

Math Board Make up an addition story about the mail carrier bringing letters to you and a classmate. Write the number sentence.

236

Chapter 6

Count and Model Numbers

Curious About Math with
Curious George

Dan and May like apples.
They buy 15 apples in all.
If Dan buys 10 apples, how
many apples does May buy?

Show What You Know

Explore Numbers 6 to 9

Count how many. Circle the number.

1.  6

7

2.  8

9

Count Groups to 20

Circle groups of 10. Write how many.

3.

___

4.

___

Make Groups of 10

Use ● . Draw to show a group of 10
in two different ways.

5.

6.

Family note: This page checks your child's understanding
of important skills needed for success in Chapter 6.

GO
Online

Assessment Options
Soar to Success Math

Vocabulary Builder

Visualize It

Draw pictures in the box to show the number.

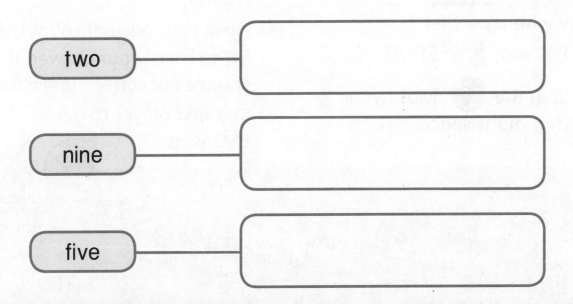

two

nine

five

Understand Vocabulary

Write a review word to name the number.

1.  _____

2. _____

3. _____

 GO Online • eStudent Edition • Multimedia eGlossary

Game Show the Numbers

Materials • 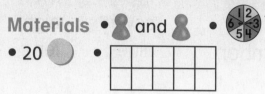 and 👤 • 🎡

• 20 🔵 • ☐☐☐☐☐
                ☐☐☐☐☐

Play with a partner.

1. Put your 👤 on START.

2. Spin the 🎡 . Move your 👤 that many spaces.

3. Read the number. Use 🔵 to show the number on a ten frame.

4. Have your partner count the 🔵 to check your answer. If you are not correct, lose a turn.

5. The first player to get to END wins.

Name _____

Count by Ones to 120

Essential Question How can knowing a counting pattern help you count to 120?

COMMON CORE STANDARD CC.1.NBT.1
Extend the counting sequence.

Listen and Draw REAL WORLD

Write the missing numbers.

21	22	23	24	25	26	27	28	29	30
31	32	33	34	35	36	37	38	39	40
41	42	43	44	45	46	47	48	49	50
51	52	53	54	55	56	57	58	59	60
61	62	63	64	65	66	67	68	69	70
71	72	73	74	75	76	77	78	79	80
81	82	83	84	85	86	87	88	89	90
91	92	93	94	95	96	97	98	99	100

Math Talk
Explain how you know which numbers are missing.

MATHEMATICAL PRACTICES

FOR THE TEACHER • Read the following problem. Debbie saw this page in a puzzle book. Two rows of numbers are missing. Use what you know about counting to write the missing numbers.

Model and Draw

Count forward.
Write the numbers.

10, __11__, ____, ____, ____

100, __101__, ____, ____, ____

110, __111__, ____, ____, ____

1	2	3	4	5	6	7	8	9	10
11	12	13	14	15	16	17	18	19	20
21	22	23	24	25	26	27	28	29	30
31	32	33	34	35	36	37	38	39	40
41	42	43	44	45	46	47	48	49	50
51	52	53	54	55	56	57	58	59	60
61	62	63	64	65	66	67	68	69	70
71	72	73	74	75	76	77	78	79	80
81	82	83	84	85	86	87	88	89	90
91	92	93	94	95	96	97	98	99	100
101	102	103	104	105	106	107	108	109	110
111	112	113	114	115	116	117	118	119	120

Share and Show

Use a Counting Chart. Count forward.
Write the numbers.

> Look for a pattern to help you write the numbers.

1. 114, ____, ____, ____, ____, ____, ____

2. 51, ____, ____, ____, ____, ____, ____

3. 94, ____, ____, ____, ____, ____, ____

4. 78, ____, ____, ____, ____, ____, ____

☑ 5. 35, ____, ____, ____, ____, ____, ____

☑ 6. 104, ____, ____, ____, ____, ____, ____

On Your Own

Use a Counting Chart. Count forward.
Write the numbers.

7. 19, ____, ____, ____, ____, ____, ____, ____, ____

8. 98, ____, ____, ____, ____, ____, ____, ____, ____

9. 60, ____, ____, ____, ____, ____, ____, ____, ____

10. 27, ____, ____, ____, ____, ____, ____, ____, ____

11. 107, ____, ____, ____, ____, ____, ____, ____, ____

12. 43, ____, ____, ____, ____, ____, ____, ____, ____

13. 68, ____, ____, ____, ____, ____, ____, ____, ____

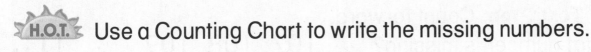 Use a Counting Chart to write the missing numbers.

14. ____, ____, ____, ____, ____, 120

15. ____, ____, ____, ____, ____, 34

PROBLEM SOLVING REAL WORLD

Write Math

Use a Counting Chart. Draw and write numbers to solve.

16. The bag has 99 pennies. Draw more pennies so there are 105 pennies in all. Write the numbers as you count.

99

17. **H.O.T.** The bag has 56 pennies. How many more pennies do you need to add to the bag to have 64 pennies?

56

_____ pennies

18. ⭐ **Test Prep** Count forward. What number is missing?

107, 108, 109, ___, 111

100	101	110	120
○	○	○	○

TAKE HOME ACTIVITY • Take a walk with your child. Count aloud together as you take 120 steps.

FOR MORE PRACTICE:
Standards Practice Book, pp. P113–P114

Name _____

Count by Tens to 120

Essential Question How do numbers change as you count by tens to 120?

COMMON CORE STANDARD CC.1.NBT.1
Extend the counting sequence.

Listen and Draw

Start on 10. Count forward by tens.
Color each number as you say it.

1	2	3	4	5	6	7	8	9	10
11	12	13	14	15	16	17	18	19	20
21	22	23	24	25	26	27	28	29	30
31	32	33	34	35	36	37	38	39	40
41	42	43	44	45	46	47	48	49	50
51	52	53	54	55	56	57	58	59	60
61	62	63	64	65	66	67	68	69	70
71	72	73	74	75	76	77	78	79	80
81	82	83	84	85	86	87	88	89	90
91	92	93	94	95	96	97	98	99	100

HOME CONNECTION • Your child used a hundred chart to count by tens. Using a hundred chart, or similar counting charts, can help children understand a counting sequence when starting from numbers other than 1.

Math Talk
Which numbers in the hundred chart did you color? Explain.

MATHEMATICAL PRACTICES

Chapter 6

two hundred forty-five **245**

Model and Draw

Start on 3. Count by tens.

1	2	3	4	5	6	7	8	9	10
11	12	13	14	15	16	17	18	19	20
21	22	23	24	25	26	27	28	29	30
31	32	33	34	35	36	37	38	39	40
41	42	43	44	45	46	47	48	49	50
51	52	53	54	55	56	57	58	59	60
61	62	63	64	65	66	67	68	69	70
71	72	73	74	75	76	77	78	79	80
81	82	83	84	85	86	87	88	89	90
91	92	93	94	95	96	97	98	99	100
101	102	103	104	105	106	107	108	109	110
111	112	113	114	115	116	117	118	119	120

THINK
When you count by tens, each number is ten more.

3, 13, 23, 33, ____, ____, ____, ____, ____, ____, ____, ____

Share and Show

Use a Counting Chart to count by tens.
Write the numbers.

1. Start on 17.

   17, ____, ____, ____, ____, ____, ____, ____, ____

2. Start on 1.

   1, ____, ____, ____, ____, ____, ____, ____, ____

3. Start on 39.

   39, ____, ____, ____, ____, ____, ____, ____, ____

Name _____

On Your Own

Use a Counting Chart. Count by tens.
Write the numbers.

4. 40, ____, ____, ____, ____, ____, ____, ____, ____

5. 15, ____, ____, ____, ____, ____, ____, ____, ____

6. 28, ____, ____, ____, ____, ____, ____, ____, ____

7. 6, ____, ____, ____, ____, ____, ____, ____, ____

8. 14, ____, ____, ____, ____, ____, ____, ____, ____

9. 32, ____, ____, ____, ____, ____, ____, ____, ____

 Solve.

10. You say me when you start on 43 and count by tens. I am after 73. I am before 93. What number am I?

_____

11. You say me when you start on 21 and count by tens. I am after 91. I am before 111. What number am I?

_____

PROBLEM SOLVING REAL WORLD

Write Math

H.O.T. Use what you know about a Counting Chart to write the missing numbers.

12.
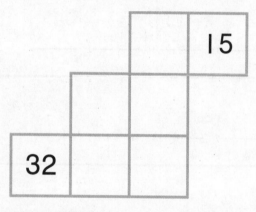

6	
16	

	28	29

13.
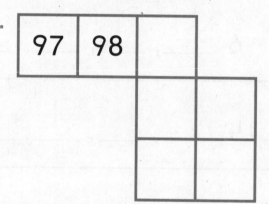

	54	55
	64	

72		

14.

		15

32		

15.

97	98	

16. ⭐ **Test Prep** Count by tens.
What numbers are missing?

3, 13, 23, ____, ____, 53

24, 25 ○   33, 34 ○   33, 43 ○   63, 73 ○

TAKE HOME ACTIVITY • Write these numbers: 2, 12, 22, 32, 42.
Ask your child to tell you the next 5 numbers.

FOR MORE PRACTICE:
Standards Practice Book, pp. P115–P116

Name _____

Understand Ten and Ones

Essential Question How can you use different ways to write a number as ten and ones?

COMMON CORE STANDARD CC.1.NBT.2b
Understand place value.

Listen and Draw REAL WORLD

Use ▣ to model the problem.
Draw the ▣ to show your work.

FOR THE TEACHER • Read the problem. Tim has 10 pennies. He gets 2 more pennies. How many pennies does Tim have now?

Math Talk
How does your picture show the pennies Tim has? **Explain.**

MATHEMATICAL PRACTICES

Chapter 6

two hundred forty-nine **249**

Model and Draw

13 is a two-**digit** number.
The 1 in 13 means 1 **ten**.
The 3 in 13 means 3 **ones**.

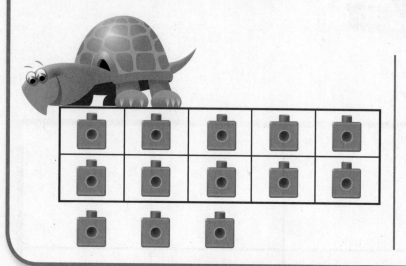

__1__ ten __3__ ones

__10__ + __3__

__13__

Share and Show

Use the model. Write the number
three different ways.

☑ 1.

____ ten ____ ones

____ + ____

____

☑ 2.

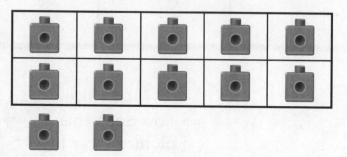

____ ten ____ ones

____ + ____

____

On Your Own

Use the model. Write the number
three different ways.

3.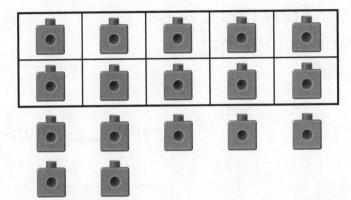

_____ ten _____ ones

_____ + _____

_____

4.

_____ ten _____ ones

_____ + _____

_____

5. **H.O.T.** Draw to show the number.
Write the missing numbers.

_____ ten _____ ones

_____ + _____

PROBLEM SOLVING REAL WORLD

Write Math

H.O.T. **Draw cubes to show the number.**
Write the number different ways.

6. David has 1 ten and 3 ones. Abby has 6 ones.
They put all their tens and ones together.
What number did they make?

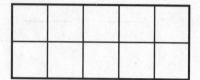

____ ten ____ ones

____ + ____

____

7. Karen has 7 ones. Jimmy has 9 ones.
They put all their ones together.
What number did they make?

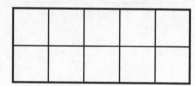

____ ten ____ ones

____ + ____

____

8. ⭐ **Test Prep** Which shows
the same number?

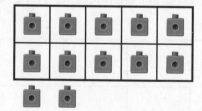

1 ten 12 ones   1 ten 7 ones   1 ten 2 ones   1 ten
○   ○   ○   ○

TAKE HOME ACTIVITY • Show your child one group of 10 pennies and
one group of 8 pennies. Ask your child to tell how many tens and ones
there are and say the number. Repeat with other numbers from 11 to 19.

FOR MORE PRACTICE:
Standards Practice Book, pp. P117–P118

Name _____

Make Ten and Ones

Essential Question How can you show a number as ten and ones?

COMMON CORE STANDARD **CC.1.NBT.2b**
Understand place value.

Listen and Draw

Use ▪ to model the problem.
Draw ▪ to show your work.

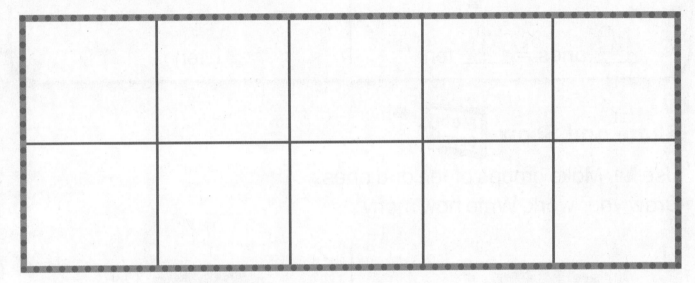

Draw to show the group of ten another way.

FOR THE TEACHER • Read the problem. Connie has 10 cubes. How can she arrange them to show 1 ten?

Math Talk
How are the pictures the same? How are the pictures different? **Explain.**
MATHEMATICAL PRACTICES

Chapter 6

two hundred fifty-three **253**

Model and Draw

You can group 10  to make 1 ten.

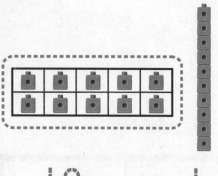

_10_ ones = _1_ ten

> Draw a quick picture to show 1 ten.

1 ten

Share and Show 📝 Math Board

Use . Make groups of ten and ones. Draw your work. Write how many.

1.

11 eleven

_1_ ten _1_ one

2.

12 twelve

____ ten ____ ones

✓ 3.

13 thirteen

____ ten ____ ones

✓ 4.

14 fourteen

____ ten ____ ones

Name _____

On Your Own

Use . Make groups of ten and ones.
Draw your work. Write how many.

5.

15
fifteen

_____ ten _____ ones

6.

16
sixteen

_____ ten _____ ones

7.

17
seventeen

_____ ten _____ ones

8.

18
eighteen

_____ ten _____ ones

9.

19
nineteen

_____ ten _____ ones

PROBLEM SOLVING REAL WORLD

Write Math

H.O.T. Solve.

10. Emily wants to write
ten and ones to show 20.
What does Emily write?

20
twenty

_____ ten _____ ones

---

11. Gina thinks of a number
that has 7 ones and 1 ten.
What is the number?

_____

---

12. Ben drew this picture
to show a number.
What is the number?

○
○
○
○
○

_____

---

13. ⭐ **Test Prep** How many tens
and ones make this number?

12
twelve

1 ten 1 one	1 ten 2 ones	1 ten 12 ones	2 tens 1 one
○	○	○	○

TAKE HOME ACTIVITY • Give your child numbers from 11 to 19.
Have your child work with pennies to show a group of ten and a
group of ones for each number.

FOR MORE PRACTICE:
Standards Practice Book, pp. P119–P120

Name _____

Tens

Essential Question How can you model and name groups of ten?

COMMON CORE STANDARDS CC.1.NBT.2a, CC.1.NBT.2c
Understand place value.

Listen and Draw REAL WORLD

Use ▣ to solve the riddle.
Draw and write to show your work.

FOR THE TEACHER • Read the following riddles. I am thinking of a number that is the same as 1 ten and 4 ones. What is my number? I am thinking of a number that is the same as 1 ten and 0 ones. What is my number?

Math Talk
Explain what you did to solve the first riddle.

MATHEMATICAL PRACTICES

Model and Draw

You can group ones to make tens.

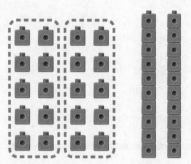

> Draw a quick picture to show the tens.

20 ones = __2__ tens __0__ ones

__2__ tens = __20__
twenty

Share and Show

Use . Make groups of ten.
Write the tens and ones.

> Draw the tens.
> Count by tens.

☑ 1.

30 ones = ____ tens ____ ones

____ tens = ____
thirty

☑ 2.

40 ones = ____ tens ____ ones

____ tens = ____
forty

258 two hundred fifty-eight

© Houghton Mifflin Harcourt Publishing Company

Name _____

On Your Own

Use . Make groups of ten.
Write the tens and ones.

Draw the tens.
Count by tens.

3. 50 ones

____ tens ____ ones

____ tens = ____
fifty

4. 60 ones

____ tens ____ ones

____ tens = ____
sixty

5. 70 ones

____ tens ____ ones

____ tens = ____
seventy

6. 80 ones

____ tens ____ ones

____ tens = ____
eighty

7. 90 ones

____ tens ____ ones

____ tens = ____
ninety

8. H.O.T. 100 ones

____ tens ____ ones

____ tens = ____
hundred

TAKE HOME ACTIVITY • Have your child count out small objects
into groups of ten, tell how many tens in all, and then say
the number word.

FOR MORE PRACTICE:
Standards Practice Book, pp. P121–P122

Name _____

Concepts and Skills

Use a Counting Chart.
Count forward. Write
the numbers. (CC.1.NBT.1)

1. 63, 64, ____, ____, ____

2. 108, 109, ____, ____, ____

Use a Counting Chart.
Count by tens. Write
the numbers. (CC.1.NBT.1)

3. 42, 52, ____, ____, ____

4. 79, 89, ____, ____, ____

5. Use the model. Write the number
   three different ways. (CC.1.NBT.2b)

____ ten ____ ones

____ + ____

____

Use 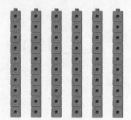. Make groups of ten and ones.
Draw your work. Write how many. (CC.1.NBT.2b)

6.

15
fifteen

____ ten ____ ones

7. ⭐ **Test Prep** What number does the
   model show? (CC.1.NBT.2a, CC.1.NBT.2c)

70   60   50   6
○   ○   ○   ○

Name _____

Tens and Ones to 50

Essential Question How can you group cubes to show a number as tens and ones?

COMMON CORE STANDARD **CC.1.NBT.2**
Understand place value.

Listen and Draw

Use to model the number.
Draw to show your work.

Tens	Ones

> **Math Talk**
> How did you figure out how many tens and ones are in 23? **Explain.**
>
> MATHEMATICAL PRACTICES

FOR THE TEACHER • Ask children to use 23 cubes and show them as tens and ones.

© Houghton Mifflin Harcourt Publishing Company

Model and Draw

The 2 in 24 means 2 tens.

Tens	Ones

__2__ tens __4__ ones = __24__

The 2 in 42 means 2 ones.

Tens	Ones

__4__ tens __2__ ones = __42__

Share and Show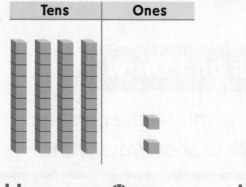

Use your MathBoard and  to show the tens and ones. Write the numbers.

1.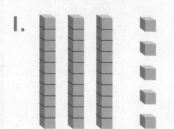

____ tens ____ ones = ____

2.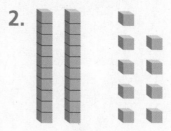

____ tens ____ ones = ____

3.

____ tens____ ones = ____

4.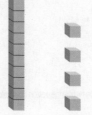

____ ten ____ ones = ____

On Your Own

Write the numbers.

5.

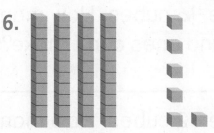

____ tens ____ ones = ____

6.

____ tens ____ ones = ____

7.

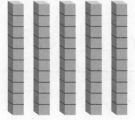

____ tens ____ ones = ____

8.

____ tens ____ ones = ____

9. **H.O.T.** Mary drew tens and ones to show 32.
She made a mistake.
Draw a correct quick picture to show 32.
Write the numbers.

Tens	Ones

Tens	Ones

____ tens ____ ones = ____

PROBLEM SOLVING

Solve. Write the numbers.

10. I have 46 cubes. How many tens and ones can I make?

_____ tens _____ ones

11. I have 32 cubes. How many tens and ones can I make?

_____ tens _____ ones

12. I have 28 cubes. How many tens and ones can I make?

_____ tens _____ ones

13. **H.O.T.** I am a number less than 50. I have 8 ones and some tens. What numbers could I be?

_____

14. ⭐ **Test Prep**   Which number does the model show?

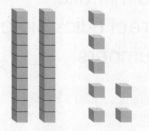

9   27   50   72
○   ○   ○   ○

TAKE HOME ACTIVITY • Write a two-digit number from 20 to 50, such as 26. Ask your child to tell which digit names the tens and which digit names the ones. Repeat with different numbers.

FOR MORE PRACTICE:
Standards Practice Book, pp. P123–P124

Name _____

Tens and Ones to 100

Essential Question How can you show numbers to 100 as tens and ones?

COMMON CORE STANDARD CC.1.NBT.2
Understand place value.

Listen and Draw

Use ▭▭▭▭▭▭▭▭▭▭ ▪ to model the number.
Draw a quick picture to show your work.

25
50
52

Math Talk
How did you figure out how many tens and ones are in 52? **Explain.**

MATHEMATICAL PRACTICES

FOR THE TEACHER • Ask children to use base-ten blocks to show how many tens and ones there are in 25, 50, and 52.

© Houghton Mifflin Harcourt Publishing Company

Model and Draw

The number just after 99 is 100.
10 tens is the same as 1 **hundred**.

Draw quick pictures to show 99 and 100.

_9_ tens _9_ ones = _99_ | _10_ tens _0_ ones = _100_

Share and Show

Use your MathBoard and 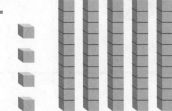 to
show the tens and ones. Write the numbers.

1.

____ tens ____ ones = ____

2.

____ tens ____ ones = ____

3.

____ tens ____ ones = ____

4.

____ tens ____ ones = ____

Name _____

On Your Own

Write the numbers.

5.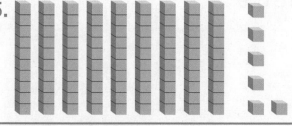

_____ tens _____ ones = _____

6.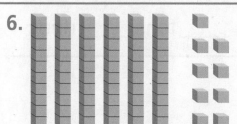

_____ tens _____ ones = _____

7.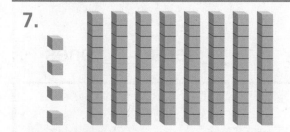

_____ tens _____ ones = _____

8.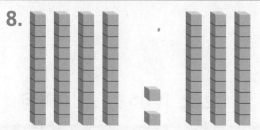

_____ tens _____ ones = _____

9.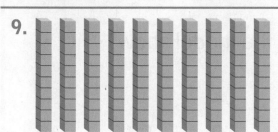

_____ tens _____ ones = _____

---

10. **H.O.T.** What number is the same as 7 tens and 20 ones?

_____

11. **H.O.T.** What number is the same as 5 tens and 13 ones?

PROBLEM SOLVING REAL WORLD

Write Math

Draw a quick picture to show the number.
Write how many tens and ones there are.

12. Edna has 82 stamps.

____ tens ____ ones

13. Amy has 79 pennies.

____ tens ____ ones

14. **H.O.T.** Moe has a group
of 70 red feathers and
30 brown feathers.

____ tens ____ ones

15. ⭐ **Test Prep** Which number does the model show?

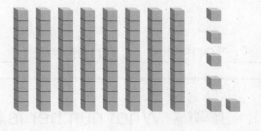

14	68	86	95
○	○	○	○

TAKE HOME ACTIVITY • Give your child numbers from 50 to 100.
Ask your child to draw a picture to show the tens and the ones in
each number and then write the number.

FOR MORE PRACTICE:
Standards Practice Book, pp. P125–P126

Problem Solving • Show Numbers in Different Ways

Essential Question How can making a model help you show a number in different ways?

COMMON CORE STANDARDS CC.1.NBT.2a, CC.1.NBT.3
Understand place value.

Gary and Jill both want 23 stickers for a class project. There are 3 sheets of 10 stickers and 30 single stickers on the table. How could Gary and Jill each take 23 stickers?

🔑 Unlock the Problem REAL WORLD

What do I need to find?

_____

__two__ different ways to make a number

What information do I need to use?

The number is ___23___.

Show how to solve the problem.

Gary	
Tens	**Ones**

_23_

(⠿)

Jill	
Tens	**Ones**

_23_

HOME CONNECTION · Showing the number with base-ten blocks helps your child explore different ways to combine tens and ones.

Try Another Problem

Use ▭▭▭▭ ▭ to show the number two different ways. Draw both ways.

• What do I need to find?
• What information do I need to use?

1. 46

Tens	Ones

⎯⎯ ◯ ⎯⎯

Tens	Ones

2. 71

Tens	Ones

⎯⎯ ◯ ⎯⎯

Tens	Ones

3. 65

Tens	Ones

⎯⎯ ◯ ⎯⎯

Tens	Ones

Math Talk
Look at Exercise 3. **Explain** why both ways show 65.

MATHEMATICAL PRACTICES

Share and Show

Use ▭▭▭▭▭ ▪ to show the number
two different ways. Draw both ways.

Write Math

4. 59

Tens	Ones

___ ◯ ___

Tens	Ones

5. 34

Tens	Ones

___ ◯ ___

Tens	Ones

6. H.O.T. Show 31 three ways.

Tens	Ones

Tens	Ones

Tens	Ones

___ ◯ ___   ___ ◯ ___

On Your Own

Write a number sentence to solve. Draw to explain.

Write Math

7. Felix invites 15 friends to his party. Some friends are girls. 8 friends are boys. How many friends are girls?

___ ◯ ___ ◯ ___ girls

 Solve. Write the numbers.

8. I am a number less than 35. I have 3 tens and some ones. What numbers can I be?

_____

9. ⭐ **Test Prep** Which is a different way to show the same number?

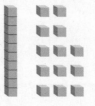

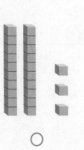 ◯

◯

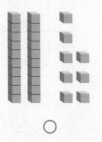 ◯

◯

TAKE HOME ACTIVITY • Have your child draw quick pictures to show the number 56 two ways.

272 two hundred seventy-two

FOR MORE PRACTICE:
Standards Practice Book, pp. P127–P128

© Houghton Mifflin Harcourt Publishing Company

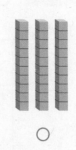
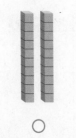
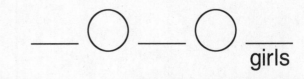

Name _____

Model, Read, and Write Numbers from 100 to 110

COMMON CORE STANDARD CC.1.NBT.1
Extend the counting sequence.

Essential Question How can you model, read, and write numbers from 100 to 110?

Listen and Draw REAL WORLD

Use .

Circle a number to answer the question.

1	2	3	4	5	6	7	8	9	10
11	12	13	14	15	16	17	18	19	20
21	22	23	24	25	26	27	28	29	30
31	32	33	34	35	36	37	38	39	40
41	42	43	44	45	46	47	48	49	50
51	52	53	54	55	56	57	58	59	60
61	62	63	64	65	66	67	68	69	70
71	72	73	74	75	76	77	78	79	80
81	82	83	84	85	86	87	88	89	90
91	92	93	94	95	96	97	98	99	100

Math Talk

Explain why 100 is to the right of 99 on the hundred chart. **Explain** why 100 is below 90.

MATHEMATICAL PRACTICES

FOR THE TEACHER • Have children locate each number on the hundred chart. What number is the same as 30 ones? What number is the same as 10 tens? What number is the same as 8 tens 7 ones? What number has 1 more one than 52? What number has 1 more ten than 65?

Model and Draw

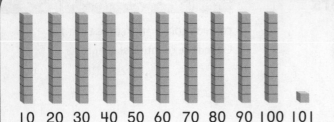

10 20 30 40 50 60 70 80 90 100 101

10 tens and 1 more = __101__

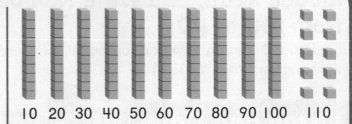

10 20 30 40 50 60 70 80 90 100 110

10 tens and 10 more = __110__

Share and Show Math Board

Use  to model the number.
Write the number.

1. 10 tens and 1 more

_____

2. 10 tens and 2 more

_____

3. 10 tens and 3 more

_____

4. 10 tens and 4 more

_____

☑5. 10 tens and 5 more

_____

☑6. 10 tens and 6 more

_____

Name _____

On Your Own

Use ▭▭▭▭▭ ▫ to model the number.
Write the number.

7. 10 tens and 7 more	8. 10 tens and 8 more	9. 10 tens and 9 more
_____	_____	_____

10. 10 tens and 10 more	11. H.O.T. 11 tens
_____	_____

Write the number.

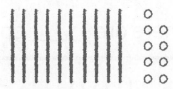

12.

_____

13.

_____

14.

_____

15.

_____

PROBLEM SOLVING

REAL WORLD

 H.O.T. Solve to find the number of apples.

THINK

 = 1 apple

= 10 apples

16.

There are _____ apples.

17.

There are _____ apples.

18.

There are _____ apples.

19. ⭐ **Test Prep** What number does the model show?

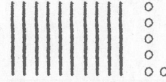

100   105   106   110
○   ○   ○   ○

© Houghton Mifflin Harcourt Publishing Company

 TAKE HOME ACTIVITY • Give your child a group of 100 to 110 pennies. Ask him or her to make as many groups of ten as possible, then tell you the total number of pennies.

FOR MORE PRACTICE:
Standards Practice Book, pp. P129–P130

Name _____

Model, Read, and Write Numbers from 110 to 120

Essential Question How can you model, read, and write numbers from 110 to 120?

COMMON CORE STANDARD CC.1.NBT.1
Extend the counting sequence.

Listen and Draw REAL WORLD

How many seashells are there?

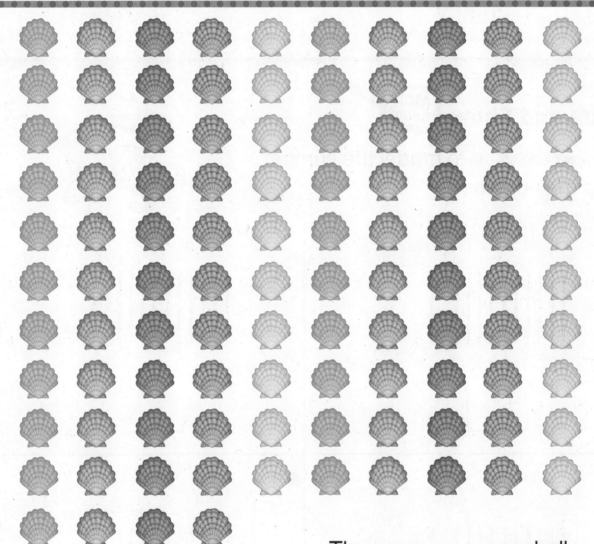

There are _____ seashells.

Math Talk
How did you decide how many seashells there are? **Explain.**

MATHEMATICAL PRACTICES

FOR THE TEACHER • Heidi has this collection of seashells. How many seashells does Heidi have?

Chapter 6

two hundred seventy-seven **277**

11 tens is 110.

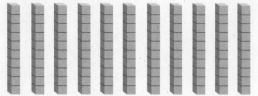

12 tens is 120.

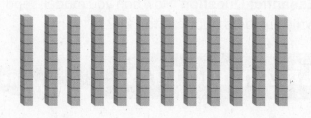

110

120

Share and Show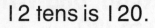

Use  to model the number.
Write the number.

1.

2.

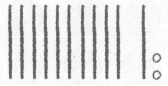

_____

☑3.

_____

☑4.

_____

Name _____

On Your Own

Use  to model the number.
Write the number.

5. _____	**6.** _____	**7.**
8. _____	**9.** _____	**10.**

 **Write the number.**

11. _____	**12.** _____	**13.** _____

PROBLEM SOLVING REAL WORLD

Write Math

H.O.T. Choose a way to solve.
Draw or write to explain.

14. Joe collects pennies. He can make
11 groups of 10 pennies.
How many pennies
does Joe have?

_____ pennies

15. Cindy collects buttons. She can
make 11 groups of 10 buttons
and one more group of 7 buttons.
How many buttons
does Cindy have?

_____ buttons

16. Lee collects marbles. He can make
11 groups of 10 marbles
and has 2 marbles left over.
How many marbles
does Lee have?

_____ marbles

17. ⭐ **Test Prep** What number
does the model show?

| | | | | | | | | | | | |

100   101   110   120
○   ○   ○   ○

TAKE HOME ACTIVITY • Give your child groups of 100 to 120 pennies. Ask
him or her to make as many groups of ten as possible, then tell you the total
number of pennies.

280 two hundred eighty

FOR MORE PRACTICE:
Standards Practice Book, pp. P131–P132

Name _____

Vocabulary

Circle the **ones** in each number.
Draw a line under the **tens** in each number. (p. 250)

1. 48

2. 84

Concepts and Skills

Use the Counting Chart.
Write the numbers. (CC.1.NBT.1)

3. Count forward.

   1 1 1 , 1 1 2 , _____ , _____ , _____

4. Count by tens.

   65, 75, _____ , _____ , _____

1	2	3	4	5	6	7	8	9	10
11	12	13	14	15	16	17	18	19	20
21	22	23	24	25	26	27	28	29	30
31	32	33	34	35	36	37	38	39	40
41	42	43	44	45	46	47	48	49	50
51	52	53	54	55	56	57	58	59	60
61	62	63	64	65	66	67	68	69	70
71	72	73	74	75	76	77	78	79	80
81	82	83	84	85	86	87	88	89	90
91	92	93	94	95	96	97	98	99	100
101	102	103	104	105	106	107	108	109	110
111	112	113	114	115	116	117	118	119	120

Write the numbers. (CC.1.NBT.2)

5.

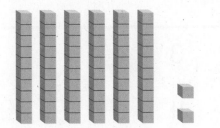

_____ tens _____ ones = _____

6.

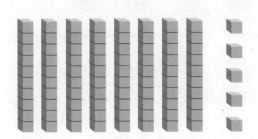

_____ tens _____ ones = _____

7. **Which shows the same number?** (CC.1.NBT.2b)

12
twelve

○ 3 tens

○ 1 ten 3 ones

○ 1 ten 2 ones

○ 3 ones

8. **Which shows the same number?** (CC.1.NBT.2b)

○ 5 tens 5 ones

○ 5 tens 1 one

○ 1 ten 5 ones

○ 1 ten 1 one

9. **Which shows the same number?** (CC.1.NBT.2b)

○ 10 + 10

○ 10 + 9

○ 10 + 5

○ 10 + 4

10. **Which number does the model show?** (CC.1.NBT.2a, CC.1.NBT.2c)

○ 3

○ 4

○ 30

○ 40

11. Which tells how many tens and ones? (CC.1.NBT.2)

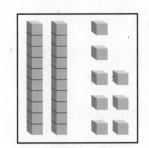

2 tens 8 ones   2 tens 9 ones   3 tens 8 ones   8 tens 2 ones
  ○   ○   ○   ○

12. What number is the same as 5 tens 6 ones? (CC.1.NBT.2)

  11   55   56   65
  ○   ○   ○   ○

13. Which way makes the same number? (CC.1.NBT.2a, CC.1.NBT.3)

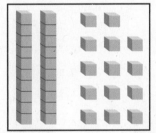

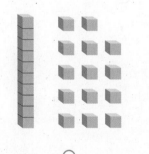   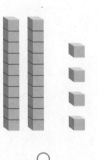   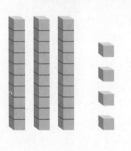   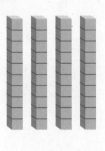

    ○   ○   ○   ○

14. What number does the model show? (CC.1.NBT.1)

99   109   110   119
○   ○   ○   ○

Performance Task (CC.1.NBT.1, CC.1.NBT.2)

Choose a number from 10 to 99.
Write your number on the penguin.

- Draw and write your number
  as tens and ones.

- Start at your number. Count forward.
  Write the next 5 numbers.

- Start at your number. Count by tens.
  Write the next 2 numbers.

Use numbers, pictures, and words
to show your work.

Compare Numbers

Curious About Math with

Curious George

How many colors do you see in the kite? Name the number that is one more.

Show What You Know

Model More

Draw lines to match.
Circle the set that has more.

1.

2.

More, Fewer

3. Circle the row that has more.

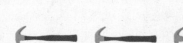

4. Circle the row that has fewer.

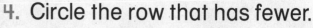

Draw Equal Groups

5. Draw a ball for each glove.

© Houghton Mifflin Harcourt Publishing Company

 Family note: This page checks your child's understanding of important skills needed for success in Chapter 7.

 GO Online Assessment Options
Soar to Success Math

Vocabulary Builder

Visualize It

Draw pictures in the box to show
more, fewer, or the **same** number.

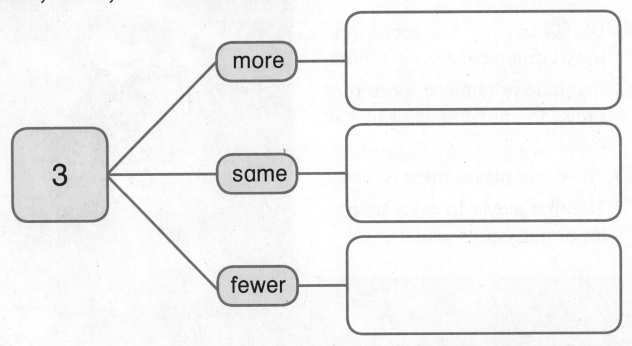

3 → more

3 → same

3 → fewer

Understand Vocabulary

Complete the sentences with review words.

1. I see 2 white cats and 4 yellow cats. I see _____ yellow cats than white cats.

2. Dave has 9 grapes. Ann has 6 grapes. Ann has _____ grapes than Dave.

3. 5 ducks and 5 swans are at the pond. There are the _____ number of ducks and swans.

GO Online
• eStudent Edition
• Multimedia eGlossary

Game Rainy Day Bingo

Materials • • 9 ● • 9 ●

Play with a partner.

① Toss the 🎲.

② Use ● to cover one space that shows a number that is 1 more.

③ If you do not have a space that shows the number, your turn is over.

④ The other player takes a turn.

⑤ The first player to cover all of his or her spaces wins.

Player 1		
4	5	2
3	6	4
2	5	7

Player 2		
6	2	3
4	7	6
5	3	7

Name _____

Algebra • Greater Than

Essential Question How can you compare two numbers to find which is greater?

COMMON CORE STANDARD CC.1.NBT.3
Understand place value.

Listen and Draw

Use ▭▭▭▭ ▪ to solve.
Draw quick pictures to show your work.

Tens	Ones

FOR THE TEACHER • Read the problem. Which number is greater, 65 or 56? Have children use base-ten blocks and draw quick pictures to solve.

Math Talk
How did you decide which number is greater? **Explain.**
MATHEMATICAL PRACTICES

Model and Draw

To compare 25 and 17, first compare the tens.

2 tens are more than 1 ten.

25 is greater than 17.

25 > 17

If the tens are the same, compare the ones.

7 ones are more than 5 ones.

17 is greater than 15.

17 > 15

Share and Show

Use your MathBoard and ⬛⬛⬛⬛ ⬛ to show each number.

	Circle the greater number.	Did tens or ones help you decide?	Write the numbers.
1.	62 (65)	tens (ones)	65 is greater than 62. 65 > 62
2.	84 48	tens ones	____ is greater than ____. ____ > ____
3.	72 70	tens ones	____ is greater than ____. ____ > ____

On Your Own

Use  if you need to.

	Circle the greater number.	Did tens or ones help you decide?	Write the numbers.
4.	32 27	tens ones	_____ is greater than _____. _____ > _____
5.	57 75	tens ones	_____ is greater than _____. _____ > _____
6.	94 98	tens ones	_____ is greater than _____. _____ > _____
7.	91 19	tens ones	_____ is greater than _____. _____ > _____
8.	68 62	tens ones	_____ is greater than _____. _____ > _____
9.	88 38	tens ones	_____ is greater than _____. _____ > _____

PROBLEM SOLVING REAL WORLD

Write Math

10. Color the balloons that show numbers greater than 56.

H.O.T.

H.O.T.

I ten 6 ones

100

59

46

80

50

65

H.O.T.

I one 6 tens

52

11. ⭐ **Test Prep** Which number is greater than 67?

19   60   66   76

○   ○   ○   ○

 TAKE HOME ACTIVITY • Write 38, 63, 68, and 83 on slips of paper. Show your child two numbers, and ask which number is greater. Repeat with different pairs of numbers.

FOR MORE PRACTICE: Standards Practice Book, pp. P137–P138

Name _____

Algebra • Less Than

Essential Question How can you compare two numbers to find which is less?

COMMON CORE STANDARD CC.1.NBT.3
Understand place value.

Listen and Draw

Use ▭▭▭▭ ▫ to solve. Draw quick pictures to show your work.

Tens	Ones

FOR THE TEACHER • Read the problem. Which number is less, 22 or 28? Have children use base-ten blocks to solve.

Math Talk
How does your drawing show which number is less? **Explain.**

MATHEMATICAL PRACTICES

Compare numbers to find which is less.

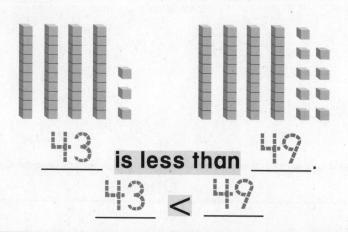

How do you know which number is less?

___43___ **is less than** ___49___.

___43___ < ___49___

Share and Show

Use your MathBoard and 🟦🟦🟦🟦🟦🟦🟦 ▫ to show each number.

	Circle the number that is less.	Did tens or ones help you decide?	Write the numbers.
1.	39 (36)	tens (ones)	__36__ is less than __39__. __36__ < __39__
2.	80 94	tens ones	____ is less than ____. ____ < ____
3.	57 54	tens ones	____ is less than ____. ____ < ____

Name _____

On Your Own

Use  if you need to.

Circle the number that is less.	Did tens or ones help you decide?	Write the numbers.
4. 47 48	tens ones	_____ is less than _____. _____ < _____
5. 82 28	tens ones	_____ is less than _____. _____ < _____
6. 96 90	tens ones	_____ is less than _____. _____ < _____
7. 23 32	tens ones	_____ is less than _____. _____ < _____
8. 65 55	tens ones	_____ is less than _____. _____ < _____
9. 79 80	tens ones	_____ is less than _____. _____ < _____

PROBLEM SOLVING REAL WORLD

Write Math

Write a number to solve.

10. Nan makes the number 46. Marty makes a number that is less than 46. What could be a number Marty makes?

_____

11. Jack makes the number 92. Kit makes a number that has fewer ones than 92. What could be a number Kit makes?

_____

12. Bill makes the number 85. Ann makes a number with fewer tens than 85. What could be a number Ann makes?

_____

13. H.O.T. Joe makes a number that has fewer tens than 31 and fewer ones than 13. What could be a number Joe makes?

_____

14. ⭐ **Test Prep** Which number is less than 72?

49   73   80   99

○   ○   ○   ○

TAKE HOME ACTIVITY • Write 47, 54, 57, and 74 on slips of paper. Show your child two numbers, and ask which number is less. Repeat with different pairs of numbers.

296 two hundred ninety-six

© Houghton Mifflin Harcourt Publishing Company

FOR MORE PRACTICE:
Standards Practice Book, pp. P139–P140

Name _____

Algebra • Use Symbols to Compare

Essential Question How can you use symbols to show how numbers compare?

COMMON CORE STANDARD CC.1.NBT.3
Understand place value.

Listen and Draw

Use 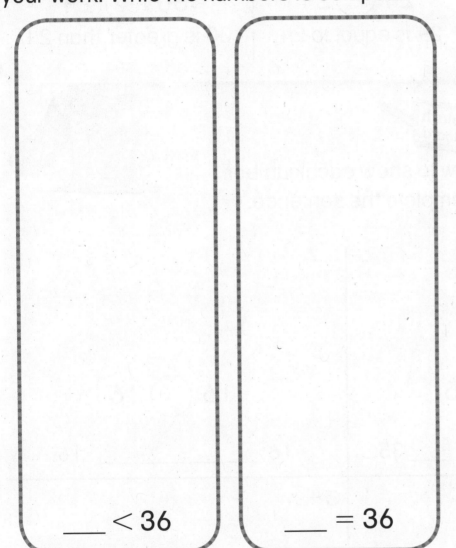 . Draw quick pictures to show your work. Write the numbers to compare.

___ < 36	___ = 36	___ > 36

Math Talk

Compare 47 and 32 in two ways. What two symbols do you use? **Explain.**

MATHEMATICAL PRACTICES

 FOR THE TEACHER • Have children use base-ten blocks to show a number less than 36, a number equal to 36, and a number greater than 36.

Model and Draw

 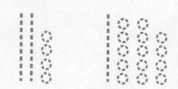 

21 $<$ 24	24 $=$ 24	30 $>$ 24
21 is less than 24.	24 is equal to 24.	30 is greater than 24.

Share and Show

Use . Draw to show each number.
Write $<$, $>$, or $=$. Complete the sentence.

1.

28 ◯ 35

28 _____ 35.

2.

16 ◯ 16

16 _____ 16.

☑ **3.**

46 ◯ 31

46 _____ 31.

☑ **4.**

51 ◯ 52

51 _____ 52.

Name _____

On Your Own

Write $<$, $>$, or $=$.
Draw a quick picture if you need to.

REMEMBER
$<$ is less than
$>$ is greater than
$=$ is equal to

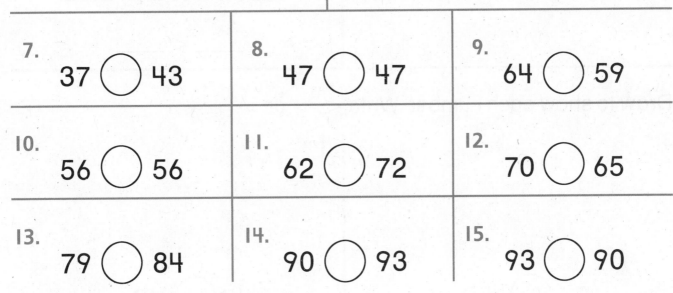

5.
45 $>$ 42

6.
38 $\bigcirc$ 50

7.
37 $\bigcirc$ 43

8.
47 $\bigcirc$ 47

9.
64 $\bigcirc$ 59

10.
56 $\bigcirc$ 56

11.
62 $\bigcirc$ 72

12.
70 $\bigcirc$ 65

13.
79 $\bigcirc$ 84

14.
90 $\bigcirc$ 93

15.
93 $\bigcirc$ 90

 Write numbers to solve.

16.
96 $=$ ___

17.
53 $>$ ___

18.
83 $<$ ___

19.
40 $<$ ___

20.
71 $>$ ___

21.
29 $=$ ___

TAKE HOME ACTIVITY • Have your child show you how to write $<$, $>$, and $=$ to compare two numbers. Ask him or her to use words to explain each comparison.

FOR MORE PRACTICE:
Standards Practice Book, pp. P141–P142

© Houghton Mifflin Harcourt Publishing Company

Mid-Chapter Checkpoint

Concepts and Skills

Circle the greater number. Write the numbers. (CC.1.NBT.3)

1.   38   83   _____ is greater than _____.

                                          _____ > _____

Circle the number that is less. Write the numbers. (CC.1.NBT.3)

2.   61   29   _____ is less than _____.

                                          _____ < _____

Draw to show each number. Write <, > or =. (CC.1.NBT.3)

3.   4.

    19 ◯ 52   44 ◯ 43

 Test Prep

5. Which is true? (CC.1.NBT.3)

    21 > 28   21 = 28   21 < 28   28 < 21
       ◯   ◯   ◯   ◯

Name _____

Problem Solving • Compare Numbers

Essential Question How can making a model help you compare numbers?

COMMON CORE STANDARD CC.1.NBT.3
Understand place value.

Cassidy has the number cards shown below. She gives away the cards with numbers less than 49 and greater than 53. Which number cards does Cassidy have now?

🔑 Unlock the Problem

What do I need to find?

the __number cards__
that Cassidy has now

What information do I need to use?

number cards < __49__

and > __53__

Show how to solve the problem.

Cassidy has number cards __51, 52__.

HOME CONNECTION • Your child made a model of the problem. The numbers crossed out are less than 49 and also greater than 53. The remaining numbers solve the problem.

Try Another Problem

Make a model to solve.

- What do I need to find?
- What information do I need to use?

1. Tony has these number cards. He gives away the cards with numbers less than 16 and greater than 19. Which number cards does Tony have now?

Tony has number cards _____.

---

2. Carol has these number cards. She keeps the cards with numbers greater than 98 and less than 95. Circle the number cards Carol keeps.

Carol keeps number cards _____.

Math Talk
Explain how you can find the number cards Tony has now.

MATHEMATICAL PRACTICES

Name _____

Share and Show

Make a model to solve.

☑ 3. Felipe has these numbers cards. He gives
away cards with numbers less than 60 and
greater than 65. Which number cards does
Felipe have now?

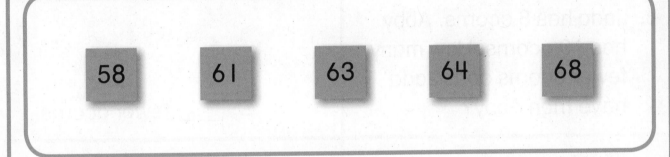

58   61   63   64   68

Felipe has number cards _____.

4. **H.O.T.** Molly underlines the number cards
greater than 76 and circles the number
cards less than 84. Which number cards
are both greater than 76 and less than 84?

72   75   78   82   85

Number cards _____ are both greater than
76 and less than 84.

On Your Own

Choose a way to solve.
Draw or write to explain.

Write Math

5. Some cows were in the field. 6 more cows walked there. Then there were 13 cows. How many cows were in the field before?	____ cows
6. Jada has 8 acorns. Abby has 10 acorns. How many fewer acorns does Jada have than Abby?	____ fewer acorns
7. H.O.T. Ed has 6 marbles. How many marbles can he put in a red cup and how many can he put in a blue cup?	___ + ___ = 6

8. ⭐ **Test Prep** Gavin crosses out the numbers that are less than 25 and greater than 29. What numbers are left?

21	23	26	28	30

21 and 23   23 and 26   26 and 28   28 and 30
○   ○   ○   ○

TAKE HOME ACTIVITY • Ask your child to tell you a number that is greater than 59 and a number less than 59.

FOR MORE PRACTICE:
Standards Practice Book, pp. P143–P144

Name _____

10 Less, 10 More

Essential Question How can you identify numbers that are 10 less or 10 more than a number?

COMMON CORE STANDARD CC.1.NBT.5
Use place value understanding and properties of operations to add and subtract.

Listen and Draw REAL WORLD

Use ▭▭▭▭ ▭ to solve. Draw quick pictures to show your work.

10 MARKERS

Pat

_____

Tony

_____

Jan

_____

FOR THE TEACHER • Read the following problem. Tony has 2 boxes of markers and 2 more markers. Pat has 10 fewer markers than Tony. Jan has 10 more markers than Tony. How many markers does each child have?

Math Talk
What number has one less 10 than 12? **Explain.**

MATHEMATICAL PRACTICES

Model and Draw

Think

23

33

Think

43

_____ is 10 less than 33.

_____ is 10 more than 33.

Share and Show ✏️ Math Board

Use mental math. Write the numbers that are 10 less and 10 more.

1. ☐ 70 ☐

2. ☐ 41 ☐

3. ☐ 58 ☐

4. ☐ 66 ☐

5. ☐ 24 ☐

6. ☐ 86 ☐

✓7. ☐ 37 ☐

✓8. ☐ 15 ☐

On Your Own

Use mental math.
Complete the chart.

	10 Less		10 More
9.	___	39	___
10.	___	75	___
11.	___	64	___
12.	___	90	___
13.	___	83	___
14.	11	___	___
15.	___	___	26

16. **H.O.T.** Solve.
    I have 89 rocks. I want to collect
    10 more. How many rocks
    will I have then?   ____ rocks

PROBLEM SOLVING REAL WORLD

Write Math

Choose a way to solve. Draw or write to show your work.

17. The plant has 4 fewer ladybugs on it than the tree. The tree has 7 ladybugs on it. How many ladybugs are on the plant?

_____ ladybugs

18. Amy has 7 ribbons. Charlotte has 9 ribbons. How many more ribbons does Charlotte have than Amy?

_____ more ribbons

19. **H.O.T.** Margo has 28 stamps. Chet has 10 more stamps than Margo. Luis has 10 more stamps than Chet. How many stamps does Luis have?

_____ stamps

20. ⭐ **Test Prep**
What number is 10 less than 76?

66	67	75	86
○	○	○	○

TAKE HOME ACTIVITY • Write a two-digit number, such as 25, 40, or 81. Ask your child to identify the numbers that are ten less than and ten more than that number. Repeat with other numbers.

FOR MORE PRACTICE:
Standards Practice Book, pp. P145–P146

Name _____

Vocabulary

Circle the number that **is greater than** 47. (p. 290)
Underline the number that **is less than** 47. (p. 294)

1.   92   29

Concepts and Skills

Write <, >, or =. (CC.1.NBT.3)

2. 80 ◯ 81	3. 19 ◯ 11	4. 26 ◯ 62
5. 35 ◯ 35	6. 89 ◯ 99	7. 78 ◯ 73
8. 63 ◯ 60	9. 42 ◯ 42	10. 15 ◯ 51
11. 57 ◯ 59	12. 10 ◯ 13	13. 38 ◯ 37
14. 22 ◯ 22	15. 75 ◯ 72	16. 96 ◯ 96

17. Aaron has 39 animal stickers. Which number is less than 39? (CC.1.NBT.3)

37   40   92   93
○   ○   ○   ○

18. Mike has 18 books. Cheryl has ten more books than Mike. How many books does Cheryl have? (CC.1.NBT.5)

8   19   20   28
○   ○   ○   ○

19. Emma jumps 25 times. Which number is greater than 25? (CC.1.NBT.3)

15   22   24   52
○   ○   ○   ○

20. Which is true? (CC.1.NBT.3)

$76 = 67$ $76 > 67$ $76 < 67$ $67 > 76$
○   ○   ○   ○

21. Leah crosses out the numbers that are less than 33 and greater than 36. What numbers are left? (CC.1.NBT.3)

31   32   34   35   37

31 and 32   32 and 34   34 and 35   35 and 37
○   ○   ○   ○

TEST PREP

22. James circles the numbers that are less than 87 and greater than 91. What numbers did he circle? (CC.1.NBT.3)

| 86 | 88 | 89 | 90 | 92 |

86 and 88   86 and 92   88 and 90   89 and 92
   ○   ○   ○   ○

---

23. Which number is greater than 17? (CC.1.NBT.3)

12   14   16   18
○   ○   ○   ○

---

24. Which is the same as the sentence? (CC.1.NBT.3)

67 is less than 73.

$67 = 73$ $67 > 73$ $67 < 73$ $67 + 73$
   ○   ○   ○   ○

---

25. Which number is ten less than 72? (CC.1.NBT.5)

82   73   71   62
○   ○   ○   ○

---

26. Which is true? (CC.1.NBT.3)

$98 > 88$ $88 > 98$ $98 < 88$ $88 = 98$
   ○   ○   ○   ○

Performance Task (CC.1.NBT.3)

Jack has some marbles. He has ten more red marbles than blue marbles. He has fewer yellow marbles than blue marbles.

How many of each color marble could Jack have?

Use numbers, pictures, or words to show your work.

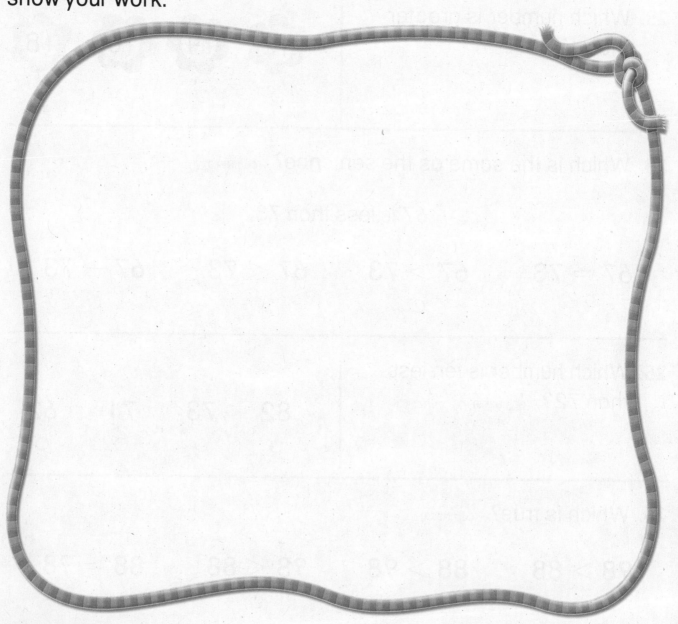

Chapter 8

Two-Digit Addition and Subtraction

Curious About Math with Curious George

There are 4 boxes of oranges on a table. Each box holds 10 oranges. How many oranges are there?

Show What You Know

Add and Subtract

Use ◼ and ◼ to add. Write the sum.
Break apart ◼ to subtract.
Write the difference.

1.

$4 + 1 =$ _____

$5 - 1 =$ _____

Count Groups to 20

Circle groups of 10. Write how many.

2.

_____

3.

_____

Use a Hundred Chart to Count

Touch and count. Color the last
number counted.

4. Start at 1 and count to 20.

5. Start at 30 and count to 56.

6. Start at 77 and count to 93.

1	2	3	4	5	6	7	8	9	10
11	12	13	14	15	16	17	18	19	20
21	22	23	24	25	26	27	28	29	30
31	32	33	34	35	36	37	38	39	40
41	42	43	44	45	46	47	48	49	50
51	52	53	54	55	56	57	58	59	60
61	62	63	64	65	66	67	68	69	70
71	72	73	74	75	76	77	78	79	80
81	82	83	84	85	86	87	88	89	90
91	92	93	94	95	96	97	98	99	100

Family note: This page checks your child's understanding
of important skills needed for success in Chapter 8.

GO Online
Assessment Options
Soar to Success Math

Vocabulary Builder

Visualize It

Sort the review words from the box.

Put Together

Take Apart

_____

_____

_____

_____

_____

_____

Understand Vocabulary

Use a review word to complete each sentence.

1. 8 is the _____ for $17 - 9$.

2. 17 is the _____ for $8 + 9$.

3. When you _____ 4 to 8,
   you find the sum.

4. When you _____ 4 from 8,
   you find the difference.

GO Online
• eStudent Edition
• Multimedia eGlossary

Game Neighborhood Sums

Materials

 • • 9 ▪ • 9 ▪ • 9 ▪

Play with a partner.

① Put your ♟ on START.

② Spin the ◑. Move that number of spaces.

③ Make a ten to help you find the sum.

④ The other player uses ▪▪▪ to check.

⑤ If you are not correct, you lose a turn.

⑥ The first player to get to END wins.

2 4 +8	Move ahead one space.	4 9 +6	4 4 +6	9 1 +6	END
4 6 +3	5 3 +7	9 7 +1	Move back one space.	3 7 +7	5 8 +5
					6 6 +4
START	2 4 +8	Move ahead one space.	6 1 +9	8 8 +2	

Name _____

Add and Subtract within 20

Essential Question What strategies can you use to add and subtract?

COMMON CORE STANDARD CC.1.OA.6
Add and subtract within 20.

Listen and Draw REAL WORLD

What is $5 + 4$?
Use a strategy to solve the addition
fact. Draw to show your work.

$5 + 4 = \underline{\hspace{1cm}}$

Math Talk
What strategy
did you use to find
the answer?
Explain.
MATHEMATICAL
PRACTICES

FOR THE TEACHER • Have children choose and
model a strategy to solve the addition fact. Then
have them draw to show their work.

Model and Draw

Think of a strategy you can use
to add or subtract.

What is $14 - 6$?

I can use a
related fact.

$\underline{6} \oplus \underline{8} = 14$

So, $14 - 6 = \underline{8}$.

Share and Show

Add or subtract.

1. $5 + 3 = $ ___	2. $10 - 5 = $ ___	3. $3 + 6 = $ ___
4. $12 - 5 = $ ___	5. $15 - 9 = $ ___	6. $5 + 7 = $ ___
7. $8 + 7 = $ ___	8. $9 - 7 = $ ___	9. $5 + 5 = $ ___
10. $12 - 7 = $ ___	11. $18 - 9 = $ ___	12. $9 + 4 = $ ___
13. $2 + 7 = $ ___	14. $5 - 1 = $ ___	15. $9 + 1 = $ ___
16. $7 - 6 = $ ___	☑17. $13 - 4 = $ ___	☑18. $2 + 6 = $ ___

© Houghton Mifflin Harcourt Publishing Company

Name _____

On Your Own

Add or subtract.

19. $\begin{array}{r} 14 \\ -\ 5 \\ \hline \end{array}$	20. $\begin{array}{r} 2 \\ +10 \\ \hline \end{array}$	21. $\begin{array}{r} 3 \\ +3 \\ \hline \end{array}$	22. $\begin{array}{r} 14 \\ -\ 8 \\ \hline \end{array}$	23. $\begin{array}{r} 8 \\ +9 \\ \hline \end{array}$	24. $\begin{array}{r} 6 \\ -3 \\ \hline \end{array}$
25. $\begin{array}{r} 6 \\ -5 \\ \hline \end{array}$	26. $\begin{array}{r} 2 \\ +8 \\ \hline \end{array}$	27. $\begin{array}{r} 0 \\ +5 \\ \hline \end{array}$	28. $\begin{array}{r} 10 \\ -\ 2 \\ \hline \end{array}$	29. $\begin{array}{r} 9 \\ +9 \\ \hline \end{array}$	30. $\begin{array}{r} 5 \\ -4 \\ \hline \end{array}$
31. $\begin{array}{r} 8 \\ -8 \\ \hline \end{array}$	32. $\begin{array}{r} 10 \\ +\ 1 \\ \hline \end{array}$	33. $\begin{array}{r} 4 \\ +7 \\ \hline \end{array}$	34. $\begin{array}{r} 9 \\ -3 \\ \hline \end{array}$	35. $\begin{array}{r} 1 \\ +8 \\ \hline \end{array}$	36. $\begin{array}{r} 17 \\ -\ 9 \\ \hline \end{array}$
37. $\begin{array}{r} 13 \\ -\ 7 \\ \hline \end{array}$	38. $\begin{array}{r} 6 \\ +5 \\ \hline \end{array}$	39. $\begin{array}{r} 10 \\ +\ 2 \\ \hline \end{array}$	40. $\begin{array}{r} 14 \\ -\ 9 \\ \hline \end{array}$	41. $\begin{array}{r} 10 \\ +10 \\ \hline \end{array}$	42. $\begin{array}{r} 11 \\ -\ 3 \\ \hline \end{array}$

43. **H.O.T.** Jamal thinks of an addition fact.
The sum is 15. One addend is 8. What
is a fact Jamal could be thinking of?

PROBLEM SOLVING REAL WORLD

Solve. Write or draw to explain.

44. There are 9 ants on a rock. Some more ants get on the rock. Now there are 18 ants on the rock. How many more ants got on the rock?

_____ more ants

45. Tom sees 8 ladybugs on a bush. Callie sees 14 ladybugs on the bush. How many more ladybugs does Callie see than Tom?

_____ more ladybugs

46. **H.O.T.** Fill in the blanks. Write a number sentence to solve.

Lin sees _____ bees. Some bees flew away. Now there are _____ bees. How many bees flew away?

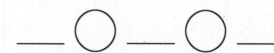

___ ◯ ___ ◯ ___

_____ bees

47. ⭐ **Test Prep**
What is the sum? $6 + 8 = $ ___

6   8   10   14
◯   ◯   ◯   ◯

TAKE HOME ACTIVITY • Have your child tell a strategy he or she would use to solve 4 + 8.

FOR MORE PRACTICE:
Standards Practice Book, pp. P151–P152

Name _____

Add Tens

Essential Question How can you add tens?

COMMON CORE STANDARD CC.1.NBT.4
Use place value understanding and
properties of operations to add and
subtract.

Listen and Draw REAL WORLD

Choose a way to show the problem.
Draw a quick picture to show your work.

FOR THE TEACHER • Read the following
problems. Barb has 20 pennies. Ed has
30 pennies. How many pennies do they have?
Kyle has 40 pennies. Kim has 50 pennies. How
many pennies do they have?

Math Talk
Explain why there
will be no ones in
your answer when
you add 20 + 30.

MATHEMATICAL
PRACTICES

How can you find 30 + 40?

$$30 \quad + \quad 40 \quad = \quad \underline{70}$$

_____ tens

Share and Show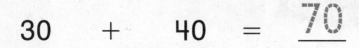

Use . Draw to show tens.
Write the sum. Write how many tens.

1. 20 + 40 = _____

_____ tens

2. 30 + 30 = _____

_____ tens

◉3. 40 + 50 = _____

_____ tens

◉4. 50 + 30 = _____

_____ tens

Name _____

On Your Own

Draw to show tens. Write the sum.
Write how many tens.

5. 40 + 40 = ____

____ tens

6. 70 + 20 = ____

____ tens

7. 10 + 80 = ____

____ tens

8. 60 + 30 = ____

____ tens

9. **H.O.T.** Draw two groups of tens you can add
to get a sum of 50. Write the number sentence.

____ ◯ ____ ◯ ____

PROBLEM SOLVING

Write Math

10. **H.O.T.** Complete the web.
Write the missing addend to
get a sum of 90.

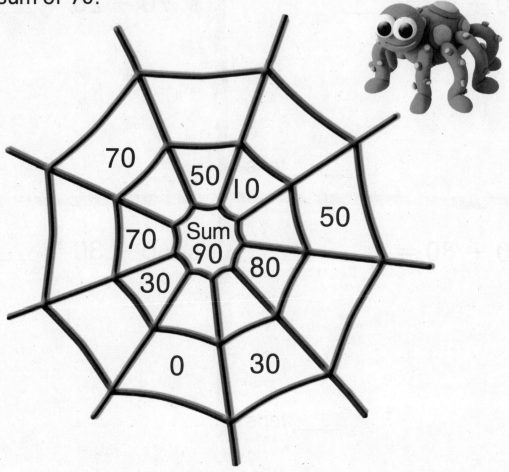

70   50   10

70   Sum   50
      90
      80
30

0   30

11. ⭐ **Test Prep** What is the sum?

$50 + 20 =$ _____ | 7   30   52   70
                          ○   ○   ○   ○

TAKE HOME ACTIVITY · Ask your child to explain
how to use tens to find 20 + 70.

FOR MORE PRACTICE:
Standards Practice Book, pp. P153–P154

Subtract Tens

Essential Question How can you subtract tens?

COMMON CORE STANDARD **CC.1.NBT.6**

Use place value understanding and properties of operations to add and subtract.

Listen and Draw REAL WORLD

Choose a way to show the problem.
Draw a quick picture to show your work.

FOR THE TEACHER • Read the following problems. Tara has 30 seashells. 20 shells are big. The rest are small. How many small shells does she have? Sammy has 50 shells. He gives 30 shells to his friend. How many shells does Sammy have now?

Math Talk

Explain how your picture shows the first problem.

MATHEMATICAL PRACTICES

How can you find 80 − 30?

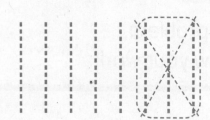

$$80 - 30 = \underline{50}$$

____ tens

Share and Show

Use ▭▭▭▭▭ ▫. Draw to show tens.
Write the difference. Write how many tens.

1. 60 − 20 = ____

____ tens

2. 70 − 30 = ____

____ tens

⊘3. 80 − 20 = ____

____ tens

⊘4. 90 − 40 = ____

____ tens

Name _____

On Your Own

Draw to show tens. Write the difference.
Write how many tens.

5. 80 − 40 = ____

6. 90 − 70 = ____

____ tens

____ tens

7. 70 − 50 = ____

8. 30 − 30 = ____

____ tens

____ tens

 **H.O.T.** Solve.

9. Jeff has 40 pennies. He gives
some to Jill. He has 10 pennies
left. How many pennies does
Jeff give to Jill?

____ pennies

 **TAKE HOME ACTIVITY** · Ask your child to explain
how to use tens to find 90 − 70.

FOR MORE PRACTICE:
Standards Practice Book, pp. P155–P156

Mid-Chapter Checkpoint

Concepts and Skills

Add or subtract. (CC.1.OA.6)

1.	2.	3.	4.	5.	6.
4 +8	15 − 7	9 −6	3 +1	10 + 6	11 − 2

Use ▭▭▭. Draw to show tens.
Write the sum. Write how many tens. (CC.1.NBT.4)

7. 30 + 50 = ____

____ tens

8. 40 + 20 = ____

____ tens

Use ▭▭▭. Draw to show tens.
Write the difference. Write how many tens. (CC.1.NBT.6)

9. 90 − 20 = ____

____ tens

10. 60 − 40 = ____

____ tens

⭐ **Test Prep**

11. What is the difference? (CC.1.NBT.6)

70 − 20 = ____

90	68	50	45
○	○	○	○

Name _____

Use a Hundred Chart to Add

Essential Question How can you use a hundred chart to count on by ones or tens?

COMMON CORE STANDARD CC.1.NBT.4
Use place value understanding and properties of operations to add and subtract.

Listen and Draw

Use the hundred chart to solve the problems.

1	2	3	4	5	6	7	8	9	10
11	12	13	14	15	16	17	18	19	20
21	22	23	24	25	26	27	28	29	30
31	32	33	34	35	36	37	38	39	40
41	42	43	44	45	46	47	48	49	50
51	52	53	54	55	56	57	58	59	60
61	62	63	64	65	66	67	68	69	70
71	72	73	74	75	76	77	78	79	80
81	82	83	84	85	86	87	88	89	90
91	92	93	94	95	96	97	98	99	100

FOR THE TEACHER • Read the following problems. Alice picks 12 flowers. Then she picks 4 more flowers. How many flowers does Alice pick? Ella picks 10 strawberries. Then she picks 20 more strawberries. How many strawberries does Ella pick?

Math Talk
Describe how you can use a hundred chart to find each sum.
MATHEMATICAL PRACTICES

Chapter 8

three hundred twenty-nine **329**

Model and Draw

Count on a hundred chart
to find a sum.

> Start at **24**.
> Count on four ones.
> **25, 26, 27, 28**

1	2	3	4	5	6	7	8	9	10
11	12	13	14	15	16	17	18	19	20
21	22	23	24	25	26	27	28	29	30
31	32	33	34	35	36	37	38	39	40
41	42	43	44	45	46	47	48	49	50
51	52	53	54	55	56	57	58	59	60
61	62	63	64	65	66	67	68	69	70
71	72	73	74	75	76	77	78	79	80
81	82	83	84	85	86	87	88	89	90
91	92	93	94	95	96	97	98	99	100

$24 + 4 = \underline{28}$

> Start at **31**.
> Count on four tens.
> **41, 51, 61, 71**

$31 + 40 = \underline{71}$

Share and Show

Use the hundred chart to add.
Count on by ones or tens.

1. $42 + 7 = \underline{\quad}$

2. $57 + 30 = \underline{\quad}$

3. $91 + 5 = \underline{\quad}$

4. $18 + 50 = \underline{\quad}$

Name _____

On Your Own

How can you use the hundred chart to find each sum?

$32 + 5 = \underline{\hspace{1cm}}$

$48 + 30 = \underline{\hspace{1cm}}$

1	2	3	4	5	6	7	8	9	10
11	12	13	14	15	16	17	18	19	20
21	22	23	24	25	26	27	28	29	30
31	32	33	34	35	36	37	38	39	40
41	42	43	44	45	46	47	48	49	50
51	52	53	54	55	56	57	58	59	60
61	62	63	64	65	66	67	68	69	70
71	72	73	74	75	76	77	78	79	80
81	82	83	84	85	86	87	88	89	90
91	92	93	94	95	96	97	98	99	100

Use the hundred chart to add.
Count on by ones or tens.

5. $13 + 70 = \underline{\hspace{1cm}}$

6. $22 + 6 = \underline{\hspace{1cm}}$

7. $71 + 3 = \underline{\hspace{1cm}}$

8. $49 + 50 = \underline{\hspace{1cm}}$

9. $53 + 4 = \underline{\hspace{1cm}}$

10. $25 + 40 = \underline{\hspace{1cm}}$

11. $2 + 84 = \underline{\hspace{1cm}}$

12. $60 + 12 = \underline{\hspace{1cm}}$

13. **H.O.T.** $31 + 20 + 40 = \underline{\hspace{1cm}}$

PROBLEM SOLVING REAL WORLD

Write Math

Choose a way to solve. Draw or write to show your work.

14. 48 leaves fall from a tree. Then 20 more leaves fall. How many leaves have fallen?

_____ leaves

15. H.O.T. Jeff is at the pond. He sees 14 turtles on a log, 2 turtles on the shore, and 3 turtles in the water. How many turtles does Jeff see?

_____ turtles

16. H.O.T. Rae put 20 books away. She put 20 more books away, then 11 more. How many books did Rae put away?

_____ books

17. ⭐Test Prep   What is the sum?

53 + 30 = ___

83	80	56	23
○	○	○	○

 TAKE HOME ACTIVITY • On a piece of paper, write 36 + 40. Ask your child to explain how to use the hundred chart to count on by tens to find the sum.

FOR MORE PRACTICE: Standards Practice Book, pp. P157–P158

HANDS ON
Lesson 8.5

Name _____

Use Models to Add

Essential Question How can models help you add ones or tens to a two-digit number?

COMMON CORE STANDARD CC.1.NBT.4
Use place value understanding and properties of operations to add and subtract.

Listen and Draw REAL WORLD

Draw to show how you can find the sum.

$14 + 5 =$ _____

Math Talk
Explain how you found the sum.

MATHEMATICAL PRACTICES

FOR THE TEACHER • Read the following problem. Amir counts 14 cars as they go by. Then he counts 5 more cars. How many cars does Amir count?

Chapter 8

three hundred thirty-three **333**

Model and Draw

Add ones to
a two-digit
number.

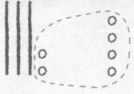

$$32 \ + \ 4 \ = \ \underline{36}$$

Add tens to
a two-digit
number.

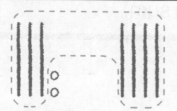

$$32 \ + \ 40 \ = \ \underline{72}$$

Share and Show

Use  . Draw to show how to
add the ones. Write the sum.

1. $27 + 2 = \underline{\hspace{1cm}}$

☑ 2. $41 + 5 = \underline{\hspace{1cm}}$

Use ▭▭▭ ▪ . Draw to show how to
add the tens. Write the sum.

3. $13 + 50 = \underline{\hspace{1cm}}$

☑ 4. $28 + 30 = \underline{\hspace{1cm}}$

Name _____

On Your Own

Use  and your MathBoard.
Add the ones or tens. Write the sum.

5. $65 + 3 =$ ____

6. $81 + 8 =$ ____

7. $54 + 20 =$ ____

8. $32 + 10 =$ ____

9. $95 + 2 =$ ____

10. $25 + 60 =$ ____

11. $2 + 54 =$ ____

12. $70 + 29 =$ ____

13. $40 + 58 =$ ____

14. $7 + 70 =$ ____

H.O.T. Make a sum of 45. Draw a quick
picture. Write the number sentence.

15. Add ones to a two-digit number.

$$\underline{\quad} + \underline{\quad} = 45$$

16. Add tens to a two-digit number.

$$\underline{\quad} + \underline{\quad} = 45$$

PROBLEM SOLVING REAL WORLD

Write Math

Choose a way to solve. Draw or write to show your work.

17. There are 7 oak trees and 32 pine trees in the park. How many trees are in the park?

_____ trees

18. Rita picks 63 strawberries. Then she picks 30 more. How many strawberries does Rita pick?

_____ strawberries

19. **H.O.T.** Kenny planted two rows of corn. He used 20 seeds in each row. He has 18 seeds left. How many seeds of corn did Kenny have?

_____ seeds

20. ⭐ **Test Prep**

What is the sum?

$$37 + 20 = \underline{\hspace{1cm}}$$

59	57	50	39
○	○	○	○

TAKE HOME ACTIVITY • Give your child the addition problems 25 + 3 and 25 + 30. Ask your child to explain how to solve each problem.

FOR MORE PRACTICE:
Standards Practice Book, pp. P159–P160

Name _____

Make Ten to Add

Essential Question How can making a ten help you add a two-digit number and a one-digit number?

COMMON CORE STANDARD CC.1.NBT.4
Use place value understanding and properties of operations to add and subtract.

Listen and Draw REAL WORLD

Use ▭▭▭▭ ▪. Draw to show how you can find the sum.

$$21 + 6 = \underline{\quad}$$

FOR THE TEACHER • Read the following problem. Sally has 21 stickers in her sticker book. She gets 6 more stickers. How many stickers does Sally have now?

Math Talk
Explain how your model shows the sum of $21 + 6$.

MATHEMATICAL PRACTICES

Make a ten to find $37 + 8$.

What can I add to 7 to make 10?

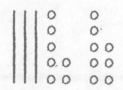

$37 + 8$

$37 + 3 + 5$

$40 + 5$

$\underline{40} + \underline{5} = \underline{45}$

So, $37 + 8 = \underline{45}$.

Share and Show Math Board

Use ▭▭. Draw to show how you make a ten. Find the sum.

1. $49 + 3 = ?$

___ + ___ = ___

So, $49 + 3 =$ ___.

On Your Own

Use ▭▭▭▭▭▭ ▪. Draw to show how
you make a ten. Find the sum.

2. $39 + 7 =$ ____

3. $72 + 9 =$ ____

4. $58 + 5 =$ ____

H.O.T. Solve. Write the numbers.

5. $46 + 7$

$46 + \boxed{} + 3$

$\boxed{} + 3$

So, $46 + 7 =$ ____.

6. $53 + 8$

$53 + \boxed{} + 1$

$\boxed{} + 1$

So, $53 + 8 =$ ____.

PROBLEM SOLVING REAL WORLD

Write Math

Choose a way to solve. Draw or write to show your work.

7. Koby puts 24 daisies and 8 tulips in a vase. How many flowers are in the vase?

_____ flowers

8. **H.O.T.** Write the missing addend.

$$46 + \boxed{} = 52$$

9. **H.O.T.** There are 27 ducklings in the water. 20 of them come out of the water. How many ducklings are still in the water?

_____ ducklings

10. ★ **Test Prep**
What is $35 + 6$?

95 ○   41 ○   40 ○   11 ○

TAKE HOME ACTIVITY • Ask your child to explain how to find the sum for $25 + 9$.

FOR MORE PRACTICE:
Standards Practice Book, pp. P161–P162

Name _____

Use Place Value to Add

Essential Question How can you model tens and ones to help you add two-digit numbers?

COMMON CORE STANDARD CC.1.NBT.4
Use place value understanding and properties of operations to add and subtract.

Listen and Draw REAL WORLD

Model the problem with ▭▭▭▭▭▭ ▪.
Draw a quick picture to show your work.

Tens	Ones

Math Talk

How many tens?
How many ones?
How many in all?
Explain.

MATHEMATICAL PRACTICES

FOR THE TEACHER • Read the following problem. Cameron has 30 shiny pennies and 25 dull pennies. How many pennies does Cameron have?

Chapter 8

three hundred forty-one **341**

How can you use tens and ones to add?

$$35$$
$$+38$$

Tens	Ones
¦¦¦ ¦¦¦	°°°°°
¦¦¦	°°°°°°°°

3 tens + 5 ones
3 tens + 8 ones
_____
__6__ tens + __13__ ones

__60__ + __13__ = __73__

$$35$$
$$+38$$
$$73$$

Share and Show

Draw a quick picture.
Use tens and ones to add.

☑ 1.

Tens	Ones

$$81$$
$$+14$$

8 tens + 1 one
1 ten + 4 ones
_____
___ tens + ___ ones

___ + ___ = ___

$$81$$
$$+14$$

On Your Own

Draw a quick picture. Use tens and ones to add.

2.

43
+37

Tens	Ones

4 tens + 3 ones
3 tens + 7 ones
_____
___ tens + ___ ones

___ + ___ = ___

43
+37

3.

62
+23

Tens	Ones

6 tens + 2 ones
2 tens + 3 ones
_____
___ tens + ___ ones

___ + ___ = ___

62
+23

4.

27
+34

Tens	Ones

2 tens + 7 ones
3 tens + 4 ones
_____
___ tens + ___ ones

___ + ___ = ___

27
+34

H.O.T. Solve.

5. 28 + 17

28 + ___ + 15

___ + 15 = ___

So, 28 + 17 = ___.

6. 59 + 13

59 + ___ + 12

___ + 12 = ___

So, 59 + 13 = ___.

PROBLEM SOLVING REAL WORLD

Write Math

7. Draw a quick picture to solve. Kim has 24 marbles. Al has 47 marbles. How many marbles do they have?

Tens	Ones

_____ marbles

8. **H.O.T.** Choose two addends from 11 to 49. Draw them. Add in any order to solve.

Addend   **Addend**

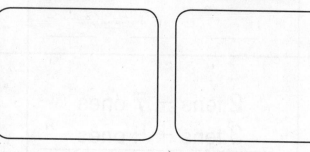

___ + ___ = ___

___ + ___ = ___

9. ⭐ **Test Prep**
How many tens and ones are in the sum?

54
+32
‾‾‾‾

○ 2 tens and 2 ones

○ 2 tens and 6 ones

○ 8 tens and 2 ones

○ 8 tens and 6 ones

TAKE HOME ACTIVITY • Write the numbers 42 and 17. Have your child tell how to find the sum by adding the tens and ones.

FOR MORE PRACTICE:
Standards Practice Book, pp. P163–P164

Name _____

Problem Solving •
Addition Word Problems

Essential Question How can drawing a picture help you explain how to solve an addition problem?

COMMON CORE STANDARD **CC.1.NBT.4**
Use place value understanding and properties of operations to add and subtract.

Kelly gets 6 new toy cars.
He already has 18 toy cars.
How many does he have now?

🔑 Unlock the Problem

What do I need to find?

_____

how many ~~toy cars~~
Kelly has now

What information do I need to use?

Kelly has ___18___ cars.

He gets ___6___ more cars.

Show how to solve the problem.

_ _ _ _ _ _ _ _ _ _ _ _ _ _ _ _ _ _

HOME CONNECTION • Being able to show and explain how to solve a problem helps your child build on their understanding of addition.

Try Another Problem

Draw and write to solve.
Explain your reasoning.

- What do I need to find?
- What information do I need to use?

1. Aisha picks 60 blueberries to make a pie. Then she picks 12 more to eat. How many blueberries does Aisha pick?

_____ blueberries

_____

- -

_____

2. Yuri collects 21 cans for the school food drive. Leo collects 36 cans. How many cans do Yuri and Leo collect?

_____ cans

_____

- -

_____

Math Talk

Explain the addition strategy you used to solve Exercise 1.

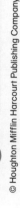

MATHEMATICAL PRACTICES

© Houghton Mifflin Harcourt Publishing Company

Name _____

Share and Show

Draw and write to solve. Explain your reasoning.

3. Tyra sees 48 geese in the field. Then she sees 17 more geese in the sky. How many geese does Tyra see?

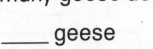

_____ geese

_____

- - - - - - - - - - - - - - - - -

_____

4. Jade paints 35 circles and 45 triangles in art class. How many shapes does Jade paint?

_____ shapes

_____

- - - - - - - - - - - - - - - - -

_____

5. **H.O.T.** It takes 23 hops to get across the yard. How many hops does it take to get across the yard and back?

_____ hops

_____

- - - - - - - - - - - - - - - - -

_____

On Your Own

Choose a way to solve. Draw or write to explain.

Write Math

6. Lisa uses 4 square beads and 8 round beads to make a bracelet. She makes another bracelet the same way. How many beads does Lisa use?

_____ beads

7. Julian sells 3 books of tickets for the school fair. Each book has 20 tickets. How many tickets does Julian sell?

_____ tickets

8. **H.O.T.** I have some red roses and pink roses. I have 14 red roses. I have 8 more pink roses than red roses. How many roses do I have?

_____ roses

9. ⭐ **Test Prep** I have 34 small shells and 14 big shells. How many shells do I have?

34   38   44   48
○   ○   ○   ○

TAKE HOME ACTIVITY • Ask your child to solve 16 + 7, 30 + 68, and 53 + 24. Ask him or her to explain how they solved each problem.

FOR MORE PRACTICE:
Standards Practice Book, pp. P165–P166

© Houghton Mifflin Harcourt Publishing Company

Name _____

Practice Addition and Subtraction

Essential Question What different ways can you use to add and subtract?

COMMON CORE STANDARDS CC.1.NBT.4, CC.1.NBT.6
Use place value understanding and properties of operations to add and subtract.

Listen and Draw REAL WORLD

Draw to show the problem.
Then solve.

FOR THE TEACHER • Read the following problem. The class collects paper bags for an art project. Ron brings 7 more bags than Ben. Ben brings 35 bags. How many bags does Ron bring?

Math Talk
How did you solve the problem? **Explain.**

MATHEMATICAL PRACTICES

Chapter 8

Model and Draw

What ways have you learned to
add and subtract?

$5 + 9 = \underline{\quad}$

> **THINK**
> $9 + 5$ is the same
> as $10 + \underline{\ ?\ }$.

$50 - 30 = \underline{\quad}$

> **THINK**
> 5 tens $-$ 3 tens.

$51 + 21 = \underline{\quad}$

> **THINK**
> 5 tens $+$ 2 tens.
> 1 one $+$ 1 one.

Share and Show

Add or subtract.

1. $30 + 60 = \underline{\quad}$	2. $73 + 5 = \underline{\quad}$	3. $10 - 4 = \underline{\quad}$
4. $29 + 4 = \underline{\quad}$	5. $9 + 9 = \underline{\quad}$	6. $5 + 6 = \underline{\quad}$
7. $25 + 54 = \underline{\quad}$	8. $15 - 8 = \underline{\quad}$	9. $40 + 10 = \underline{\quad}$
10. $40 - 10 = \underline{\quad}$	11. $14 - 7 = \underline{\quad}$	12. $90 - 70 = \underline{\quad}$
13. $86 + 12 = \underline{\quad}$	14. $1 + 9 = \underline{\quad}$	15. $6 + 7 = \underline{\quad}$
16. $9 - 2 = \underline{\quad}$	☑ 17. $8 + 31 = \underline{\quad}$	☑ 18. $50 + 11 = \underline{\quad}$

Name _____

On Your Own

Add or subtract.

19. 12 − 3	**20.** 10 +10	**21.** 7 +42	**22.** 41 +36
23. 8 +10	**24.** 16 + 7	**25.** 6 − 6	**26.** 3 +8
27. 64 + 3	**28.** 60 −30	**29.** 2 +7	**30.** 5 −1
31. 13 − 5	**32.** 52 +40	**33.** 3 +2	**34.** 30 +50
35. 8 +4	**36.** 18 − 8	**37.** 20 +13	**38.** 70 −50
39. 29 + 2	**40.** 34 +24	**41.** 20 +70	**42.** 11 − 7

PROBLEM SOLVING

REAL WORLD

Write Math

Solve. Write or draw to explain.

43. Jane drew some stars. Then she drew 9 more stars. Now there are 19 stars. How many stars did Jane draw first?

_____ stars

44. Adel drew 10 more stars than Charlie. Charlie drew 24 stars. How many stars did Adel draw?

_____ stars

45. H.O.T. Write three ways to get a sum of 49.

_____ ◯ _____ = 49

_____ ◯ _____ = 49

_____ ◯ _____ = 49

46. ⭐ **Test Prep** What is the sum? $40 + 38 =$ _____

38 ◯   48 ◯   70 ◯   78 ◯

TAKE HOME ACTIVITY • Have your child explain how he or she solved Exercise 43.

FOR MORE PRACTICE:
Standards Practice Book, pp. P167–P168

Name _____

Vocabulary

Write how many **tens** there are
in the sum or difference. (p. 322)

1. $70 - 40 = 30$

_____ tens

2. $20 + 30 = 50$

_____ tens

Concepts and Skills

Use the hundred chart
to add. Count on by
ones or tens. (CC.1.NBT.4)

3. $22 + 6 =$ _____

4. $41 + 40 =$ _____

5. $2 + 31 =$ _____

6. $80 + 15 =$ _____

1	2	3	4	5	6	7	8	9	10
11	12	13	14	15	16	17	18	19	20
21	22	23	24	25	26	27	28	29	30
31	32	33	34	35	36	37	38	39	40
41	42	43	44	45	46	47	48	49	50
51	52	53	54	55	56	57	58	59	60
61	62	63	64	65	66	67	68	69	70
71	72	73	74	75	76	77	78	79	80
81	82	83	84	85	86	87	88	89	90
91	92	93	94	95	96	97	98	99	100

7. What is the difference?
(CC.1.NBT.6)

$$50 - 40 = \underline{\quad}$$

9   10   54   90
○   ○   ○   ○

---

8. What is the sum? (CC.1.NBT.4)

$$18 + 50 = \underline{\quad}$$

58   60   68   88
○   ○   ○   ○

---

9. Which shows a way
you can make a ten
to find $26 + 7$? (CC.1.NBT.4)

$20 + 10$ $30 + 3$ $30 + 13$ $40 + 3$
○   ○   ○   ○

---

10. Pam has 20 crayons.
She gets a new box
of 64 crayons. How
many crayons does   24   30   66   84
Pam have now? (CC.1.NBT.4)   ○   ○   ○   ○

11. What is the sum?
(CC.1.NBT.4)

$10 + 70 = $ _____

8 ○   17 ○   71 ○   80 ○

12. What is the sum?
(CC.1.NBT.4)

$65 + 9 = $ _____

47 ○   70 ○   74 ○   95 ○

13. What is the sum?
(CC.1.NBT.4)

$$\begin{array}{r} 54 \\ + 32 \\ \hline \end{array}$$

22 ○   26 ○   82 ○   86 ○

14. What is the sum?
(CC.1.NBT.4)

$43 + 5 = $ _____

45 ○   48 ○   75 ○   93 ○

15. What is the sum?
(CC.1.NBT.4)

$$\begin{array}{r} 18 \\ + 41 \\ \hline \end{array}$$

51 ○   58 ○   59 ○   69 ○

Jamie is baking cookies. She bakes 24 chocolate chip cookies and 18 oatmeal cookies. How many cookies does Jamie bake?

Use numbers, pictures, or words to show your work.

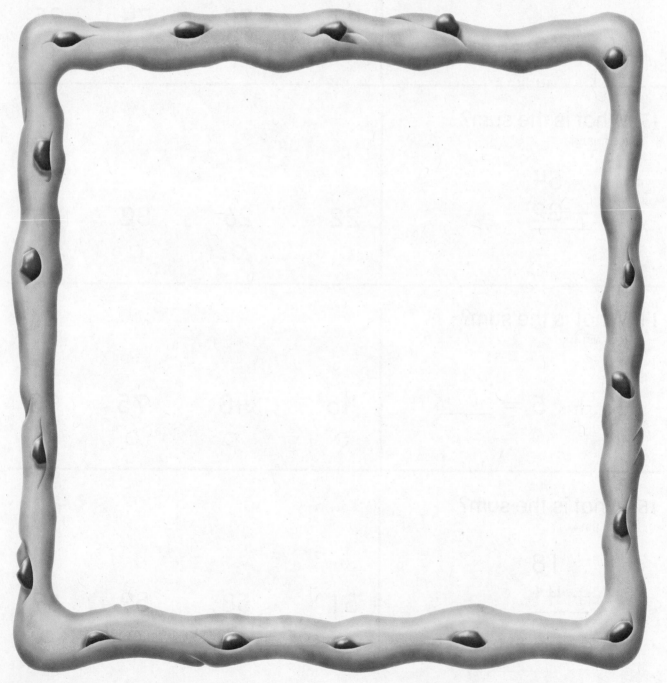

All Kinds of
Weather

written by Margie Sigman

COMMON CORE

CRITICAL AREA Developing understanding of linear measurement and measuring lengths as iterating length units

357

In rainy weather,

We play together.

Things We Use for Rainy Weather

raincoats

umbrellas

Use ● to complete the graph.

How many raincoats do you see? _____

How many umbrellas do you see? _____

SCIENCE

Describe rainy weather.

359

In sunny weather,

We play together.

Things We Use for Sunny Weather

sun hats

sunglasses

✿ Use ● to complete the graph.

How many sunglasses do you see? _____

How many sun hats do you see? _____

SCIENCE

Describe sunny weather.

Whatever the weather,

We play together.

SCICENCE

Describe the weather shown here.

Write About the Story

Use ●. Show some sun hats and sunglasses in each category on the graph.

Things We Use for Sunny Weather

sun hats

sunglasses

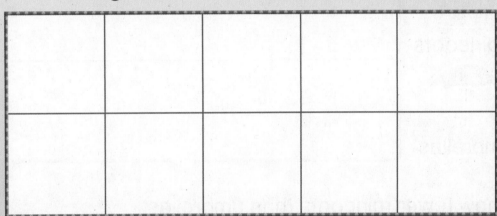

Write
Math
Write a sentence telling how many sun hats there are.
Write a sentence telling how many sunglasses there are.

_____
_____
_____
_____
_____
_____
_____
_____

More or Fewer?

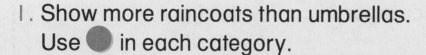

1. Show more raincoats than umbrellas.
   Use ⬤ in each category.

Things We Use for Rainy Weather

raincoats

umbrellas

2. Show fewer raincoats than umbrellas.
   Use ⬤ in each category.

Things We Use for Rainy Weather

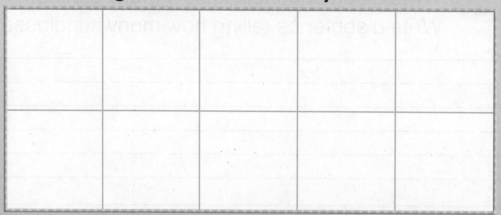

raincoats

umbrellas

Write a story problem about raincoats and umbrellas. Tell how to classify each item in the correct category.

Chapter 9 Measurement

Curious About Math with
Curious George

What objects in the
picture are shorter
than the arch?

Name _____

Bigger and Smaller

Circle the bigger object. | Circle the smaller object.

1.

2.

Compare Length

Circle the longer object.
Draw a line under the shorter object.

3.

4.

Numbers 1 to 10

Write each number in order to 10.

5.

1 ☐ ☐ ☐ ☐ ☐ ☐ ☐ ☐ 10

 Family note: This page checks your child's understanding of important skills needed for success in Chapter 9.

 Assessment Options
Soar to Success Math

© Houghton Mifflin Harcourt Publishing Company

Vocabulary Builder

Review Words	
nine	ten
eleven	twelve
long	longer
short	shorter

Visualize It

Sort the review words from the box.

length

long
_____

_____

_____

_____

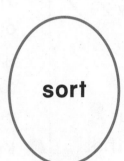

sort

numbers

nine
_____

_____

_____

_____

Understand Vocabulary

Complete the sentences with the correct word.

1. A crayon is _____ than a marker.

2. A toothbrush is _____ than a paper clip.

Write the name below the number.

3.   9   10   11   12

_____   _____   _____   _____

GO
Online
• eStudent Edition
• Multimedia eGlossary

Game Measure UP!

Materials

- 12 ⬤ ⬤
- 2 (eraser)
- 2 (pencil)
- 2 (marker)
- 2 (crayon)
- 2 ✂ (scissors)
- 2 (paintbrush)

Play with a partner.

1. Put 🧑🧑 on START.
2. Spin the 🌀. Move your 🧑 that many spaces. Take that object.
3. Your partner spins, moves, and takes that object.
4. Compare the lengths of the two objects.
5. The player with the longer object places a ⬤ on the space. If both objects are the same length, both players put a ⬤ on the board.
6. Keep playing until one person gets to END. The player with the most ⬤ wins.

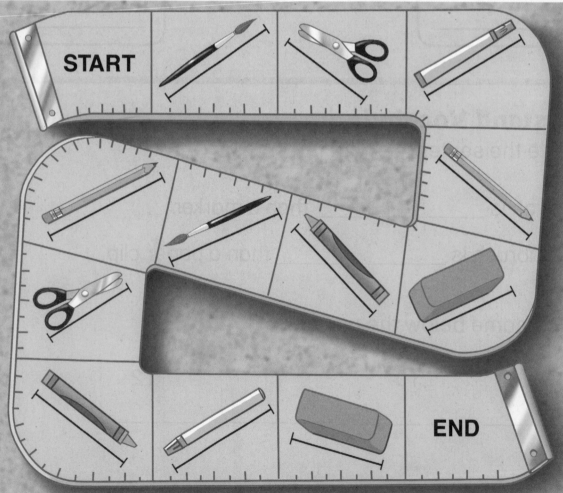

START

END

Name _____

Order Length

Essential Question How do you order objects by length?

COMMON CORE STANDARD CC.1.MD.1
Measure lengths indirectly and by iterating length units.

Listen and Draw REAL WORLD

Use objects to show the problem.
Draw to show your work.

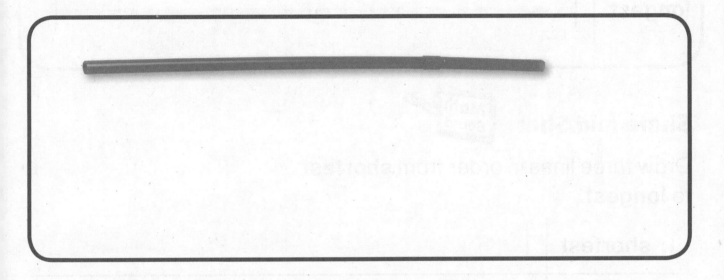

 FOR THE TEACHER • Read the problem. Have children use classroom objects to act it out. Rosa has something that is longer than the drinking straw. She has another object that is shorter than the key. What objects might she have?

Math Talk
Compare the straw and the key. Which is longer? Which is shorter? **Explain.**

MATHEMATICAL PRACTICES

Chapter 9

three hundred sixty-nine **369**

Order three pieces of yarn from **shortest** to **longest**. Draw the missing piece of yarn.

shortest |━━━━━━━━━━━━━|

|

longest |═══════════════════════════|

Share and Show

Draw three lines in order from **shortest** to **longest**.

I. **shortest** |

2. |

3. **longest** |

Draw three lines in order from **longest** to **shortest**.

4. **longest** |

5. |

6. **shortest** |

On Your Own

Draw three crayons in order from **shortest** to **longest**.

7. **shortest**	|
8.	|
9. **longest**	|

Draw three crayons in order from **longest** to **shortest**.

10. **longest**	|
11.	|
12. **shortest**	|

13. **H.O.T.** Complete each sentence.

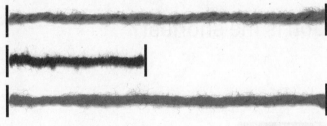

The _____ yarn is the shortest.

The _____ yarn and the _____ yarn are the same length.

PROBLEM SOLVING

REAL WORLD

Write Math

Solve.

14. Draw four objects in order from shortest to longest.

Objects

15. H.O.T. The string is shorter than the ribbon. The chain is shorter than the ribbon. Circle the longest object.

string

ribbon

chain

16. ⭐ **Test Prep** Which ribbon is the shortest?

TAKE HOME ACTIVITY • Show your child three different lengths of objects, such as three pencils or spoons. Ask him or her to order the objects from shortest to longest.

372 three hundred seventy-two

FOR MORE PRACTICE:
Standards Practice Book, pp. P173–P174

Indirect Measurement

Essential Question How can you compare lengths of three objects to put them in order?

COMMON CORE STANDARD CC.1.MD.1
Measure lengths indirectly and by iterating length units.

Listen and Draw  REAL WORLD

Clue 1: A yellow string is shorter than a blue string.

Clue 2: The blue string is shorter than a red string.

Clue 3: The yellow string is shorter than the red string.

yellow |

blue |

red |

Math Talk
Explain how the clues helped you draw the strings in the correct order.

MATHEMATICAL PRACTICES

 FOR THE TEACHER • Read the clues. Have children use the MathBoard to draw each clue. Then have children draw the strings in order from shortest to longest.

Chapter 9

Use the clues. Write **shorter** or **longer**
to complete the sentence. Then draw to
prove your answer.

Clue 1: A green pencil is longer than an orange pencil.

Clue 2: The orange pencil is longer than a brown pencil.

So, the green pencil is _longer_ than the brown pencil.

brown

orange

green

Share and Show Math Board

Use the clues. Write **shorter** or **longer**
to complete the sentence. Then draw
to prove your answer.

✓ 1. Clue 1: A red line is shorter than a blue line.
   Clue 2: The blue line is shorter than a purple line.

   So, the red line is _____ than the purple line.

red

blue

purple

On Your Own

Use the clues. Write **shorter** or **longer**
to complete the sentence. Then draw
to prove your answer.

2. Clue 1: A green line is shorter than a pink line.
   Clue 2: The pink line is shorter than a blue line.

   So, the green line is _____ than the blue line.

green	
pink	
blue	

3. Clue 1: An orange line is longer than a yellow line.
   Clue 2: The yellow line is longer than a red line.

   So, the orange line is _____ than the red line.

red	
yellow	
orange	

PROBLEM SOLVING REAL WORLD

Write Math

4. **H.O.T.** The ribbon is longer than the yarn. The yarn is longer than the string. The yarn and the pencil are the same length. Draw the lengths of the objects next to their labels.

ribbon	
yarn	
pencil	
string	

5. ⭐ **Test Prep** A green line is shorter than the orange line. The orange line is shorter than a blue line. Which is correct?

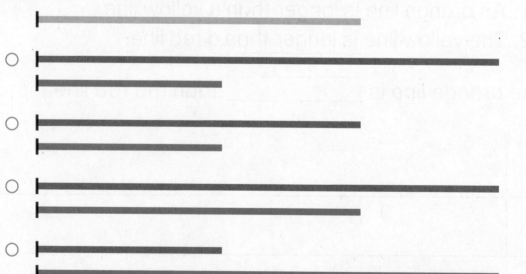

TAKE HOME ACTIVITY · Show your child the length of one object. Then show your child an object that is longer and an object that is shorter than the first object.

FOR MORE PRACTICE:
Standards Practice Book, pp. P175–P176

Use Nonstandard Units to Measure Length

Essential Question How do you measure length using nonstandard units?

HANDS ON
Lesson 9.3

COMMON CORE STANDARD CC.1.MD.2
Measure lengths indirectly and by iterating length units.

Listen and Draw

Draw to show the problem.

 FOR THE TEACHER • Read the problem. Jimmy sees that his boat is about 6 color tiles long. Draw Jimmy's boat. Draw the color tiles to show how you measured.

Math Talk
How do you draw the boat to be the right length? **Explain.**

MATHEMATICAL PRACTICES

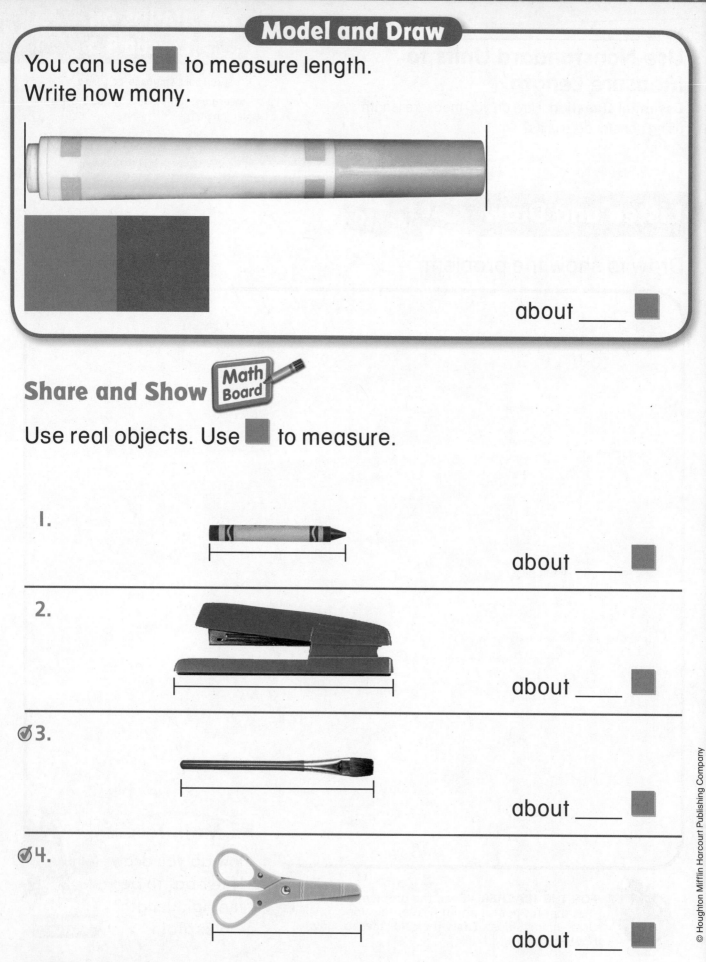

Model and Draw

You can use ⬛ to measure length.
Write how many.

about ____ ⬛

Share and Show Math Board

Use real objects. Use ⬛ to measure.

1.

about ____ ⬛

2.

about ____ ⬛

☑3.

about ____ ⬛

☑4.

about ____ ⬛

On Your Own

Use real objects. Use  to measure.

5.

about _____ ⬛

6.

about _____ ⬛

7.

about _____ ⬛

8.

about _____ ⬛

9. H.O.T. The green yarn is about 2 ⬛ long.
About how long is the blue yarn?

about _____ ⬛

PROBLEM SOLVING REAL WORLD

Write Math

Solve.

10. Mark measures a real glue stick with .
About how long is a glue stick?
Circle the answer that is most reasonable.

about 1   about 4 ☐   about 10 ☐

---

11. **H.O.T.** Bo has 4 ribbons. Circle the ribbon
that is less than 3 ☐ long but more than
1 ☐ long.

---

12. ⭐ **Test Prep** Use ☐. Ray measures
the key with ☐. About how long is the key?

○ about 1 ☐ long
○ about 2 ☐ long
○ about 3 ☐ long
○ about 4 ☐ long

TAKE HOME ACTIVITY • Give your child paper clips or other small
objects that are the same length. Have him or her estimate the lengths
of objects around the house and then measure to check.

FOR MORE PRACTICE:
Standards Practice Book, pp. P177–P178

Name _____

Make a Nonstandard Measuring Tool

Essential Question How do you use a nonstandard measuring tool to measure length?

COMMON CORE STANDARD CC.1.MD.2
Measure lengths indirectly and by iterating length units.

Listen and Draw REAL WORLD

Circle the name of the child who measured correctly.

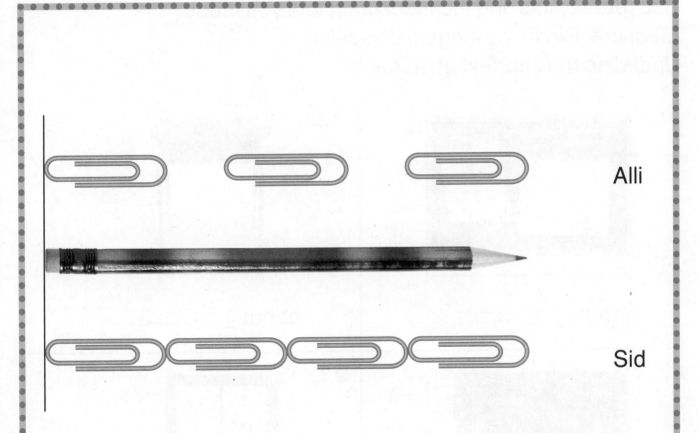

Alli

Sid

 FOR THE TEACHER • Read the problem. Sid and Alli measure the same pencil. Sid says it is about 4 paper clips long. Alli says it is about 3 paper clips long. Circle the name of the child who measured correctly.

 **Math Talk**
Explain how you know who measured correctly.

MATHEMATICAL PRACTICES

Chapter 9

three hundred eighty-one **381**

Make your own paper clip measuring tool like the one on the shelf. Measure the length of a door. About how long is the door?

about _____

Share and Show

Use real objects and the measuring tool you made.
Measure. Circle the longest object.
Underline the shortest object.

1.

about _____ ⬭

2.

about _____ ⬭

☑ 3.

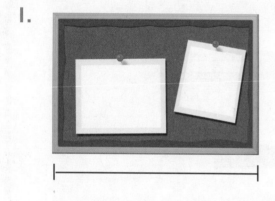

about _____ ⬭

☑ 4.

about _____ ⬭

Name _____

On Your Own

Use the measuring tool you made.
Measure real objects.

5.

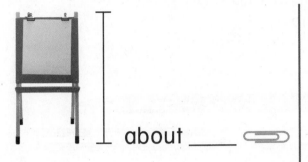

about ____ ◯=

6.

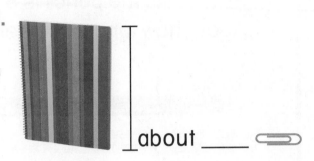

about ____ ◯=

7.

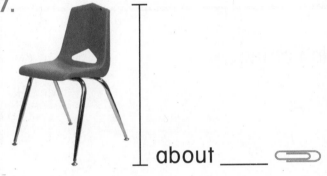

about ____ ◯=

8.

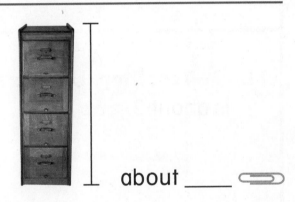

about ____ ◯=

9. **H.O.T.** Cody measured his
real lunch box. It is about
10 ◯= long. About how
long is Cody's real pencil?

Cody's lunch box
and pencil

about ____ ◯=

PROBLEM SOLVING REAL WORLD

Write Math

Solve.

10. **H.O.T.** Lisa tried to measure the pencil.
She thinks the pencil is 5 paper clips long.
About how long is the pencil?

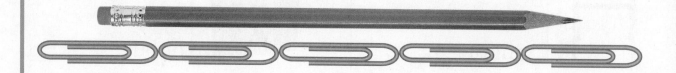

about ____

11. ⭐ **Test Prep** Use . Which string
is about 3  long?

○

○ (long string)

○

○ (medium string)

 TAKE HOME ACTIVITY • Have your child measure different objects around the
house using a paper clip measuring tool.

FOR MORE PRACTICE:
Standards Practice Book, pp. P179–P180

Name _____

Problem Solving • Measure and Compare

Essential Question How can acting it out help you solve measurement problems?

COMMON CORE STANDARD CC.1.MD.2
Measure lengths indirectly and
by iterating length units.

The blue ribbon is about 4  long. The red ribbon is 1  long. The green ribbon is 2  longer than red ribbon. Measure and draw the ribbons in order from **shortest** to **longest**.

🔑 Unlock the Problem

What do I need to find?

order the ribbons from
shortest to
longest

What information do I need to use?

Measure the
ribbons using paper clips.

Show how to solve the problem.

© Houghton Mifflin Harcourt Publishing Company

HOME CONNECTION • Have your child act out a measurement problem by finding the lengths of 3 objects and order them from shortest to longest.

Try Another Problem

Zack has 3 ribbons. The yellow ribbon is about 4 ⬭ long. The orange ribbon is 3 ⬭ shorter than the yellow ribbon. The blue ribbon is 2 ⬭ longer than the yellow ribbon.

Measure and draw the ribbons in order from **longest** to **shortest**.

1. |

about ____ ⬭

2. |

about ____ ⬭

3. |

about ____ ⬭

Math Talk

How many paper clips shorter is the orange ribbon than the blue ribbon? **Explain.**

MATHEMATICAL PRACTICES

© Houghton Mifflin Harcourt Publishing Company

Name _____

Share and Show

Solve. Draw or write to explain.

☑ 4. Lisa measures her shoe to be about
5 ⬭ long. Measure and draw an
object that is 3 ⬭ shorter than her
shoe. Measure and draw an object
that is 2 ⬭ longer than her shoe.

5. **H.O.T.** Noah measures a marker to be
about 4 ⬭ long and a pencil to be
about 6 ⬭ long. Draw an object that
is 1 ⬭ longer than the marker and
1 ⬭ shorter than the pencil.

TAKE HOME ACTIVITY • Have your child explain how he or she solved
Exercise 4.

© Houghton Mifflin Harcourt Publishing Company

FOR MORE PRACTICE:
Standards Practice Book, pp. P181–P182

Name _____

☑️ Mid-Chapter Checkpoint

Concepts and Skills

Draw three crayons in order from **shortest**
to **longest**. (CC.1.MD.1)

1.

shortest		
longest		

Use ■ to measure. (CC.1.MD.2)

2.

about _____ ■

3. ⭐ **Test Prep** Kiley measures a package
with her paper clip measuring tool.
About how long is the package? (CC.1.MD.2)

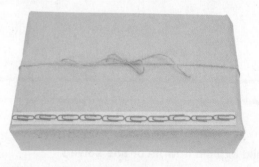

○ about 1 ⌇

○ about 5 ⌇

○ about 10 ⌇

○ about 20 ⌇

Name _____

Time to the Hour

Essential Question How do you tell time to the hour on a clock that has only an hour hand?

COMMON CORE STANDARD CC.1.MD.3
Tell and write time.

Listen and Draw REAL WORLD

Start at 1.

Write the missing numbers.

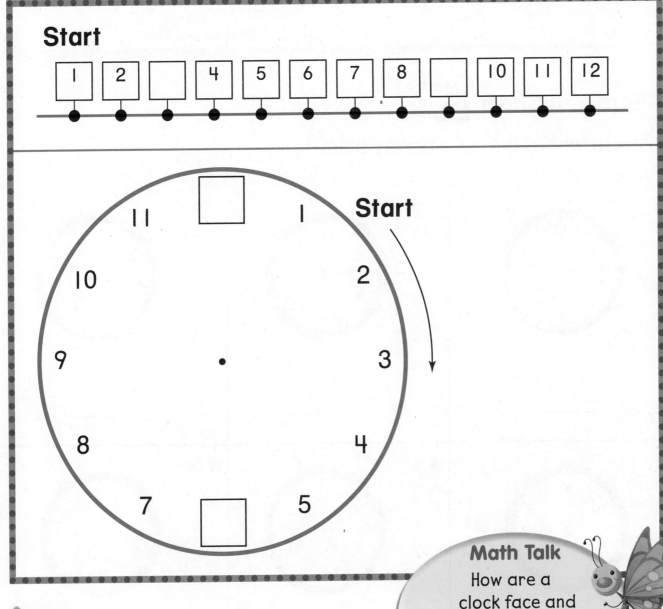

Start

Start

HOME CONNECTION • A clock face with only an hour hand can make it easier for your child to learn to tell time.

Math Talk
How are a clock face and ordering numbers alike? **Explain.**

MATHEMATICAL PRACTICES

Chapter 9

three hundred eighty-nine **389**

Model and Draw

What does this clock show?

The **hour hand** points to the 3.
It is 3 o'clock.

Say three o'clock.
Write 3:00 .

Share and Show

Look at where the hour hand points.
Write the time.

1. 	2. 	3. 
_____	_____	_____
4. 	✓ 5. 	✓ 6. 
_____	_____	_____

On Your Own

Look at where the hour hand points.
Write the time.

7.

_____

8.

_____

9.

_____

10.

_____

11.

_____

12.

_____

13.

_____

14.

_____

15.

_____

PROBLEM SOLVING REAL WORLD

16. Which time is **not** the same? Circle it.

1:00   1 o'clock

17. **H.O.T.** Manny leaves for school at 8 o'clock. Write and draw to show 8 o'clock.

_____

18. ⭐ **Test Prep**

Look at the hour hand. What is the time?

○ 12:00

○ 2:00

○ 1 o'clock

○ 3 o'clock

TAKE HOME ACTIVITY • Have your child describe what he or she did in this lesson.

FOR MORE PRACTICE:
Standards Practice Book, pp. P183–P184

Name _____

Time to the Half Hour

Essential Question How do you tell time to
the half hour on a clock that has only an hour hand?

COMMON CORE STANDARD CC.1.MD.3
Tell and write time.

Listen and Draw

Circle **4:00**, **5:00**, or **between 4:00 and 5:00**
to describe the time shown on the clock.

4:00

between 4:00 and 5:00

5:00

4:00

between 4:00 and 5:00

5:00

4:00

between 4:00 and 5:00

5:00

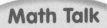

Math Talk
Use **before** and
after to **describe**
the time shown on
the middle clock.

MATHEMATICAL
PRACTICES

FOR THE TEACHER • Have children look at the
hour hand on each clock to decide which choice
best describes the time shown.

Chapter 9

three hundred ninety-three **393**

Model and Draw

As an **hour** passes, the hour hand moves from one number to the next number.

The hour hand is halfway between the 7 and the 8.

When a **half hour** has passed, the hour hand points halfway between two numbers.

half past 7:00

Share and Show

Look at where the hour hand points.
Write the time.

1.

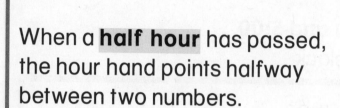

_____

2.

_____

☑3.

_____

☑4.

_____

On Your Own

Look at where the hour hand points.
Write the time.

5.

_____
- - - - - - - - - - - - - - - -
_____

6.

_____
- - - - - - - - - - - - - - - -
_____

7.

_____
- - - - - - - - - - - - - - - -
_____

8.

_____
- - - - - - - - - - - - - - - -
_____

9.

_____
- - - - - - - - - - - - - - - -
_____

10.

_____
- - - - - - - - - - - - - - - -
_____

PROBLEM SOLVING REAL WORLD

Write Math

11. Tim plays soccer at half past 9:00. He eats lunch at half past 1:00. He sees a movie at half past 2:00.

Look at the clock.
Write what Tim does.

_____

Tim _ .

12. **H.O.T.** Tyra has a piano lesson at 5:00. The lesson ends at half past 5:00. How much time is Tyra at her lesson? Circle your answer.

half hour

hour

13. ⭐ **Test Prep**
Look at the hour hand. What is the time?

○ half past 5:00
○ 5:00
○ half past 4:00
○ 4:00

TAKE HOME ACTIVITY · Say a time, such as half past 10:00. Ask your child to describe where the hour hand points at this time.

FOR MORE PRACTICE:
Standards Practice Book, pp. P185–P186

Name _____

Tell Time to the Hour and Half Hour

Essential Question How are the minute hand and hour hand different for time to the hour and time to the half hour?

COMMON CORE STANDARD CC.1.MD.3
Tell and write time.

Listen and Draw  REAL WORLD

Each clock has an hour hand and a minute hand.
Use what you know about the hour hand
to write the missing numbers.

It is 1:00.

The hour hand points to the _____.

The minute hand points to the _____.

It is half past 1:00.

The hour hand points between the _____ and the _____.

The minute hand points to the _____.

Math Talk
Look at the top clock. **Explain** how you know which is the minute hand.

MATHEMATICAL PRACTICES

HOME CONNECTION • While children may easily read time on a digital clock, learning to tell time on an analog clock helps to develop important concepts of time.

Model and Draw

An hour has 60 minutes.

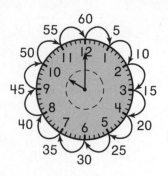

The clocks show 10:00.

A half hour has 30 minutes.

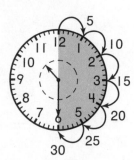

The clocks show half past 10:00. The **minute hand** has moved from the 12 to the 6.

30 minutes after 10:00

Share and Show

 Math Board

Write the time.

1.

☑ 2.

☑ 3.

© Houghton Mifflin Harcourt Publishing Company

Name _____

On Your Own

Write the time.

4.

5.

6.

7.

8.

9.

H.O.T. Circle your answer.

10. Sara goes to the park when both the hour hand and the minute hand point to the 12. What time does Sara go to the park?

    1:00   12:00   12:30

11. Mel goes to the park at 3 o'clock. He stays for 2 hours. What time does Mel leave the park?

    1 o'clock   3 o'clock   5 o'clock

PROBLEM SOLVING

REAL WORLD

Write Math

Solve.

12. Matt wakes up at 6 o'clock. Linda wakes up 30 minutes later. Draw to show what time Linda wakes up.

13. David left school at 3:30. Circle the clock that shows 3:30.

14. H.O.T. The hour hand points halfway between the 2 and 3. Draw the hour hand and the minute hand. Write the time.

15. ⭐ **Test Prep** What time is it?

○ 6:30

○ 7:30

○ 8:00

○ 8:30

 TAKE HOME ACTIVITY · At times on the half hour, have your child show you the minute hand and the hour hand on a clock and tell what time it is.

FOR MORE PRACTICE:
Standards Practice Book, pp. P187–P188

Name _____

Practice Time to the Hour and Half Hour

Essential Question How do you know whether to draw and write time to the hour or half hour?

COMMON CORE STANDARD CC.1.MD.3
Tell and write time.

Circle the clock that matches the problem.

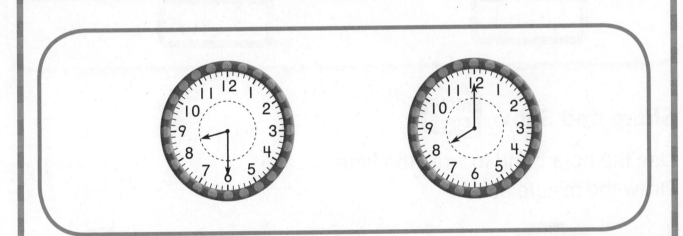

FOR THE TEACHER • Read the following problems. Barbara goes to the store at 8:00. Circle the clock that shows 8:00. Children use the top work space to solve. Then have children solve this problem: Barbara takes Ria for a walk at 1:30. Circle the clock that shows 1:30.

Math Talk
Describe how you know which clock shows 1:30.

MATHEMATICAL PRACTICES

Where should you draw the
minute hand to show the time?

9:00

9:30

Share and Show  Math Board

Use the hour hand to write the time.
Draw the minute hand.

1.

2.

3.

4.

⚆ 5.

⚆ 6.

On Your Own

Use the hour hand to write the time.
Draw the minute hand.

7.

8.

9.

10.

11.

12.

13. Explain What is the error? Zoey tried
to show 6:00. Explain how to change
the clock to show 6:00.

_____

- -

_____

_____

- -

_____

PROBLEM SOLVING REAL WORLD

Write Math

Solve.

14. Vince looks at the clock on the wall. It shows 4:00. He goes to a baseball game 30 minutes later. Draw to show what time Vince goes to a baseball game.

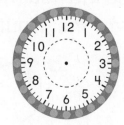

15. Missy watched a game for an hour. Write how many minutes Missy watched a game.

_____ minutes

16. H.O.T. Brandon has lunch at 12:00. Then he has math class 30 minutes later. Then he has art class 30 minutes after math class. Draw what time Brandon has art class.

17. ⭐ Test Prep Which clock shows 11:30?

○   ○   ○   ○

TAKE HOME ACTIVITY • Show your child the time on a clock. Ask him or her what time it will be in 30 minutes.

FOR MORE PRACTICE:
Standards Practice Book, pp. P189–P190

Chapter 9 Review/Test

Vocabulary

Circle the clock that shows time to the **half hour**. (p. 394)

Underline the clock that shows time to the **hour**. (p. 394)

1.

Concepts and Skills

Use ▪ to measure. (CC.1.MD.2)

2.

about ____ ▪

Draw three crayons in order from **longest**
to **shortest**. (CC.1.MD.1)

3.

longest	
shortest	

4. Mike measures a box with .
About how long is the box? (CC.1.MD.2)

about 3 ⊂⊃   about 5 ⊂⊃   about 10 ⊂⊃   about 20 ⊂⊃
○   ○   ○   ○

5. Karen measures the crayon with ■. About how long is the crayon? (CC.1.MD.2)

about 1 ■   about 3 ■   about 5 ■   about 7 ■
○   ○   ○   ○

6. A red line is longer than a purple line.
The purple line is longer than a yellow line.
Which is correct? (CC.1.MD.1)

406 four hundred six

7. **What is the time?** (CC.1.MD.3)

- ○ 7:00
- ○ half past 7:00
- ○ 8:00
- ○ half past 8:00

8. **Look at the hour hand. What time is it?** (CC.1.MD.3)

- ○ 7:00
- ○ 8:00
- ○ 9 o'clock
- ○ 10 o'clock

9. The red line is about 4 ⊂⊃ long. The blue line is
1 ⊂⊃ longer than the red line. The green line is
2 ⊂⊃ shorter than the red line. Which is correct? (CC.1.MD.2)

○

○

○

○

Performance Task (CC.1.MD.1, CC.1.MD.2)

Choose three objects to measure.

- Measure the length of each object with ▪.
- Order the objects from shortest to longest.

Write each measurement.
Use pictures, words, or numbers to
show how you ordered the lengths
of the objects.

Show your work.

Chapter
10
Represent Data

Curious About Math with
Curious George

How many days will it
snow or rain this week
where you live? How
can you find out?

Name _____

Make a Concrete Graph

Sort a handful of ■ and ■. Make a concrete graph.

Square Colors							
■							
■							

1. How many ■ are there? _____

More, Fewer

2. Color the squares to show a set of fewer.

🏎️	🏎️	🏎️	🏎️	

Draw Equal Groups

3. Draw a ◯ below each picture to show the same number of objects.

✺	✺	✺		

Family note: This page checks your child's understanding of important skills needed for success in Chapter 10.

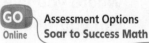

Assessment Options
Soar to Success Math

© Houghton Mifflin Harcourt Publishing Company

Name _____

Review Words

graph
more
fewer
most
fewest

Vocabulary Builder

Visualize It

Complete the chart.

Mark each row with a ✔.

Word	I Know	Sounds Familiar	I Do Not Know
graph			
more			
fewer			
most			
fewest			

Understand Vocabulary

Use the review words. Label the groups.

1.

_____   _____

2.

_____   _____

GO Online
• eStudent Edition
• Multimedia eGlossary

Game

Graph Game

Materials • 16 🔲 • 16 🔲 • 16 🔲

Play with a partner.

1 Spin the 🕐.

2 Put 1 cube of that color in the correct row of your graph.

3 Take turns. Play until each partner has 5 turns.

4 The player who went last spins again to get a color.

5 The player with more cubes of that color wins. Spin again if you both have the same number of cubes of that color.

Player 1

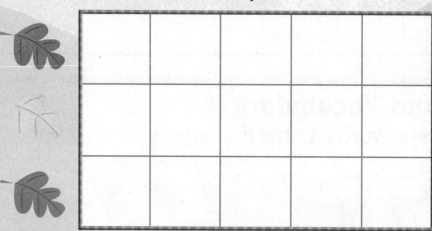

Player 2

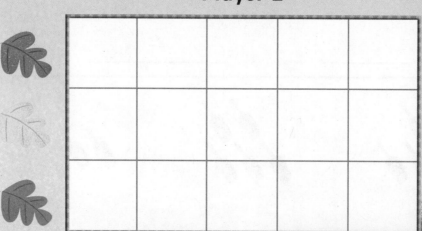

Name _____

Read Picture Graphs

Essential Question What do the pictures in a picture graph show?

COMMON CORE STANDARD CC.1.MD.4
Represent and interpret data.

Listen and Draw  REAL WORLD

Use . Draw to show the cubes.

Write how many more .

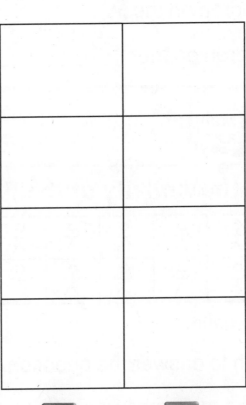

_____ more

 FOR THE TEACHER • Read the following problem. There are 2 green cubes and 4 blue cubes. How many more blue cubes are there than green cubes?

Math Talk
Describe how you can use your picture to compare the cubes.
MATHEMATICAL PRACTICES

Chapter 10

four hundred thirteen **413**

Model and Draw

Children at the Playground
swings
slide

A **picture graph** uses pictures to show information.

Each  **stands for 1 child.**

There are __4__ children on the .

There are ____ children on the .

There are more children on the ____________.

Share and Show

Our Favorite Activity at the Fair
animals
rides

Each  **stands for 1 child.**

Use the picture graph to answer the question.

1. Which activity did more children choose? Circle.  

2. How many children chose ? ____ children

✓ 3. How many children chose ? ____ children

✓ 4. How many fewer children chose  than ? ____ fewer children

Name _____

On Your Own

What We Drink for Lunch									
milk	🧍	🧍	🧍	🧍	🧍	🧍	🧍	🧍	
juice	🧍	🧍	🧍						
water	🧍	🧍	🧍	🧍	🧍				

Each 🧍 stands for 1 child.

Use the picture graph to answer the question.

5. How many children

drink 🥛?

_____ children

6. How many children in all

drink 🧃 and 💧?

_____ children

7. What do most children drink

for lunch? Circle.

8. How many more children

drink 🥛 than 🧃?

_____ more children

9. How many fewer children

drink 💧 than 🥛?

_____ fewer children

10. How many children in all

drink 🥛, 🧃, and 💧.

_____ children

11. ☀H.O.T.☀ 4 new children join the class.

They drink 🧃 at lunch. Now, how many

more children drink 🧃 than 💧?

_____ more children

PROBLEM SOLVING REAL WORLD

Write Math

Our Favorite Animal at the Zoo

🦓	zebras	�	�	�	�	�			
🦁	lions	�	�	�	�	�	�	�	�
🦭	seals	�							

Each � stands for 1 child.

Write a number sentence to solve the problem.

12. How many children chose 🦓 and 🦭 altogether?

___ ◯ ___ ◯ ___

____ children

13. How many more children chose 🦁 than 🦭 ?

___ ◯ ___ ◯ ___

____ more children

14. **H.O.T.** How many more children chose 🦁 than 🦓 and 🦭 altogether?

___ ◯ ___ ◯ ___

____ more children

15. ⭐ **Test Prep** Use the graph at the top. How many children chose 🦁 ?

9 children   8 children   5 children   1 child

◯   ◯   ◯   ◯

TAKE HOME ACTIVITY · Keep track of the weather for one week by drawing a picture each day to show if it is sunny, cloudy, or rainy. At the end of the week, ask your child what the weather was like for most of the week.

FOR MORE PRACTICE:
Standards Practice Book, pp. P195–P196

© Houghton Mifflin Harcourt Publishing Company

Name _____

Make Picture Graphs

Essential Question How do you make a picture graph to answer a question?

COMMON CORE STANDARD CC.1.MD.4
Represent and interpret data.

Listen and Draw REAL WORLD

Use ⬤ to solve the problem.
Draw to show your work.

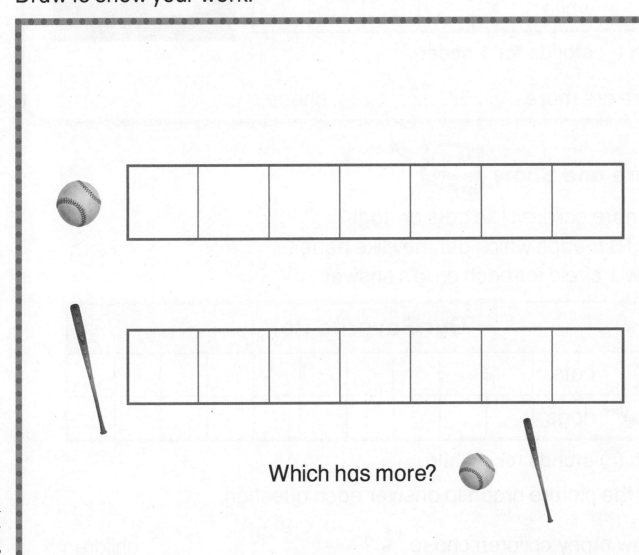

Which has more?

FOR THE TEACHER • Read the following problem. Asaf has 6 baseballs. He has 4 bats. Does he have more baseballs or bats? Have children draw circles to show the baseballs and bats. Then have them circle the object with more.

Math Talk
Describe what the picture graph shows.

MATHEMATICAL PRACTICES

Chapter 10

Model and Draw

Are there more black or white sheep in the picture? Make a picture graph to find out.

Sheep in the Meadow						
 black	◯					
🐑 white						

Each ◯ stands for 1 sheep.

There are more _____ sheep.

Share and Show

Do more children like cats or dogs?
Ask 10 friends which pet they like better.
Draw 1 circle for each child's answer.

Our Favorite Pet										
🐱 cats										
🐕 dogs										

Each ◯ stands for 1 child.

Use the picture graph to answer each question.

1. How many children chose ? ____ children

_____

✓ 2. How many children chose 🐕 ? ____ children

_____

✓ 3. Which pet did more children choose? Circle.

Name _____

On Your Own

Which activity do the most children like best?
Ask 10 friends. Draw 1 circle for each child's answer.

Our Favorite Activity										
📖 reading										
💻 computer										
⚽ sports										

Each ◯ stands for 1 child.

Use the picture graph to answer the question.

4. How many children chose 📖?

   _____ children

5. How many children chose 💻 and ⚽?

   _____ children

6. Which activity did the most children choose? Circle.

7. Did all your classmates make picture graphs that look the same? Write **yes** or **no**.

   _____

   _____

8. 🌅 H.O.T. Write your own question about the graph.

   _____

   _____

   _____

   _____

PROBLEM SOLVING REAL WORLD

Write Math

Matt made this picture graph to show the paint colors his friends like best.

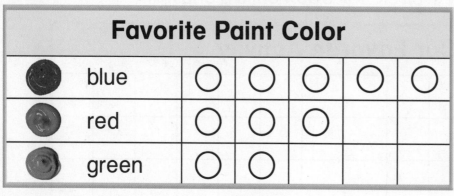

Favorite Paint Color

	blue	○	○	○	○	○
	red	○	○	○		
	green	○	○			

Each ○ stands for 1 child.

9. How many children chose a paint color?

    ____ children

10. How many fewer children chose than ?

    ____ fewer children

11. **H.O.T.** Matt adds his own choice to the graph. Now, two colors have the same number of circles. Circle the color Matt chose.

    blue   red   green

12. ⭐ **Test Prep** Use the graph at the top. How many children chose 🔵 and 🔴?

    2   3   5   8
    ○   ○   ○   ○

TAKE HOME ACTIVITY • Ask your child to make a picture graph showing how many glasses of water each family member drinks in a day. Discuss how to find who drinks the most water.

FOR MORE PRACTICE:
Standards Practice Book, pp. P197–P198

© Houghton Mifflin Harcourt Publishing Company

Name _____

Read Bar Graphs

Essential Question How can you read a bar graph to find the number that a bar shows?

COMMON CORE STANDARD CC.1.MD.4
Represent and interpret data.

Listen REAL WORLD

Write a question about the graph.
Use ⬤ to help solve the problem.

Type of Sneaker We Are Wearing										
👟 laces	◯	◯	◯	◯	◯	◯	◯	◯	◯	◯
👟 no laces	◯	◯	◯	◯	◯	◯				

Each ◯ stands for 1 child.

_____

_____

_____

_____

FOR THE TEACHER • Read the following problem. Emma's class made this picture graph. What question could Emma's class answer using the graph? Write the question and the answer.

Math Talk
Describe how the class made this picture graph.

MATHEMATICAL PRACTICES

Chapter 10

Model and Draw

In a **bar graph,** each bar shows information. You can compare the lengths of the bars.

What title describes this graph?

> Touch the end of a bar. Look down to see the number of children.

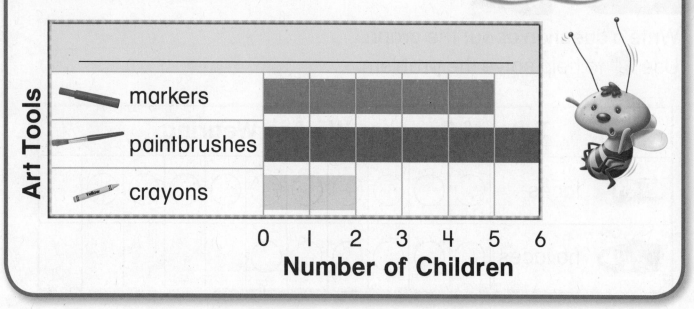

Art Tools

markers

paintbrushes

crayons

0 1 2 3 4 5 6

Number of Children

Share and Show Math Board

Use the bar graph to answer the question.

1. How many children chose ?

   _____ children

2. How many children chose [crayon]?

   _____ children

3. How many more children chose [marker] than [crayon]?

   _____ more children

✓ 4. Which art tool did the fewest children choose? Circle.

✓ 5. Which art tool did the most children choose? Circle.

422 four hundred twenty-two

© Houghton Mifflin Harcourt Publishing Company

Name _____

On Your Own

Use the bar graph to answer the question.

6. How many children chose 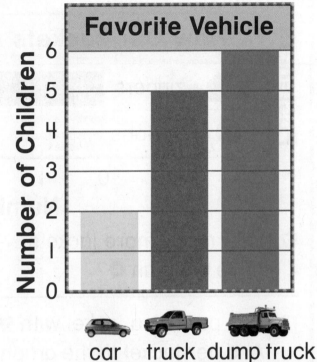?

   ____ children

7. How many children chose 🚛 ?

   ____ children

8. How many children in all chose 🚗 and 🚛 ?

   ____ children

9. How many more children chose 🚙 than 🚗 ?

   ____ more children

10. Which vehicle did the most children choose? Circle.

11. **H.O.T.** Order the vehicles from least to most votes. Write 1 for the least votes and 3 for the most votes.

    ____   ____   ____

PROBLEM SOLVING REAL WORLD

Write Math

Use the bar graph to answer the question.

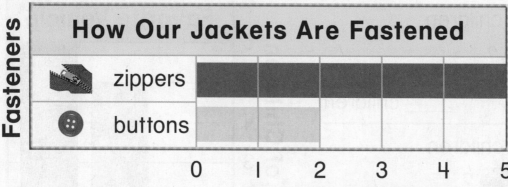

How Our Jackets Are Fastened

Fasteners

zippers

buttons

0 1 2 3 4 5
Number of Jackets

12. How many more jackets
have 🤐 than 🔘?   _____ more jackets

13. Kim puts on a jacket with 🔘.
Add her jacket to the graph.
Now how many jackets have 🔘?   _____ jackets

14. H.O.T. Ed adds a row to the graph to
show jackets with snaps. 2 fewer
jackets have snaps than have zippers.
How many jackets have snaps?   _____ jackets

15. ⭐ **Test Prep** Use the graph at the top.
How many jackets have 🤐?

2 jackets   5 jackets   7 jackets   10 jackets
  ○   ○   ○   ○

TAKE HOME ACTIVITY · Have your child look through newspapers and
magazines for examples of bar graphs. Talk about what information is shown
in each graph you find.

FOR MORE PRACTICE:
Standards Practice Book, pp. P199–P200

© Houghton Mifflin Harcourt Publishing Company

Make Bar Graphs

Essential Question How does a bar graph help you compare information?

COMMON CORE STANDARD CC.1.MD.4
Represent and interpret data.

Listen and Draw  REAL WORLD

Use to model the problem.
Color 1 box for each food item
to complete the graph.

Kinds of Food	Food Sold at the Soccer Game							
🍕 pizza								
🌭 hot dogs								
🌮 tacos								

0   1   2   3   4   5   6   7
Number of Food Items Sold

 FOR THE TEACHER • Read the following problem. Dan keeps track of the food he sells at the soccer game. He sells all of the food on the table. Make a bar graph to show the food Dan sells.

Math Talk
How do you know that you counted each food in the picture? **Explain.** 
MATHEMATICAL PRACTICES

Model and Draw

Are there more  or 🌻 in the garden?

Make a bar graph to find out.

Color 1 box for each flower in the picture.

Kinds of Flowers

Flowers in the Garden								
🌼 daisies								
🌻 sunflowers								

0   1   2   3   4   5   6   7

Number of Flowers

There are more _____ in the garden.

Share and Show

Do more children write with their left hand or right hand?

Ask 10 friends which hand they use. Make a bar graph.

Writing Hand

Hand We Use to Write										
🖐 left										
🖐 right										

0   1   2   3   4   5   6   7   8   9   10

Number of Children

✓ 1. Which hand do more children use to write? _____

Name _____

On Your Own

Do children like , ◼, or ◉ best?
Ask 10 friends which toy they like best.

2. Make a bar graph. Write a title and labels for your graph.

		0	1	2	3	4	5	6	7	8	9	10
🧸	bear											
◼	blocks											
◉	marbles											

3. Which toy did the most children choose? Circle.

  ◉

4. How many children chose ◼?

_____ children

5. 🌞 H.O.T. 🌞 How are picture graphs and bar graphs alike?

_____

_____

_____

TAKE HOME ACTIVITY · Your child has learned how to make picture graphs and bar graphs. Ask your child to explain how bar graphs are different from picture graphs.

FOR MORE PRACTICE:
Standards Practice Book, pp. P201–P202

✓ Mid-Chapter Checkpoint

Concepts and Skills

Use the bar graph to answer the question. (CC.1.MD.4)

Ways to Get to School

How We Get to School

	0	1	2	3	4	5	6	7	8
Car									
Bike									
Bus									

Number of Children

1. How many children take the bus to school? _____ children

Use the picture graph to answer the question. (CC.1.MD.4)

Do you wear glasses?

yes	◯	◯	◯					
no	◯	◯	◯	◯	◯	◯	◯	◯

Each ◯ stands for 1 child.

2. How many children do not wear glasses?

_____ children

3. How many children wear glasses?

_____ children

4. ⭐ **Test Prep** How many fewer children answered yes than no about wearing glasses? (CC.1.MD.4)

3 fewer children	4 fewer children	5 fewer children	8 fewer children
◯	◯	◯	◯

Name _____

Read Tally Charts

Essential Question How do you count the tallies on a tally chart?

COMMON CORE STANDARD CC.1.MD.4
Represent and interpret data.

Listen and Draw · REAL WORLD

Use ● to solve the problem.
Draw to show your work.
Write how many.

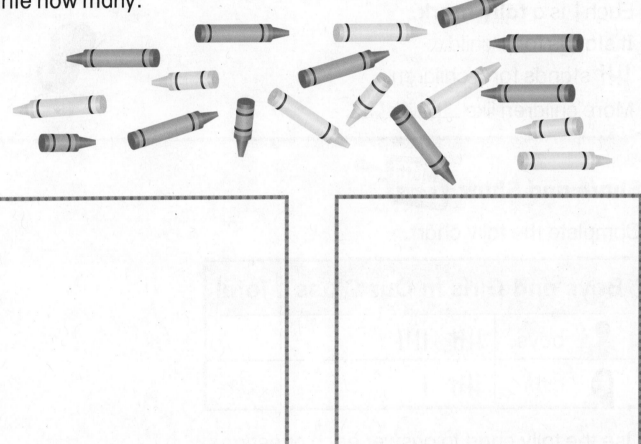

_____

 FOR THE TEACHER • Read the following problem. Jane is sorting her crayons. Draw to show how she can sort the crayons into two groups.

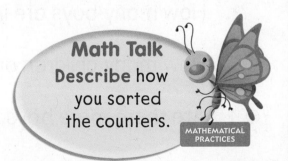
Math Talk
Describe how you sorted the counters.
MATHEMATICAL PRACTICES

Chapter 10

four hundred twenty-nine **429**

Model and Draw

Do more children like chicken or pizza better?

Food We Like		Total
 chicken	III	3
pizza	ⅢⅠ III	

Each | is a **tally mark.**

It stands for 1 child.

ⅢⅠ stands for 5 children.

More children like ___pizza___.

You can use a **tally chart** to collect information.

Share and Show

Complete the tally chart.

Boys and Girls in Our Class		Total
boys	ⅢⅠ IIII	
girls	ⅢⅠ I	

Use the tally chart to answer each question.

1. How many girls are in the class? _____ girls

2. How many boys are in the class? _____ boys

☑ 3. How many children are in the class in all? _____ children

☑ 4. Are there more boys or girls in the class? _____

Name _____

On Your Own

Complete the tally chart.

Our Favorite Sport		Total
⚾ t-ball	卌	
⚽ soccer	卌 ||	
🥏 swimming	|||	

Use the tally chart to answer the question.

5. How many children chose ? _____ children

6. How many children chose ? _____ children

7. How many more children chose ⚾ than 🥏? _____ more children

8. Which sport did the most children choose? Circle.

9. 🌅 **H.O.T.** Write your own question about the tally chart.

_____

- -

_____

10. 🌅 **H.O.T.** Sam asked some other children which sport they like. They all chose 🥏. Now the most children chose 🥏. How many children did Sam ask? _____ children

PROBLEM SOLVING REAL WORLD

Write Math

Color We Like Best		Total
🔴 red	||||	
🔵 blue	₩₩₩ ₩₩₩	
🟢 green	||||	

Remember to write the total.

Complete each sentence about the tally chart.
Write **greater than**, **less than**, or **equal to**.

11. The number of tallies for 🔵 is _____ the number of tallies for 🔴.

_____

12. The number of tallies for 🔴 is _____ the number of tallies for 🟢.

_____

13. The number of tallies for 🟢 is _____ the number of tallies for 🔵.

_____

14. **H.O.T.** The number of tallies for 🔵 is _____ the number of tallies for both 🔴 and 🟢.

15. ⭐ **Test Prep** Which tally marks show the number 10?

\|\|\|\| ₩₩₩   ₩₩₩ ₩₩₩   ₩₩₩ ₩₩₩ ₩₩₩

○   ○   ○   ○

TAKE HOME ACTIVITY · Together with your child, make a tally chart showing how many times you all say the word "eat" during a meal. Then have your child write the number.

FOR MORE PRACTICE:
Standards Practice Book, pp. P203–P204

Name _____

Make Tally Charts

Essential Question Why is a tally chart a good way to show information that you have collected?

COMMON CORE STANDARD CC.1.MD.4
Represent and interpret data.

 **Listen** REAL WORLD

Complete the tally chart.

Our Favorite Game		Total
card game	IIII	
puzzle	III	
board game	IIII IIII	

Use the tally chart to answer the question.

Which game did the most children choose? Circle.

Which game did the fewest children choose? Circle.

 FOR THE TEACHER • Read the following problem. Ava asks the children in her class which of three games they like the best. She makes a tally mark to show each child's answer. Which game did the most children choose? Which did the fewest children choose?

Math Talk
How do you know which game is the favorite? **Explain.**
MATHEMATICAL PRACTICES

Chapter 10

Model and Draw

How can you make a tally chart to show the boats at the lake?

> Decide if each boat has a sail.

Boats at the Lake		Total
boats with sails	‖	
boats without sails		

Share and Show Math Board

Use the picture to complete the tally chart. Then answer each question.

Fish in the Tank		Total
 zebra fish		
angel fish		

1. How many 🐟 are in the tank?

_____ 🐟

☑ 2. How many more 🐟 than 🐠 are there?

_____ more

☑ 3. How many 🐟 and 🐠 are in the tank?

_____ fish

Name _____

On Your Own

Which of these snacks do most children like the best?
Ask 10 friends. Make 1 tally mark for each child's answer.

Our Favorite Snack		Total
pretzel		
apple		
yogurt		

Use the tally chart to answer each question.

4. How many children chose ?

_____ children

5. How many children chose ?

_____ children

6. Which snack do most children like best? Circle.

7. **H.O.T.** What if 6 children out of the 10 chose ? Which snack would be the favorite? Circle it.

8. **Explain** Write your own question about the tally chart.

_____

_ _ _ _ _ _ _ _ _ _ _ _ _ _ _ _ _ _ _ _

_____

PROBLEM SOLVING REAL WORLD

Jenna asked 10 friends to choose their favorite subject. She will ask 10 more children.

Our Favorite School Subject		Total
math	ЖН I	
reading	II	
science	II	

9. Predict. Which subject will children most likely choose?

_____

10. Predict. Which subject will children least likely choose?

_____

11. H.O.T. How can you prove if your prediction is good? Try it.

_____
_____

12. ⭐ **Test Prep** Which fruit did the most children choose?

Fruit We Like			Total
	apple	IIII	4
	banana	ЖН	5
	grapes	II	2

TAKE HOME ACTIVITY • With your child, survey friends and family to find out their favorite food. Draw tally marks to record the results and then prepare the food.

FOR MORE PRACTICE:
Standards Practice Book, pp. P205–P206

Name _____

Problem Solving • Represent Data

Essential Question How can showing information in a graph help you solve problems?

COMMON CORE STANDARD CC.1.MD.4
Represent and interpret data.

Brad sees many animals at the park. How can you find how many animals Brad sees?

🔑 Unlock the Problem REAL WORLD

What do I need to find?	**What information do I need to use?**
how many ~~animals~~ Brad sees	the number of ~~rabbits~~, ~~birds~~, and ~~deer~~ in the picture

Show how to solve the problem.

Animals Brad Sees							
🐰 rabbit							
🐦 bird							
🦌 deer							

0   1   2   3   4   5   6   7
Number of Animals

____ + ____ + ____ = ____ animals

HOME CONNECTION • Your child learned how to represent data from a picture in a bar graph. Have your child explain why it is easier to use data in a bar graph than in a picture.

Chapter 10

four hundred thirty-seven **437**

Try Another Problem

Make a graph to solve.

- What do I need to find?
- What information do I need to use?

1. Jake has 4 more train cars than Ed. Ed has 3 train cars. Ben has 2 fewer train cars than Ed. How many train cars does Jake have?

_____ train cars

Our Train Cars

Children									
Jake									
Ed									
Ben									

0   1   2   3   4   5   6   7   8
Number of Train Cars

2. Marla has 8 dolls. Three dolls have blue eyes. The rest have brown. How many dolls have brown eyes?

_____ dolls

Dolls Marla Has

Eye Color								
blue eyes								
brown eyes								

0   1   2   3   4   5   6   7   8
Number of Dolls

Math Talk

Describe how the bar graph helps you solve Exercise 2.

MATHEMATICAL PRACTICES

© Houghton Mifflin Harcourt Publishing Company

Share and Show

Find out about the eye color of your classmates.

3. Write a question you can ask your friends.

   _____

☑4. Ask 10 friends your question.
   Make a tally chart.

		Total

☑5. Use the tally chart to make a bar graph.

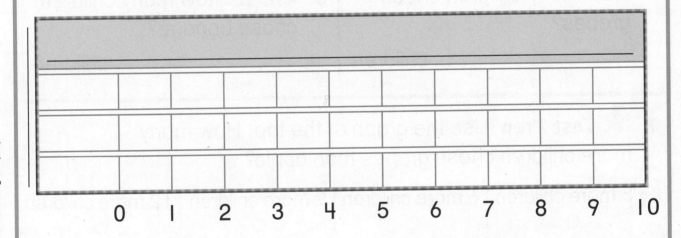

6. **Explain** What did you learn from the graph?

   _____

On Your Own

Write Math

What is your favorite fruit? Nina asked 20 children this question. Then she made a bar graph. But Nina spilled paint on the graph.

REMEMBER Nina asked 20 people.

7. How many children chose grapes?

_____ children

8. H.O.T. How many children chose banana?

_____ children

9. ⭐ **Test Prep** Use the graph at the top. How many more children chose grapes than apple?

| 3 more children | 6 more children | 9 more children | 12 more children |
| ○ | ○ | ○ | ○ |

TAKE HOME ACTIVITY • Work with your child to make a tally chart and a bar graph showing the favorite color of 10 family members or friends. Talk about the results.

FOR MORE PRACTICE:
Standards Practice Book, pp. P207–P208

Chapter 10 Review/Test

Vocabulary

1. Circle the **picture graph**. (p. 414)

2. Use the picture graph to complete the **bar graph**. (p. 422)

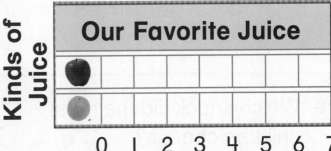

Each 🧍 stands for 1 child.

Concepts and Skills

Use the graphs above to answer the question. (CC.1.MD.4)

3. How many children chose ?   _____ children

_____

4. How many children chose ?   _____ children

_____

5. How many more children chose
   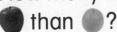 than 🟠?   _____ more children

_____

6. Which juice did more children
   choose? Circle it.

7. How many children chose soccer? (CC.1.MD.4)

Our Favorite Sport		Total
t-ball	III	3
⚽ soccer	卌 I	

3   4   6   9
○   ○   ○   ○

---

8. Which snack did the most children choose? (CC.1.MD.4)

Our Favorite Snack	
🍌 banana	卌
🥨 pretzel	III
🧃 raisins	II

🍌   🥨   🧃   🍎
○   ○   ○   ○

---

9. How many children chose RED ? (CC.1.MD.4)

Color We Like						
RED red	☘	☘	☘	☘	☘	
BLUE blue	☘	☘	☘	☘	☘	☘

○ 3 children
○ 5 children
○ 6 children
○ 9 children

Each ☘ stands for I child.

Name _____

10. How many more days this month had 💧 than ☀ ? (CC.1.MD.4)

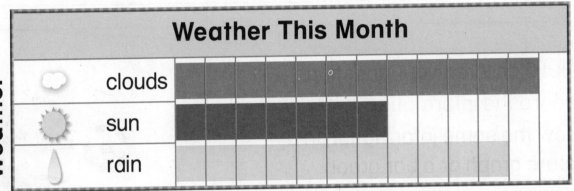

Weather This Month

Kinds of Weather

		Number of Days
☁	clouds	
☀	sun	
💧	rain	

0 1 2 3 4 5 6 7 8 9 10 11 12 13
Number of Days

○ 1 more day   ○ 5 more days

○ 4 more days   ○ 11 more days

11. Sam makes a tally chart to show how many cars and trucks he has. Which group of tally marks shows how many cars Sam has? (CC.1.MD.4)

Sam's Cars and Trucks		Total
🚗	cars	8
🚚	trucks	‖‖	6

卌 I	卌 III	卌 IIII	卌 卌
○	○	○	○

Performance Task (CC.1.MD.4)

Write a question to ask your class.

_____

- -

_____

- Ask 10 children your question.
- Record the information in a tally chart.
- Show the same information in a picture graph or a bar graph.

Use words, numbers, or pictures to tell which thing is the favorite.

Geometry

On the Move

written by Jennifer Earnshaw

COMMON CORE

CRITICAL AREA Reasoning about attributes of, and composing and decomposing geometric shapes

The train car waits for the engine.

Name some shapes you see.

Social Studies

What will this train bring?

The big truck travels up the road.

Name some shapes you see.

Social Studies

What will this truck bring?

The ship loads at the dock.

Name some shapes you see.

Social Studies

What will this ship bring?

These trucks drive across town.

Name some shapes you see.

Social Studies

What will these trucks bring?

449

The airplane arrives at the airport.

Name some shapes you see.

Social Studies

What will this airplane bring?

Write About the Story

Think of another kind of truck that takes goods from one place to another. Draw a picture. Use circles, squares, triangles, or rectangles in your drawing.

truck

Write Math ▷ Write about your drawing.

_____

_____

_____

_____

_____

_____

Figure It Out

1. Draw an airplane.
Use some triangles and
circles in your drawing.

2. Draw a train.
Use some rectangles and
circles in your drawing.

 Choose two shapes to use to draw
a ship. Draw the ship.

452

Chapter 11

Three-Dimensional Geometry

Curious About Math with Curious George

What three-dimensional shapes do you see in the sand castle?

Name _____

Alike and Different

Circle the objects that are alike.

1.

2.

Identify Three-Dimensional Shapes

Color the blue. Color the  red.

Color the  yellow.

3.

4.

5.

Sort by Size

Mark an X on the object that does not belong.

6.

 Family note: This page checks your child's understanding of important skills needed for success in Chapter 11.

GO Online — Assessment Options
Soar to Success Math

Vocabulary Builder

Visualize It

Write review words to name the shapes.

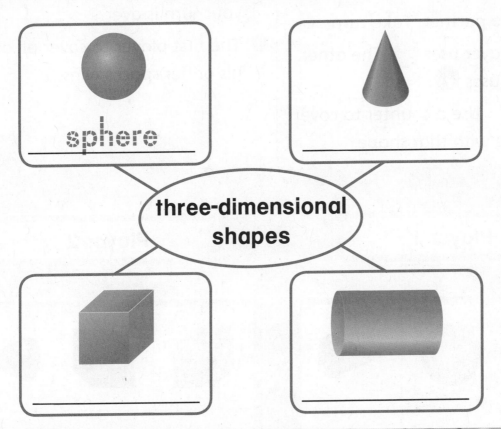

three-dimensional shapes

sphere
_____

_____

_____

_____

Understand Vocabulary

Look at the three-dimensional shapes.
Color the sphere . Color the cube 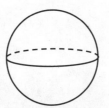.
Color the cylinder 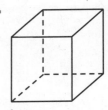.

I.

2.

3.

GO Online • eStudent Edition
• Multimedia eGlossary

Game Shape Match Bingo

Materials • 9 • 9 •

Play with a partner. Take turns.

1 One player uses ◯. The other player uses ◯.

2 Spin ◉. Use a counter to cover a space with that shape.

3 If you cannot cover a space, your turn is over.

4 The first player to cover all of his or her spaces wins.

Player 1	**Player 2**

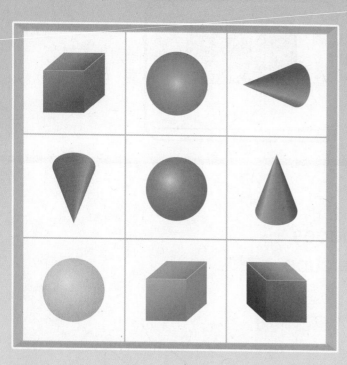 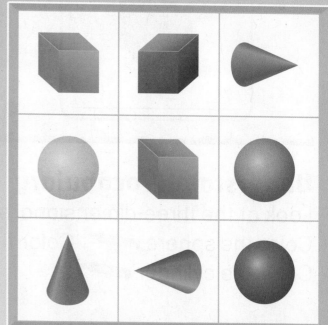

Name _____

Three-Dimensional Shapes

Essential Question How can you identify
and describe three-dimensional shapes?

COMMON CORE STANDARD CC.1.G.1
Reason with shapes and their
attributes.

Listen and Draw

Draw to sort the three-dimensional shapes.

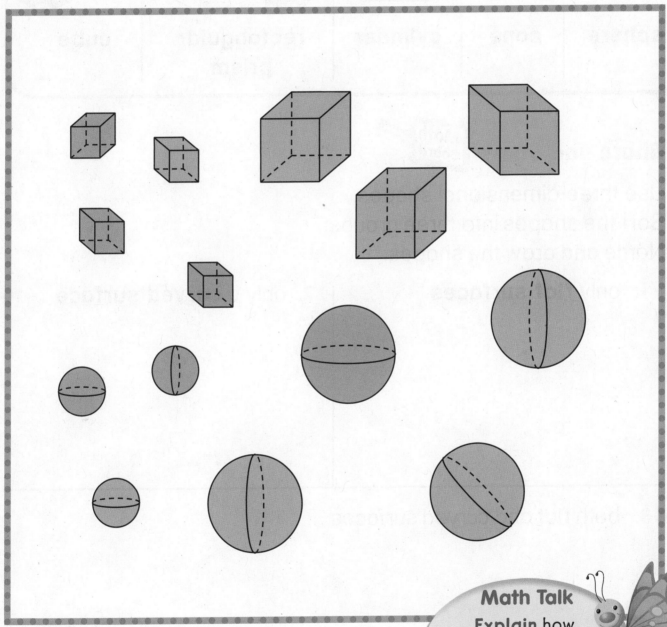

 FOR THE TEACHER • Have children sort the
three-dimensional shapes into two groups.
Have them draw around each group to show
how they sorted.

Math Talk
Explain how
you sorted
the shapes.

MATHEMATICAL
PRACTICES

Chapter 11

These are three-dimensional shapes.

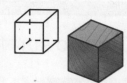

Why is a cube a special kind of rectangular prism?

sphere

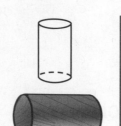

cone

cylinder

rectangular prism

cube

Share and Show Math Board

Use three-dimensional shapes.
Sort the shapes into three groups.
Name and draw the shapes.

1. only **flat surfaces**

2. only a **curved surface**

☑ 3. both flat and curved surfaces

Name _____

On Your Own

Use three-dimensional shapes. Write the number of flat surfaces for each shape.

4. A rectangular prism has __6__ flat surfaces.

_____

5. A cube has _____ flat surfaces.

_____

6. A cylinder has _____ flat surfaces.

_____

7. A cone has _____ flat surface.

 Write to name each shape.

Exercises 4–7 can help you write the shape names.

8.

sphere

9.

_____

10.

_____

11.

_____

12.

_____

PROBLEM SOLVING REAL WORLD

Write Math

Circle the objects that match the clues.

13. Josh drew an object that has only flat surfaces.

14. Kelly drew objects that have both flat and curved surfaces.

15. H.O.T. Sandy drew some rectangular prisms.

 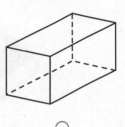  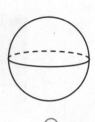
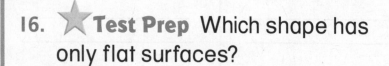

16. ⭐ **Test Prep** Which shape has only flat surfaces?

○   ○   ○   ○

TAKE HOME ACTIVITY · Ask your child to name real objects shaped like a sphere, a rectangular prism, and a cylinder.

460 four hundred sixty

FOR MORE PRACTICE:
Standards Practice Book, pp. P213–P214

Name _____

Combine Three-Dimensional Shapes

Essential Question How can you combine three-dimensional shapes to make new shapes?

COMMON CORE STANDARD CC.1.G.2
Reason with shapes and their attributes.

Listen and Draw REAL WORLD

Trace to draw the new shape.
Write to name the new shape.

Mandy	Carl

_____

- - - - - - - - - - - - -

_____

_____

- - - - - - - - - - - - -

_____

FOR THE TEACHER • Have children trace the shapes to solve the problems. Mandy stacks one cylinder on top of another cylinder. Carl stacks one cube on top of another cube. What new shapes did Mandy and Carl make?

Math Talk
Describe the new shapes Mandy and Carl made.

MATHEMATICAL PRACTICES

Model and Draw

You can put shapes together to make a new shape.

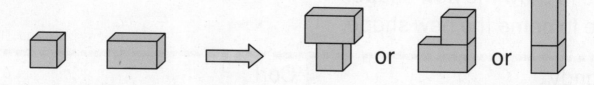

What other new shapes could you make?

Share and Show

Use three-dimensional shapes.

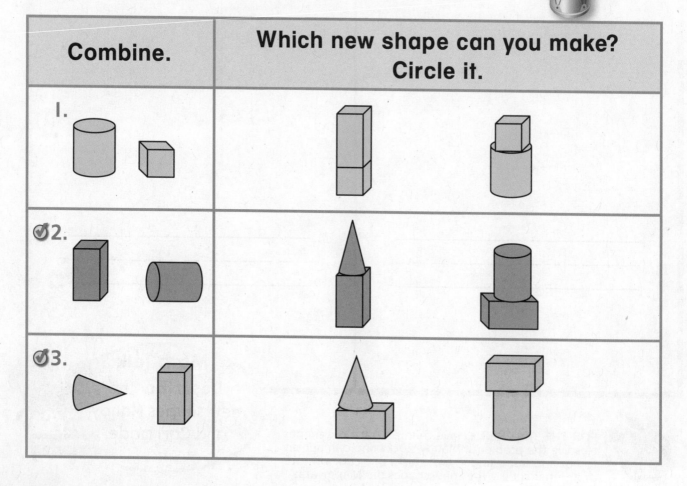

Combine.	Which new shape can you make? Circle it.
1.	
☑2.	
☑3.	

On Your Own

Use three-dimensional shapes.

Combine.	Which new shape can you make? Circle it.
4.	
5.	
6.	
7.	
8. H.O.T.	

PROBLEM SOLVING REAL WORLD

 Write Math

H.O.T. Circle the shapes you could use to model the ice cream cone and birdhouse.

9.

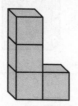

10.

11. **H.O.T.** Circle the ways that make the same shape.

12. ⭐ **Test Prep** Which new shape can you make?

Combine and .

  ○

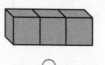 ○

○

  ○

TAKE HOME ACTIVITY · Ask your child to show you two different new shapes he or she can make by combining a soup can and a cereal box.

464 four hundred sixty-four

Name _____

Make New Three-Dimensional Shapes

Essential Question How can you use a combined shape to build new shapes?

COMMON CORE STANDARD CC.1.G.2
Reason with shapes and their attributes.

Listen and Draw REAL WORLD

Draw to copy the shape.

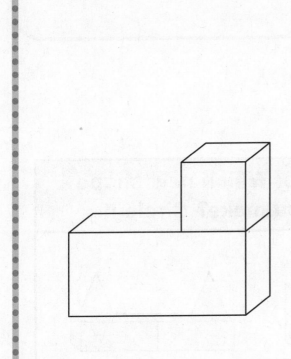

FOR THE TEACHER • Jeff put a box on top of another box. Draw to copy the new shape Jeff made.

Math Talk
Describe how to draw to copy the new shape.

MATHEMATICAL PRACTICES

Chapter 11

Model and Draw

Step 1
Build.

Step 2
Repeat.

Step 3
Combine.

Circle a new shape you can make. **Explain** why you cannot make the other shape.

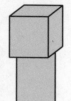
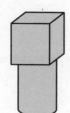

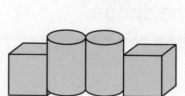
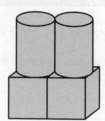

Share and Show

Use three-dimensional shapes.

Build and Repeat.	Combine. Which new shape can you make? Circle it.
1.	
☑2.	
☑3.	

© Houghton Mifflin Harcourt Publishing Company

Name _____

On Your Own

Use three-dimensional shapes.

Build and Repeat.	Combine. Which new shape can you make? Circle it.
4.	
5.	
6.	

7. **H.O.T.** Look at the shape.

How many ⬛ are used to make the shape?

_____  make the shape.

How many ⬛ are used to make the shape?

_____ ⬛ make the shape.

 TAKE HOME ACTIVITY • Ask your child to explain how he or she solved Exercise 4.

FOR MORE PRACTICE:
Standards Practice Book, pp. P217–P218

Name _____

Concepts and Skills

1. Circle the rectangular prisms. (CC.1.G.1)
2. Draw a line under the shapes that have both flat and curved surfaces. (CC.1.G.1)

Use three-dimensional shapes. (CC.1.G.2)

Combine.	Which new shape can you make? Circle it.
3. 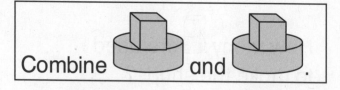	

4. ⭐ **Test Prep** Which new shape can you make? (CC.1.G.2)

Combine 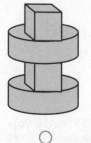 and 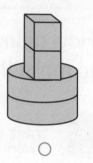 .

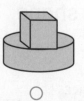 ○

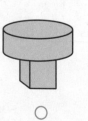 ○

○

○

Problem Solving • Take Apart Three-Dimensional Shapes

Essential Question How can acting it out help you take apart combined shapes?

COMMON CORE STANDARD CC.1.G.2
Reason with shapes and their attributes.

Mike has 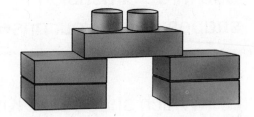, and . He chose some shapes to build a bridge. Which shapes did Mike use to build the bridge?

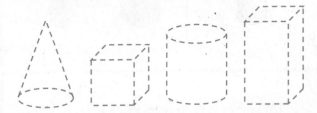

Unlock the Problem REAL WORLD

What do I need to find?

which __shapes__ Mike chose to build the bridge

What information do I need to use?

Mike has these shapes.

Show how to solve the problem.

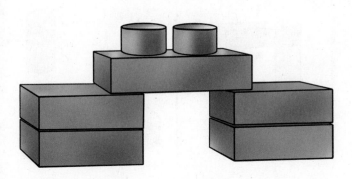

HOME CONNECTION • Your child is investigating how shapes can be taken apart. Being able to decompose shapes into smaller parts provides a foundation for future work with fractions.

Try Another Problem

Kim used shapes to build this castle.

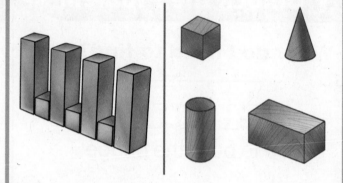

Use three-dimensional shapes. Circle your answer.

1. Which shapes did Kim use to build the tower?

 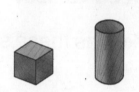

2. Which shapes did Kim use to build this wall?

3. Which shapes did Kim use to build this wall?

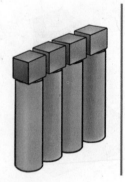 

4. Which shapes did Kim use to build the gate?

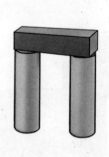

Math Talk

Describe how you know which shapes Kim used to build the tower.

MATHEMATICAL PRACTICES

© Houghton Mifflin Harcourt Publishing Company

Name _____

Share and Show

Use three-dimensional shapes.
Circle your answer.

Write Math

☑5. Zack used shapes to build this gate. Which shapes did Zack use?

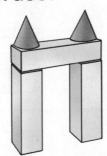

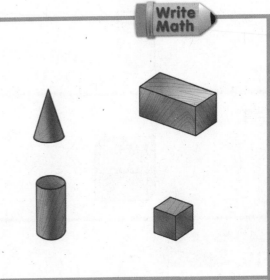

☑6. Chris used shapes to build this wall. Which shapes did Chris use?

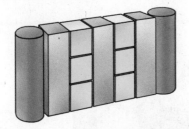

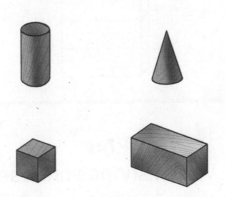

7. **H.O.T.** Rosa uses ▢, △, ⬭, and 🪵 to build a tower. Draw to show a tower Rosa could build.

Chapter 11 • Lesson 4

four hundred seventy-one **471**

On Your Own

Circle the ways that show the same shape.

8.

   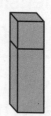

9.

 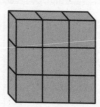 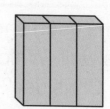

10. H.O.T.

11. ⭐ **Test Prep**
Which shapes are used
to make the towers?

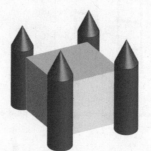

○   ○   ○   ○

TAKE HOME ACTIVITY • Use real items such as a soup can
(cylinder) and a cereal box (rectangular prism) to build a shape.
Ask your child to name the shapes you used.

FOR MORE PRACTICE:
Standards Practice Book, pp. P219–P220

Name _____

Two-Dimensional Shapes on Three-Dimensional Shapes

Essential Question What two-dimensional shapes do you see on the flat surfaces of three-dimensional shapes?

COMMON CORE STANDARD CC.1.G.1
Reason with shapes and their attributes.

Listen and Draw REAL WORLD

Use a cone.

Math Talk
What other shape could you use to draw the same kind of picture? **Explain.**

MATHEMATICAL PRACTICES

FOR THE TEACHER • Read the following problem and have children use the workspace to act it out. Lee places a cone on a piece of paper and draws around its flat surface. What did Lee draw?

Chapter 11

Model and Draw

Trace around the flat surfaces of the three-dimensional shape to find the two-dimensional shapes.

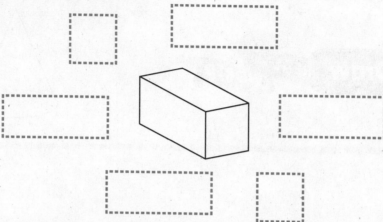

Share and Show

Use three-dimensional shapes. Trace around the flat surfaces. Circle the shapes you draw.

1.

2.

3.

Name _____

On Your Own

Circle the objects you could trace to draw the shape.

4.

5.

6.

7.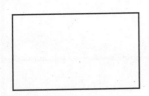

8. H.O.T. Draw a shape you would make if you traced this object.

PROBLEM SOLVING REAL WORLD

Write Math

Circle the shape that the pattern will make if you fold it and tape it together.

9.

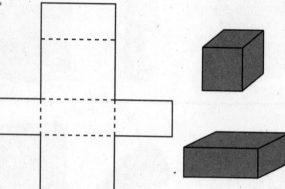

10.

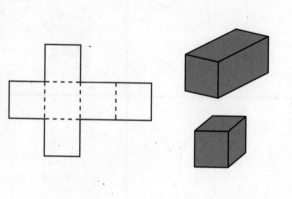

11. H.O.T.

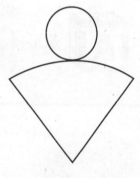

12. ★ **Test Prep** Which flat surface does a cube have?

   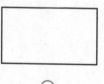

○   ○   ○   ○

TAKE HOME ACTIVITY · Collect a few three-dimensional objects, such as boxes, that are shaped like rectangular prisms or cubes. Ask your child what two-dimensional shapes are on those objects.

476 four hundred seventy-six

FOR MORE PRACTICE:
Standards Practice Book, pp. P221–P222

Chapter 11 Review/Test

Vocabulary (p. 458)

1. Color the **cube** with 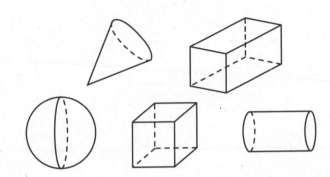 .

2. Color the **cone** with ✏ .

3. Color the **cylinder** with ✏ .

Concepts and Skills (CC.1.G.1)

4. Circle the objects that have only flat surfaces.

5. Draw a line under the object that has both curved and flat surfaces.

Use three-dimensional shapes.
Write the number of flat surfaces. (CC.1.G.1)

6. A rectangular prism has _____ flat surfaces.

---

7. Circle the objects you could trace to draw the shape. (CC.1.G.1)

8. Which shape has only flat surfaces? (CC.1.G.1)

      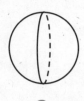

○   ○   ○   ○

9. Which shape has only 2 flat surfaces? (CC.1.G.1)

rectangular prism   sphere   cone   cylinder
○   ○   ○   ○

10. Which new shape can you make? (CC.1.G.2)

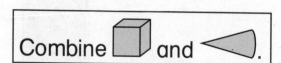

Combine and.

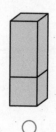   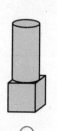      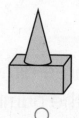

○   ○   ○   ○

11. Which new shape can you make? (CC.1.G.2)

Combine and.

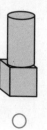   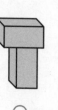

○   ○   ○   ○

TEST PREP

12. Which new shape
can you make? (CC.1.G.2)

Combine 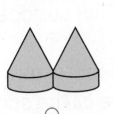 and .

○   ○   ○   ○

13. Which shape was **not** used
to build this sandcastle? (CC.1.G.2)

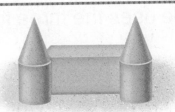

○   ○   ○   ○

14. Which shape can you draw if you trace
around the flat surface of a ? (CC.1.G.1)

□   ○   △   ▯

○   ○   ○   ○

15. Which shape can you draw if you trace
around a flat surface of a cube? (CC.1.G.1)

△   ○   ▭   □

○   ○   ○   ○

© Houghton Mifflin Harcourt Publishing Company

Performance Task (CC.1.G.1, CC.1.G.2)

Shane has these blocks.

cone   cube   sphere

cylinder   rectangular prism

- He stacks two blocks to build a tower. One block has a curved surface. The other has only flat surfaces.

- Then he builds two more towers. His three towers are all the same.

- He uses the three towers to make a wall.

Use blocks. Make a wall that Shane could build. Draw your wall. Write the names of the two shapes you use.

Two-Dimensional Geometry

Curious About Math with
Curious George

Shapes can be found in many places. What shapes might you see on a playground?

Name _____

Show What You Know ✓

Sort by Shape

Circle the shape that belongs in each group.

1.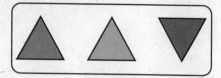

2.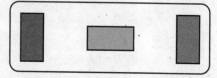

Sort Shapes

Circle the shapes with 4 sides.

3.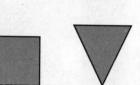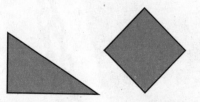

Identify Two-Dimensional Shapes

Color each square blue. Color each rectangle yellow.
Color each circle red.

4.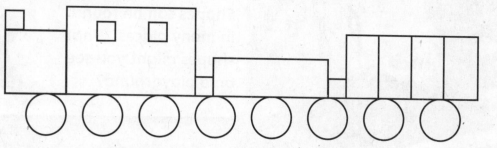

 Family note: This page checks your child's understanding of important skills needed for success in Chapter 12.

 Assessment Options
Soar to Success Math

Vocabulary Builder

Visualize It

Complete the chart.
Mark each row with a ✓.

Word	I Know	Sounds Familiar	I Do Not Know
circle			
hexagon			
rectangle			
square			
triangle			

Understand Vocabulary

Write the number of each shape.

1. _____ circles

2. _____ squares

3. _____ triangles

Game Rocket Shapes

Materials

 • 6 ■ • 8 ● • 14 ▲

Play with a partner.
Take turns.

1 Spin the .

2 Name the shape you spin.

3 Place that shape on the rocket if you can.

4 If you cannot place the shape, your turn is over.

5 The first player to cover a whole rocket wins.

Player 1

Player 2

Name _____

Sort Two-Dimensional Shapes

Essential Question How can you use attributes to sort two-dimensional shapes?

COMMON CORE STANDARD CC.1.G.1
Reason with shapes and their attributes.

Listen and Draw REAL WORLD

Draw to sort the shapes.
Write the sorting rule.

_____
— — — — — — — — —
_____

_____
— — — — — — — — —

 FOR THE TEACHER • Read the following aloud.
Devon wants to sort these shapes to show a group
of triangles and a group of rectangles. Draw and
write to show how Devon sorts the shapes.

Math Talk
Are there shapes
that did not go
in your groups?
Explain.

MATHEMATICAL
PRACTICES

Chapter 12

four hundred eighty-five **485**

Model and Draw

Here are some ways to sort
two-dimensional shapes.

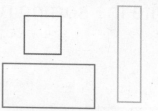
A **square** is a
special kind of
rectangle.

<u>curved</u> and
closed shapes

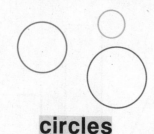

circles

closed shapes
with ____ **sides**

triangles

closed shapes
with ____ **vertices**

rectangles

Share and Show 🖊 Math Board

Read the sorting rule. Circle the
shapes that follow the rule.

THINK
Vertices are where
the sides meet.

1. 4 vertices

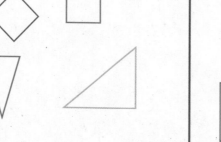

2. **not** curved

☑3. only 3 sides

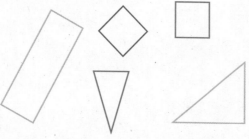

☑4. more than 3 sides

486 four hundred eighty-six

Name _____

On Your Own

Circle the shapes that follow the rule.

5. curved

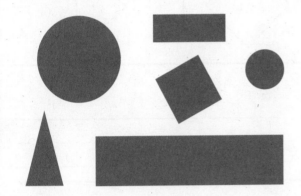

6. only 3 vertices

7. 4 sides

8. 4 sides are the same length

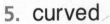 **H.O.T.** Draw 2 different two-dimensional shapes
that follow both parts of the sorting rule.

9. 3 sides and 3 vertices

10. 2 sides are long and
2 sides are short

PROBLEM SOLVING REAL WORLD

Write Math

Ted sorted these shapes three different ways. Write sorting rules to tell how Ted sorted.

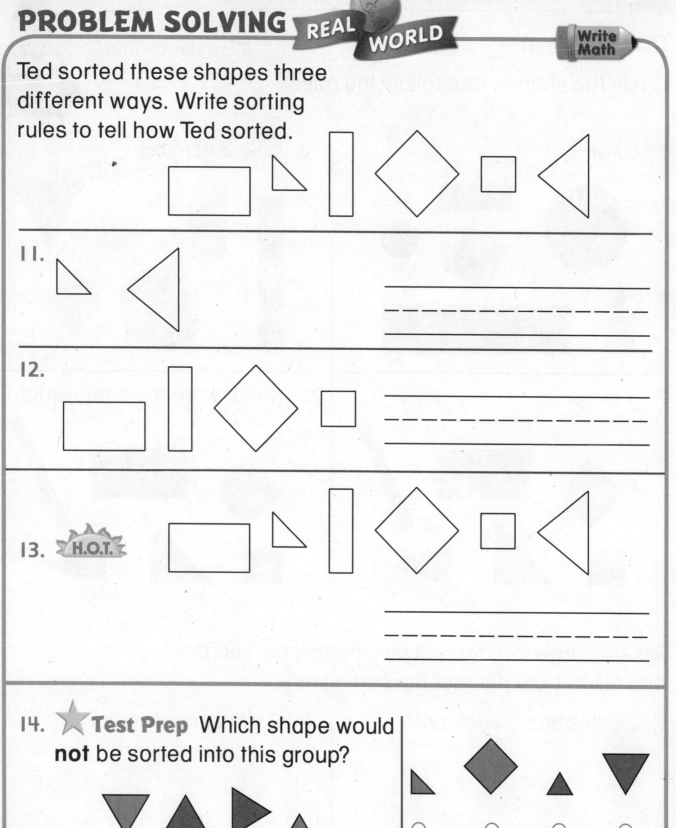

11.

12.

13. H.O.T.

14. ⭐ **Test Prep** Which shape would **not** be sorted into this group?

TAKE HOME ACTIVITY • Gather some household objects such as photos, coins, and napkins. Ask your child to sort them by shape.

FOR MORE PRACTICE:
Standards Practice Book, pp. P227–P228

Name _____

Describe Two-Dimensional Shapes

Essential Question What attributes can you use to describe two-dimensional shapes?

COMMON CORE STANDARD CC.1.G.1
Reason with shapes and their attributes.

Listen and Draw

Use two-dimensional shapes. Sort them into two groups. Draw to show your work.

curved	straight

Math Talk
Explain how you sorted the shapes into two groups. Name the shapes in each group.

MATHEMATICAL PRACTICES

FOR THE TEACHER • Have children sort two-dimensional shapes into groups that are curved and straight. Have them draw the shapes to show how they sorted.

Model and Draw

Some shapes have straight sides and vertices.

side

trapezoid

hexagon

vertex

Share and Show

Use two-dimensional shapes. Draw and write to complete the chart.

	Shape	Draw the shape.	Number of Straight Sides	Number of Vertices
1.	hexagon			
2.	rectangle			
3.	square			
✓ 4.	trapezoid			
✓ 5.	triangle			

490 four hundred ninety

Name _____

On Your Own

Use to trace each straight side.
Use to circle each vertex.
Write the number of sides and vertices.

6.

_____ sides

_____ vertices

7.
_____ sides

_____ vertices

8.

_____ sides

_____ vertices

9.

_____ sides

_____ vertices

10.
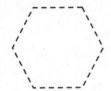
_____ sides

_____ vertices

11.
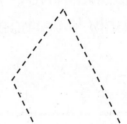
_____ sides

_____ vertices

 Draw a picture to solve.

12. I am a shape with 3 straight sides and 3 vertices.

13. I am a shape with 4 straight sides that are the same length and 4 vertices.

PROBLEM SOLVING REAL WORLD

Write Math

Draw shapes to match the clues.

14. Jake draws a shape that has fewer than 5 sides. It has 3 vertices.	
15. Meg draws a shape with 4 sides. She labels it as a trapezoid.	
16. **H.O.T.** Ben draws two different shapes. They each have only 4 vertices.	

17. ⭐**Test Prep** How many vertices does a hexagon have?

   3   4   5   6

   ○   ○   ○   ○

TAKE HOME ACTIVITY · Have your child draw a square, a trapezoid, and a triangle. For each shape, have him or her show you the sides and vertices and tell how many of each.

FOR MORE PRACTICE:
Standards Practice Book, pp. P229–P230

Name _____

Combine Two-Dimensional Shapes

Essential Question How can you put two-dimensional shapes together to make new two-dimensional shapes?

COMMON CORE STANDARD CC.1.G.2
Reason with shapes and their attributes.

Listen and Draw

Use pattern blocks. Draw to show your work.

Math Talk
Describe the new shape Karen made.

MATHEMATICAL PRACTICES

FOR THE TEACHER • Have children use pattern blocks to act out the following problem. Karen has some pattern blocks. She puts two triangles together. Draw a new shape Karen could make.

© Houghton Mifflin Harcourt Publishing Company

Chapter 12

How many  do you need to make a ⬡ ?

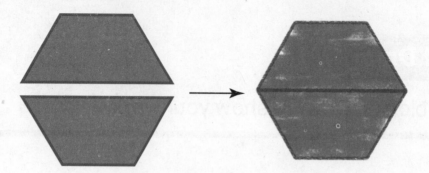

_2_ ⬠ make a ⬡ .

Share and Show [Math Board]

Use pattern blocks. Draw to show the blocks.
Write how many blocks you used.

1. How many ◆ make a ⬡ ?

2. How many ▲ make a ⬟ ?

_____ ◆ make a ⬡ .

_____ ▲ make a ⬟ .

Name _____

On Your Own

Use pattern blocks. Draw to show the blocks.
Write how many blocks you used.

3. How many ▲ make a ⬡ ?

    ____ ▲ make a ⬡ .

4. How many ▲ make a ◆ ?

    ____ ▲ make a ◆ .

 Solve. Circle a block to show your answer.

5. Use me two times to
   make this shape. Which
   block am I?

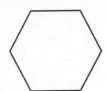

6. Use me two times to
   make this shape. Which
   block am I?

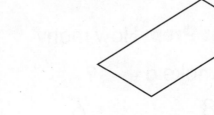

PROBLEM SOLVING REAL WORLD

Write Math

H.O.T. Use pattern blocks.
Draw to show your answer.

7. 2 ▲ make a ◆.

How many ▲ make 3 ◆?

_____ ▲ make 3 ◆.

8. ⭐ **Test Prep** How many ◆ do you
use to make a ?

| 8 | 6 | 3 | 2 |
| ○ | ○ | ○ | ○ |

TAKE HOME ACTIVITY • Have your child explain how
he or she solved Exercises 1 and 2.

FOR MORE PRACTICE:
Standards Practice Book, pp. P231–P232

© Houghton Mifflin Harcourt Publishing Company

Name _____

Combine More Shapes

Essential Question How can you combine
two-dimensional shapes to make new shapes?

COMMON CORE STANDARD CC.1.G.2
Reason with shapes and their
attributes.

Listen and Draw

Use shapes to fill each outline.
Draw to show your work.

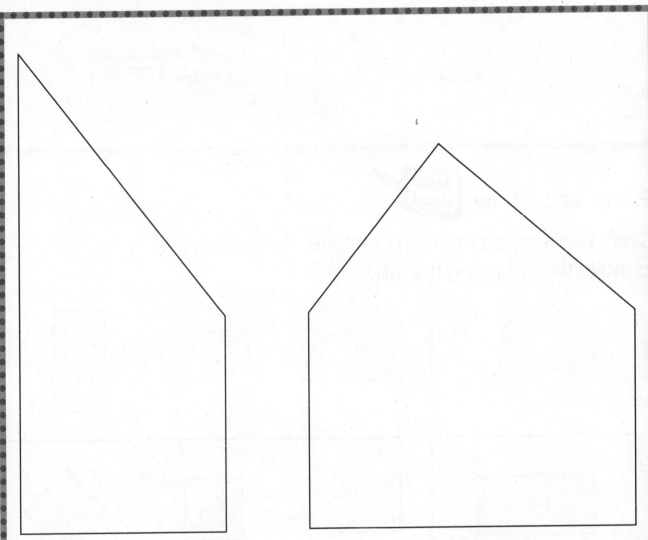

FOR THE TEACHER • Have children use two
shapes to fill the outline on the left, and draw a
line to show the two shapes. Then have children
use three shapes to fill the outline on the right,
again drawing lines to show the shapes.

Math Talk
Use the outline on
the left to **describe**
how two shapes can
make another
shape.

MATHEMATICAL
PRACTICES

Chapter 12

four hundred ninety-seven **497**

Model and Draw

Combine shapes to
make a new shape.

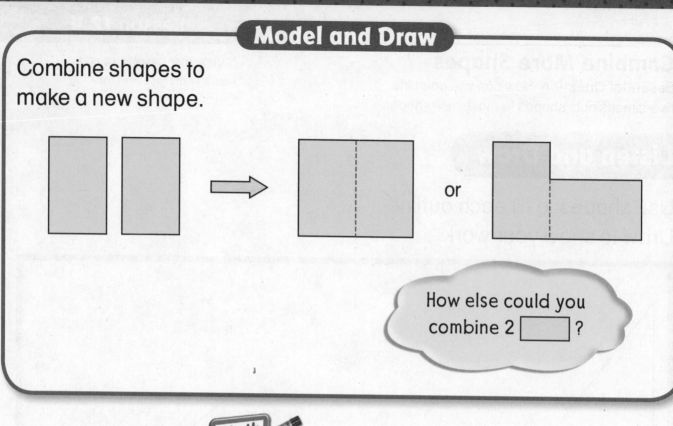

How else could you
combine 2 ☐ ?

Share and Show Math Board

Circle two shapes that can combine
to make the shape on the left.

1.

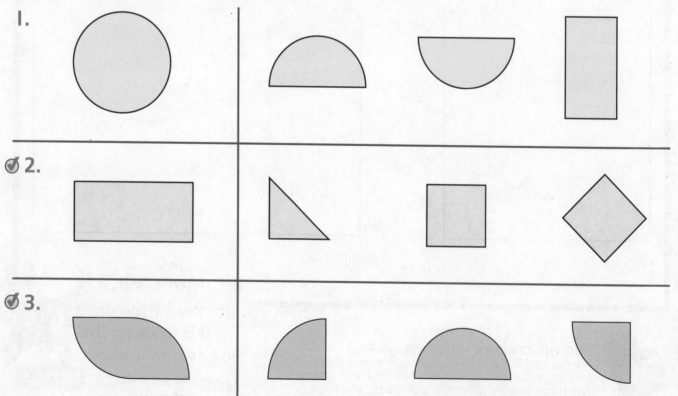

✓ 2.

✓ 3.

© Houghton Mifflin Harcourt Publishing Company

Name _____

On Your Own

Circle two shapes that can combine
to make the shape on the left.

4.

5.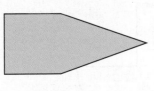

6.

7. Explain how to use Shape 1 and Shape 2
to make the New Shape.

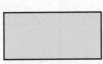      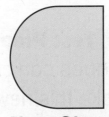

Shape 1   **Shape 2**   **New Shape**

_____

_____

_____

_____

PROBLEM SOLVING

REAL WORLD

Write Math

H.O.T. Draw lines to show how the shapes on the left combine to make the new shape.

8.

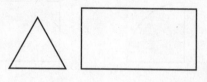

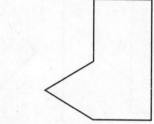

9.

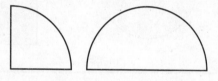

10.

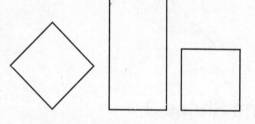

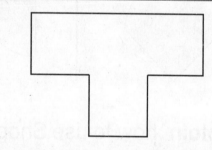

11. ⭐ **Test Prep** Which shapes can combine to make this new shape?

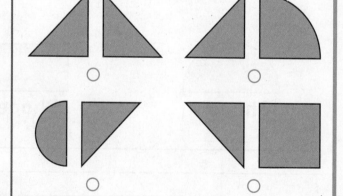

TAKE HOME ACTIVITY • Ask your child to draw a new shape he or she can make by combining two triangles.

FOR MORE PRACTICE:
Standards Practice Book, pp. P233–P234

Name _____

Problem Solving • Make New Two-Dimensional Shapes

Essential Question How can acting it out help you make new shapes from combined shapes?

COMMON CORE STANDARD CC.1.G.2
Reason with shapes and their attributes.

Cora wants to combine shapes to make a circle. She has ◺. How can Cora make a circle?

🔑 Unlock the Problem

What do I need to find?

how Cora can make a

circle

What information do I need to use?

Cora uses this shape.

Show how to solve the problem.

Step 1 Use shapes. Combine to make a new shape.

 and  make

Step 2 Then use the new shape.

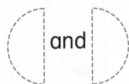 and   make

 HOME CONNECTION • Recognizing how shapes can be put together and taken apart provides a foundation for future work with fractions.

© Houghton Mifflin Harcourt Publishing Company

Try Another Problem

Use shapes to solve.
Draw to show your work.

1. Use ☐ to make a larger ☐.

   Step 1 Combine shapes to make a new shape.

   ☐ and ☐

   Step 2 Then use the new shape.

   and

2. Use to make a ☐.

   Step 1 Combine shapes to make a new shape.

    and

   Step 2 Then use the new shape.

   and

Math Talk

Describe how you made the rectangle in Exercise 2.

MATHEMATICAL PRACTICES

Name _____

Share and Show

Use shapes to solve.
Draw to show your work.

✓3. Use ◺ to make a ☐.

Step 1 ▶ Combine shapes to make a new shape.

△ and △ **make** ▶ ▭

Step 2 ▶ Then use the new shape.

and **make** ▶ ◇

4. **H.O.T.** Use ⬡ and △ to make a ▱.

Step 1 ▶ Combine shapes to make a new shape.

⬡ and △ **make** ▶ △

Step 2 ▶ Then use the new shape.

and **make** ▶ ▱

TAKE HOME ACTIVITY • Have your child
explain how he or she solved Exercise 3.

Chapter 12 • Lesson 5

FOR MORE PRACTICE:
Standards Practice Book, pp. P235–P236

five hundred three **503**

Name _____

 Mid-Chapter Checkpoint

Concepts and Skills

Write the number of sides
and vertices. (CC.1.G.1)

1. 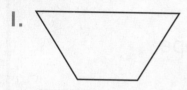 ____ sides

____ vertices

2. ____ sides

____ vertices

Circle the shapes that can combine
to make the new shape. (CC.1.G.2)

3.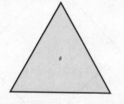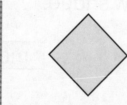

4.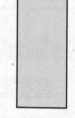

5. ⭐ **Test Prep**

Which new shape could you
make? (CC.1.G.2)

Step 1
Combine and to make 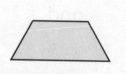.

Step 2
Then use and 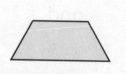.

 ○

 ○

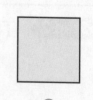 ○

 ○

504 five hundred four

Chapter 12

© Houghton Mifflin Harcourt Publishing Company

Name _____

Find Shapes in Shapes

Essential Question How can you find shapes in other shapes?

COMMON CORE STANDARD CC.1.G.2
Reason with shapes and their attributes.

Listen and Draw

Use pattern blocks. What shape can you make with 1 ⬡ and 2 △? Draw to show your shape.

Math Talk
Can you use the same pattern blocks to make a different shape? **Explain.**

MATHEMATICAL PRACTICES

FOR THE TEACHER • Have children explore making new shapes with the given pattern blocks. Discuss different shapes that can be made using the same pattern blocks.

Which two pattern blocks make this shape?

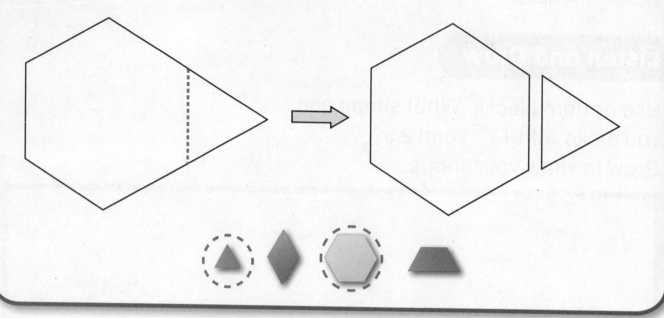

Share and Show

Use two pattern blocks to make the shape.
Draw a line to show your model.
Circle the blocks you use.

✓1.

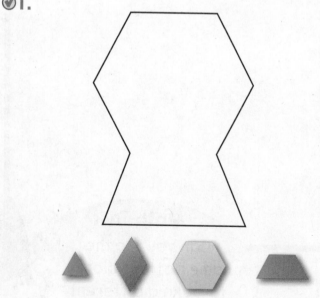

✓2.

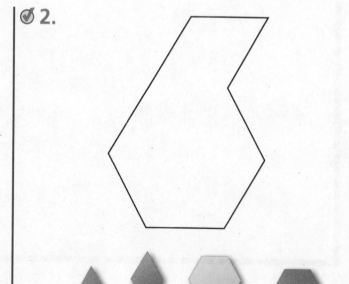

Name _____

On Your Own

Use two pattern blocks to make the shape.
Draw a line to show your model.
Circle the blocks you use.

3.
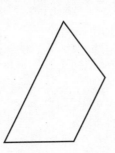

4.
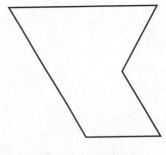

5.
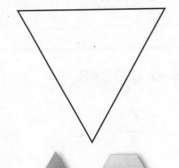

6.
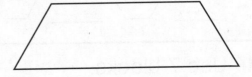

7. **H.O.T.** Use three pattern blocks to make the shape.
Draw lines to show your model.
Circle the blocks you use.

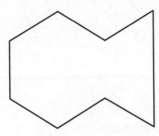

PROBLEM SOLVING

H.O.T. Make the shape below. Use the number of pattern blocks listed in the exercise. Write how many of each block you use.

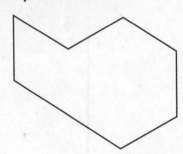

8. Use 3 blocks.

____ △ ____ ▱

____ ▽ ⬡

9. Use 5 blocks.

____ △ ____ ▱

____ ▽ ⬡

10. Use 7 blocks.

____ △ ____ ▱

____ ▽ ⬡

11. Use 8 blocks.

____ △ ____ ▱

____ ▽ ⬡

12. ⭐ **Test Prep** Which two pattern blocks can you use to make this shape?

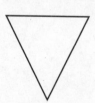

○   ○   ○   ○

TAKE HOME ACTIVITY • Have your child use this page to explain how to find shapes within the given shape.

FOR MORE PRACTICE:
Standards Practice Book, pp. P237–P238

Name _____

Take Apart Two-Dimensional Shapes

Essential Question How can you take apart two-dimensional shapes?

COMMON CORE STANDARD CC.1.G.2
Reason with shapes and their attributes.

Listen and Draw REAL WORLD

Color rectangles orange.
Color triangles purple.

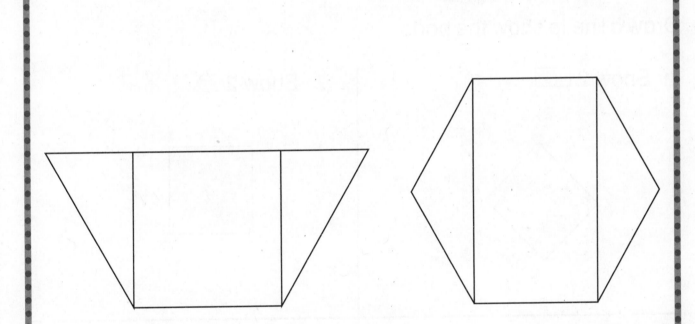

 FOR THE TEACHER • Read the following aloud. Karen put some triangles and rectangles together. She drew pictures to show what she made. Color to show how Karen put the shapes together.

Math Talk
What shapes did Karen make? **Explain.**
MATHEMATICAL PRACTICES

Chapter 12

five hundred nine **509**

You can draw to show parts of a shape.

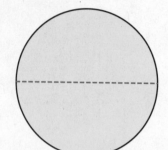 shows  and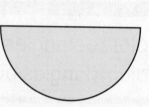

Share and Show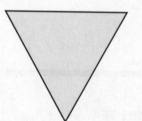

Draw a line to show the parts.

1. Show 2 ▭.

2. Show 2 △.

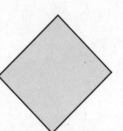

☑ 3. Show 2 ◻.

☑ 4. Show 2 △.

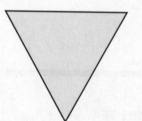

Name _____

On Your Own

Draw a line to show the parts.

5. Show 2 .

6. Show 2 .

7. Show 1 ▭ and 1 ◻.

8. Show 1 △ and 1 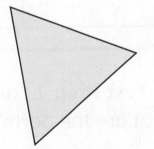.

Draw two lines to show the parts.

9. Show 3 △.

10. Show 2 △ and 1 ▱.

PROBLEM SOLVING

 Write Math

H.O.T. How many squares are there?

11.

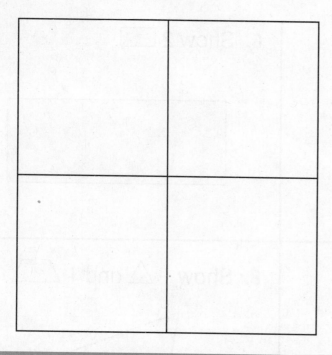

_____ squares

12. ★ **Test Prep** Look at the picture.
What are the parts?

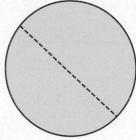

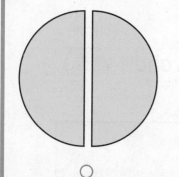 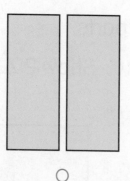 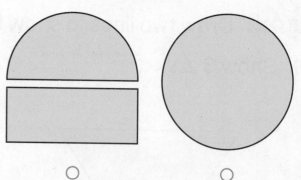

TAKE HOME ACTIVITY • Ask your child to explain how
he or she solved Exercise 11.

FOR MORE PRACTICE:
Standards Practice Book, pp. P239–P240

Name _____

Equal or Unequal Parts

Essential Question How can you identify equal and unequal parts in two-dimensional shapes?

COMMON CORE STANDARD CC.1.G.3
Reason with shapes and their attributes.

Listen and Draw

Draw to show the parts.

Show 2 △.

Show 3 △.

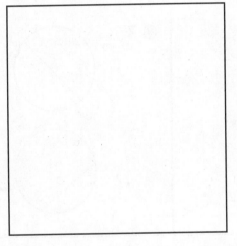

FOR THE TEACHER • Have children draw lines to show two triangles in one square and three triangles in the other square.

Math Talk
Describe how the triangles shown in each square compare.

MATHEMATICAL PRACTICES

Chapter 12

Model and Draw

These show **equal parts**, or **equal shares**.

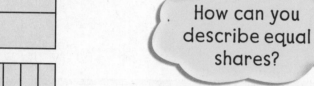
How can you describe equal shares?

These show **unequal parts**, or **unequal shares**.

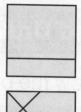

Share and Show

 Math Board

Circle the shape that shows equal parts.

THINK
Are the parts the same size?

1.
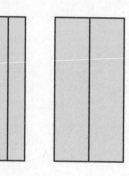

2.
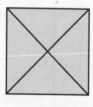

☑ 3.

Circle the shape that shows unequal parts.

4.

5.
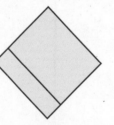

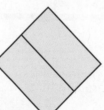

☑ 6.
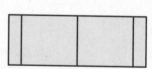

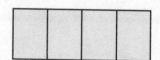

Name _____

On Your Own

Color the shapes that show unequal shares.

7.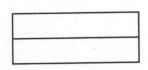

8.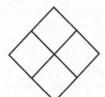

Color the shapes that show equal shares.

9.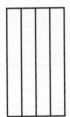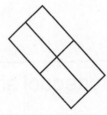

10.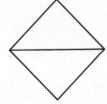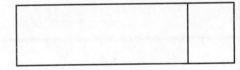

H.O.T. Write the number of equal shares.

11.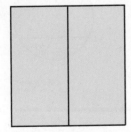

____ equal shares

12.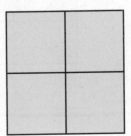

____ equal shares

PROBLEM SOLVING

 Write Math

  H.O.T. Draw lines to show the parts.

13. 2 equal parts

14. 2 unequal parts

15. 4 equal shares

16. 4 unequal shares

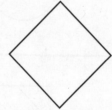

17. ⭐ **Test Prep** Which shows equal shares?

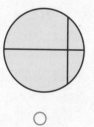   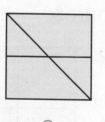   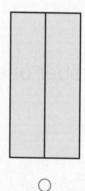   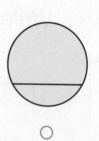

○   ○   ○   ○

 TAKE HOME ACTIVITY • Draw a circle on a piece of paper. Ask your child to draw a line so the circle shows 2 equal shares.

FOR MORE PRACTICE:
Standards Practice Book, pp. P241–P242

Name _____

Halves

Essential Question How can a shape be separated into two equal shares?

COMMON CORE STANDARD CC.1.G.3
Reason with shapes and their attributes.

Listen and Draw REAL WORLD

Draw to solve.

FOR THE TEACHER • Have children draw to solve this problem: Two friends share the sandwich on the left. How can they cut the sandwich so each gets an equal share? Then have children solve this problem: Two other friends share the sandwich on the right. How could this sandwich be cut a different way so each friend gets an equal share?

Math Talk
Will all four friends get the same amount of sandwich? **Explain.**

MATHEMATICAL PRACTICES

The 2 equal shares
make 1 whole.

2 equal shares

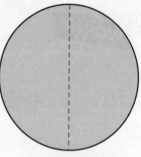

Is **half of** the circle larger or smaller than the whole circle?

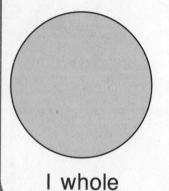

1 whole

2 **halves**

Share and Show

Draw a line to show halves.

1.

✓ 2.

3.

✓ 4.

On Your Own

Circle the shapes that show halves.

5.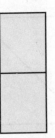

6.

7.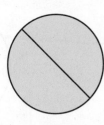

8.

9.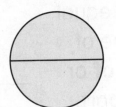

10.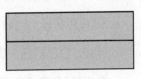

11.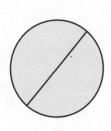

12.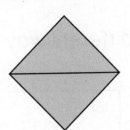

13.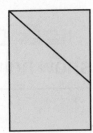

14. **H.O.T.** Use the picture.
Write numbers to solve.

The picture shows _____ halves.

The _____ equal shares make _____ whole.

PROBLEM SOLVING REAL WORLD

Write Math

Draw or write to solve.

15. Color half of each shape.

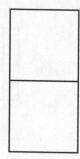
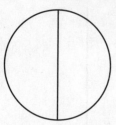
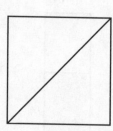

16. Linus cut a circle into equal shares. He traced one of the parts. Write **half of** or **halves** to name the part.

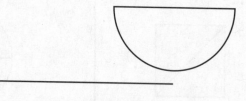

_____

_ _ _ _ _ _ _ _ _ _

_____ a circle

17. H.O.T. Draw three different ways to show halves.

18. ⭐ **Test Prep** Which shows halves?

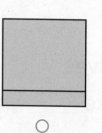
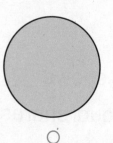
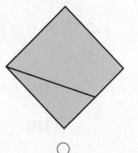
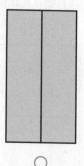

○   ○   ○   ○

TAKE HOME ACTIVITY • Draw a rectangle on a piece of paper. Ask your child to draw a line to show halves.

FOR MORE PRACTICE:
Standards Practice Book, pp. P243–P244

Name _____

Fourths

Essential Question How can a shape be separated into four equal shares?

COMMON CORE STANDARD CC.1.G.3
Reason with shapes and their attributes.

Listen and Draw REAL WORLD

Use what you know about halves.
Draw to solve. Write how many.

There are ____ equal shares.

FOR THE TEACHER • Read the following problem. Two friends will share a pizza. Then two more friends come. Now four friends will share the pizza. How can the pizza be cut so each friend gets an equal share? How many equal shares are there?

Math Talk
How did you decide how to cut the pizza? **Explain.**

MATHEMATICAL PRACTICES

Chapter 12

Model and Draw

The 4 equal shares make 1 whole.

4 equal shares

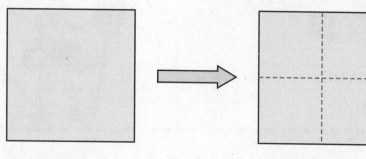

1 whole

4 **fourths**, or
4 **quarters**

How can you describe one of the 4 equal shares?

Share and Show

Color a **fourth of** the shape.

1.

2.

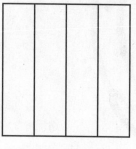

☑ 3.

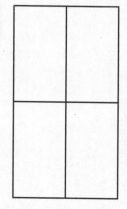

Color a **quarter of** the shape.

4.

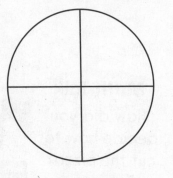

5.

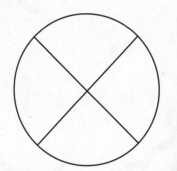

☑ 6.

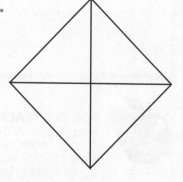

Name _____

On Your Own

Circle the shapes that show fourths.

7. 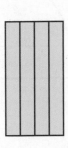	8. 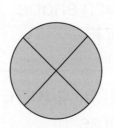	9. 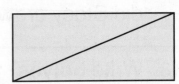
10. 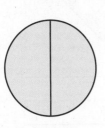	11. 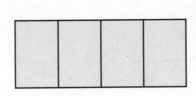	12. 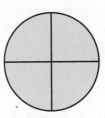
13. 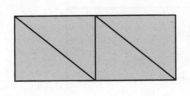	14. 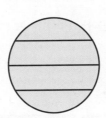	15. 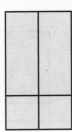

16. **H.O.T.** Draw three different ways to show fourths.

PROBLEM SOLVING REAL WORLD

 Write Math

Solve.

17. Stacy drew a picture to show a quarter of a circle. Which shape did Stacy draw? Circle it.

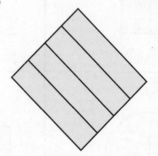

18. Write **halves, fourths,** or **quarters** to name the equal shares.

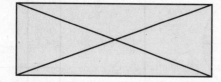

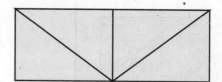

19. **H.O.T.** Circle the shape that shows quarters.

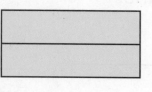 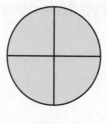

20. ⭐ **Test Prep** Which shows fourths?

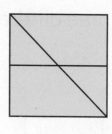 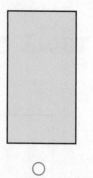

○   ○   ○   ○

 TAKE HOME ACTIVITY • Draw a circle on a piece of paper. Ask your child to draw lines to show fourths.

FOR MORE PRACTICE:
Standards Practice Book, pp. P245–P246

Name _____

Vocabulary

Draw a line to show **halves**. (p.518)

1.

2.

3.

Concepts and Skills

4. Circle the shapes that have only 3 vertices.

(CC.1.G.1)

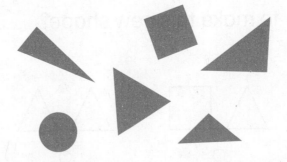

Use pattern blocks. Draw to show the blocks.
Write how many blocks you use. (CC.1.G.2)

5.

 ____ make a ____ .

6.

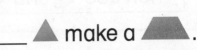 ____ ▲ make a ◤ .

---

7. Color the shapes that show equal shares. (CC.1.G.3)

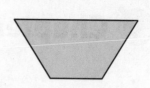

8. How many straight sides does a trapezoid have? (CC.1.G.1)

2	4	5	6
○	○	○	○

---

9. Which shapes can combine to make this new shape? (CC.1.G.2)

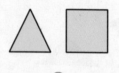   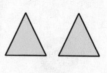   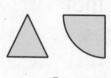   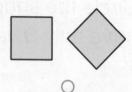

  ○   ○   ○   ○

---

10. Which new shape could you make? (CC.1.G.2)

 Step 1

Combine and ⬦ to make 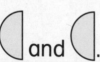.

Step 2

Then use and ⬦.

      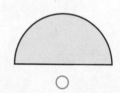

---

11. Which two pattern blocks can you use to make this shape? (CC.1.G.2)

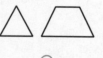      

  ○   ○   ○   ○

© Houghton Mifflin Harcourt Publishing Company

Name _____

12. Look at the picture.
What are the parts? (CC.1.G.2)

○   ○   ○   ○

13. Which shape shows unequal parts? (CC.1.G.3)

○   ○   ○   ○

14. Which shading shows half of a square?

(CC.1.G.3)

○   ○   ○   ○

15. Which shape shows fourths? (CC.1.G.3)

○   ○   ○   ○

16. Which shading shows a quarter of
a rectangle? (CC.1.G.3)

○   ○   ○   ○

Performance Task (CC.1.G.1, CC.1.G.3)

Use the following clues to draw a shape.

- The shape has only straight sides.
- The shape has more than 3 sides.
- The shape has fewer than 5 vertices.
- The shape can be cut into fourths.

Draw to show the shape. Draw lines
to show how the shape can be cut.
Write how many equal shares there are.

Picture Glossary

add sumar

$$3 + 2 = 5$$

addend sumando

$$1 + 3 = 4$$

addend

addition sentence enunciado de suma

$2 + 1 = 3$ is an **addition sentence**.

bar graph gráfica de barras

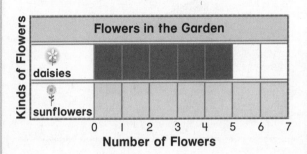

circle círculo

compare comparar

Subtract to **compare** groups.

$$5 - 1 = 4$$

There are more ●.

cone cono

count back contar hacia atrás

$8 - 1 = 7$

Start at 8.

Count back 1.

You are on 7.

count on contar hacia adelante

$4 + 2 = 6$

Say 4.

Count on 2.

5, 6

cube cubo

curved surface superficie curva

Some three-dimensional shapes have a **curved surface**.

cylinder cilindro

© Houghton Mifflin Harcourt Publishing Company

difference diferencia

$$4 - 3 = 1$$

The **difference** is 1.

---

digit dígito

13 is a two-**digit** number.

The 1 in 13 means 1 ten.
The 3 in 13 means 3 ones.

---

doubles dobles

$$5 + 5 = 10$$

doubles minus one dobles
menos uno

$$5 + 5 = 10, \text{so } 5 + 4 = 9$$

---

doubles plus one dobles
más uno

$$5 + 5 = 10, \text{so } 5 + 6 = 11$$

---

equal parts partes iguales

These show **equal parts**,
or equal shares.

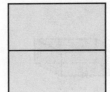 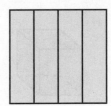

© Houghton Mifflin Harcourt Publishing Company

equal shares porciones iguales

These show equal parts, or **equal shares**.

fewer menos

3 **fewer**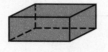

flat surface superficie plana

Some three-dimensional shapes have only **flat surfaces**.

fourth of cuarto de

A **fourth of** this shape is shaded.

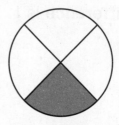

fourths cuartos

 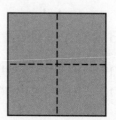

I whole   4 **fourths**, or 4 quarters

half hour media hora

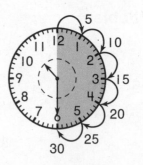

A **half hour** has 30 minutes.

half of mitad de

Half of this shape is shaded.

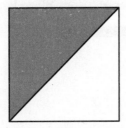

halves mitades

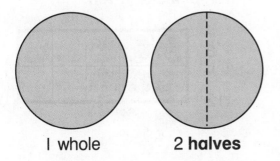

I whole   2 **halves**

hexagon hexágono

hour hora

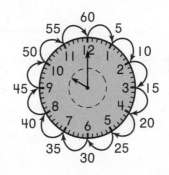

An **hour** has 60 minutes.

hour hand horario

hour hand →

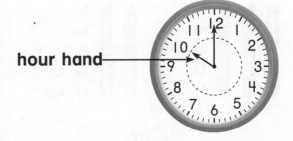

hundred centena

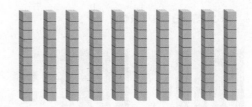

10 tens is the same as 1 **hundred**.

is equal to (=) es igual a

2 plus 1 **is equal to** 3.

$$2 + 1 = 3$$

longest el más largo

longest

is greater than es mayor que

35 **is greater than** 27.

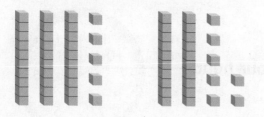

$$35 > 27$$

make a ten formar una decena

Move 2 counters into the ten frame. **Make a ten**.

$$\begin{array}{r} 8 \\ + 4 \\ \hline 12 \end{array}$$

is less than es menor que

43 **is less than** 49.

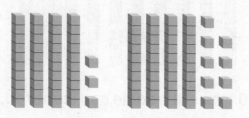

$$43 < 49$$

minus (−) menos

4 **minus** 3 is equal to 1.

$$4 - 3 = 1$$

© Houghton Mifflin Harcourt Publishing Company

minute hand minutero

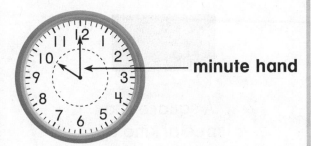

← **minute hand**

ones unidades

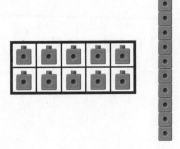

10 **ones** = 1 ten

minutes minutos

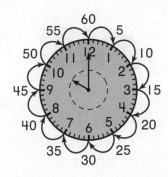

An hour has 60 **minutes.**

order orden

You can change the **order** of the addends.

1 + 3 = 4   3 + 1 = 4

more más

5 − 1 = 4

There are **more** ●.

picture graph gráfica con dibujos

Our Favorite Activity at the Fair							
🐴 animals	⚲	⚲	⚲	⚲	⚲		
🎡 rides	⚲	⚲	⚲	⚲	⚲	⚲	⚲

Each ⚲ stands for 1 child.

plus (+) más

2 **plus** 1 is equal to 3.
$$2 + 1 = 3$$

---

quarter of cuarta parte de

A **quarter of** this shape
is shaded.

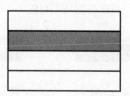

---

quarters cuartas partes

I whole

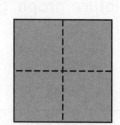

4 fourths,
or 4 **quarters**

rectangle rectángulo

A square is a
special kind of
rectangle.

---

rectangular prism prisma
rectangular

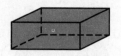

A cube is a special
kind of rectangular
prism.

---

related facts operaciones
relacionadas

$$4 + 5 = 9 \qquad 9 - 5 = 4$$

$$5 + 4 = 9 \qquad 9 - 4 = 5$$

shortest el más corto

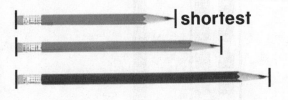

side lado

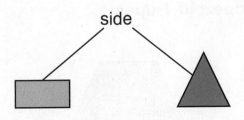

sphere esfera

square cuadrado

subtract restar

Subtract to find out how many.

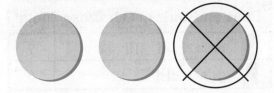

subtraction sentence
enunciado de resta

$4 - 3 = 1$ is a **subtraction sentence**.

sum suma o total

2 plus 1 is equal to 3.

The **sum** is 3.

ten decena

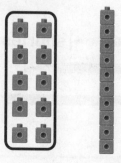

10 ones = 1 **ten**

tally chart tabla de conteo

Boys and Girls in Our Class			Total
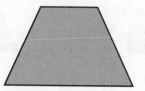	boys	⊮⊮⊮ IIII	9
	girls	⊮⊮⊮ I	6

trapezoid trapecio

tally mark marca de conteo

⊮⊮⊮

Each **tally mark** | stands for 1.
⊮⊮⊮ stands for 5.

triangle triángulo

unequal parts partes desiguales

These show **unequal parts**, or unequal shares.

 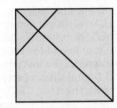

unequal shares porciones desiguales

These show unequal parts, or **unequal shares**.

 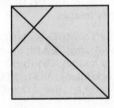

vertex vértice

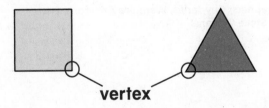

vertex

zero 0 cero

When you add **zero** to any number, the sum is that number.

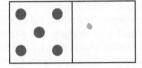

$$5 + \mathbf{0} = 5$$

© Houghton Mifflin Harcourt Publishing Company

Photo Credits